3rd Edition Extra

with business skills lessons and self-assessment

Elementary
MARKET LEADER

Business English Course Book
with MyEnglishLab

David Cotton   David Falvey   Simon Kent

with Nina O'Driscoll

Contents

	DISCUSSION	TEXTS	LANGUAGE WORK	SKILLS	CASE STUDY
UNIT 1 INTRODUCTIONS ➡ page 6	Introduce yourself	Listening: An interview with a consultant Reading: From small town to global leader	Nationalities *to be* *a/an* with jobs *wh-* questions	Introducing yourself and others	A job fair in Singapore: Decide on the successful candidate for a job Writing: e-mail
UNIT 2 WORK AND LEISURE ➡ page 14	Discuss what people want from work	Reading: Business diary: Eugene Kaspersky – *Financial Times* Listening: An interview with Ros Pomeroy	Days, months, dates Leisure activities Present simple Adverbs and expressions of frequency	Talking about work and leisure	Hudson Design Inc.: Resolve issues with unhappy staff Writing: e-mail
UNIT 3 PROBLEMS ➡ page 22	Talk about problems at work	Listening: An interview with a specialist in change leadership Reading: call-centre interviews	Adjectives *too/enough* Present simple: negatives and questions *have* *some* and *any*	Telephoning: solving problems	High-Style Business Rentals: Respond to negative customer feedback Writing: e-mail

WORKING ACROSS CULTURES: 1 EATING OUT		➡ page 30
REVISION UNIT A		➡ page 32
BUSINESS SKILLS: 1.1 SMALL TALK; 1.2 TELEPHONING		➡ page A1

	DISCUSSION	TEXTS	LANGUAGE WORK	SKILLS	CASE STUDY
UNIT 4 TRAVEL ➡ page 36	Talk about business travel	Listening: An interview with a business traveller Reading: Hilton Tokyo – hotel description	Travel details *can/can't* *there is / there are*	Making bookings and checking arrangements	The Gustav Conference Centre: Coordinate the needs of three different companies Writing: e-mail
UNIT 5 FOOD AND ENTERTAINING ➡ page 44	Discuss food from different countries	Reading: India likes fast-food chains – *Financial Times* Listening: An interview with a specialist in change leadership	Eating out *some/any* Countable and uncountable nouns	Making decisions	Which restaurant? Choose the right place to eat for some important clients Writing: e-mail
UNIT 6 BUYING AND SELLING ➡ page 52	Talk about buying different products	Reading: Uniqlo: a global success story Listening: An interview with a management consultant	Choosing a product Choosing a service Past simple Past time references	Describing a product	NP Innovations: Decide on a new product Writing: e-mail

WORKING ACROSS CULTURES: 2 COMMUNICATION STYLES		➡ page 60
REVISION UNIT B		➡ page 62
BUSINESS SKILLS: 2.1 MEETINGS; 2.2 PRESENTATIONS		➡ page A5

WRITING FILE
➡ page 126

ACTIVITY FILE
➡ page 130

CONTENTS

	DISCUSSION	TEXTS	LANGUAGE WORK	SKILLS	CASE STUDY
UNIT 7 PEOPLE → page 66	Talk about how you like to work	Listening: Interview with a management consultant Reading: Women at the top: Andrea Jung – *Financial Times*	Describing people Past simple: negatives and questions Question forms	Dealing with problems	Tell us about it: Give advice on problems at work Writing: reply to a problem message
UNIT 8 ADVERTISING → page 74	Do an advertising quiz	Reading: Volkswagen's Black Beetle ad – *Financial Times* Listening: An interview with an organisation development consultant	Advertising and markets Comparatives and superlatives *much / a lot, a little / a bit*	Participating in discussions	Excelsior Chocolate Products: Devise an advertising campaign Writing: product launch plan
UNIT 9 COMPANIES → page 82	Do a companies quiz	Listening: An interview with a specialist in change leadership Reading: New markets for Gamesa	Describing companies Present continuous Present simple or present continuous	Starting a presentation	Presenting your company: Prepare a short presentation Writing: company profile

WORKING ACROSS CULTURES: 3 DOING BUSINESS INTERNATIONALLY	→ page 90
REVISION UNIT C	→ page 92
BUSINESS SKILLS: 3.1 NEGOTIATIONS; 3.2 MEETINGS	→ page A9

	DISCUSSION	TEXTS	LANGUAGE WORK	SKILLS	CASE STUDY
UNIT 10 COMMUNICATION → page 96	Do a communications quiz	Listening: An interview with a management consultant Reading: I'm a fan of Facebook, but not of video calls – *Financial Times*	Internal communication Talking about future plans *will*	Making arrangements	Blakelock Engineering: Decide who should leave a company Writing: e-mail
UNIT 11 CULTURES → page 104	Look at some tips for doing business in another country	Listening: Three people talk about cultural mistakes Reading: Lessons in cultural difference – *Financial Times*	Company cultures *should/shouldn't could/would*	Identifying problems and agreeing action	The wind of change: Assess ideas for changing a company culture Writing: action minutes
UNIT 12 JOBS → page 112	Discuss jobs	Listening: An interview with an organisation development consultant Reading: profile on a professional networking site	Skills and abilities Present perfect Past simple and present perfect	Interview skills	Nelson & Harper Inc.: Interview candidates for a job Writing: letter

WORKING ACROSS CULTURES: 4 TEAM WORKING	→ page 120
REVISION UNIT D	→ page 122
BUSINESS SKILLS: 4.1 INTERVIEWS; 4.2 PRESENTATIONS	→ page A13

GRAMMAR REFERENCE → page 145	**AUDIO SCRIPTS** → page 158	**GLOSSARY** → page 168

Introduction

What is *Market Leader*, and who is it for?

Market Leader is a multi-level business English course for businesspeople and students of business English. It has been developed in association with the *Financial Times*, one of the leading sources of business information in the world. It consists of 12 units based on topics of great interest to everyone involved in international business.

This third edition of the Elementary level features completely updated content and a significantly enhanced range of authentic resource material, reflecting the latest trends in the business world. If you are in business, the course will greatly improve your ability to communicate in English in a wide range of business situations. If you are a student of business, the course will develop the communication skills you need to succeed in business and will enlarge your knowledge of the business world. Everybody studying this course will become more fluent and confident in using the language of business and should increase their career prospects.

The authors

David Falvey (left) has over 25 years' teaching and managerial experience in the UK, Japan and Hong Kong. He has also worked as a teacher trainer at the British Council in Tokyo, and was Head of the English Language Centre and Principal Lecturer at London Metropolitan University.

David Cotton (centre) has over 45 years' experience teaching and training in EFL, ESP and English for Business, and is the author of numerous business English titles, including *Agenda*, *World of Business*, *International Business Topics* and *Keys to Management*. He is also one of the authors of the best-selling *Business Class*. He was previously a Senior Lecturer at London Metropolitan University.

Simon Kent (right) has over 25 years' teaching experience, including three years as an in-company trainer in Berlin at the time of German reunification. He has spent the majority of his career to date in higher education in the UK where he has taught on and directed programmes of business, general and academic English.

INTRODUCTION

What is in the units?

STARTING UP

You are offered a variety of interesting activities in which you discuss the topic of the unit and exchange ideas about it.

VOCABULARY

You will learn important new words and phrases which you can use when you carry out the tasks in the unit. You can find definitions and examples, and listen to the pronunciation of new vocabulary in the i-Glossary feature on the DVD-ROM. The DVD-ROM also contains practice exercises. A good business dictionary, such as the *Longman Business English Dictionary*, will also help you to increase your business vocabulary.

READING

You will read authentic articles on a variety of topics from the *Financial Times* and other newspapers and books on business. You will develop your reading skills and learn essential business vocabulary. You will also be able to discuss the ideas and issues in the articles.

LISTENING

You will hear authentic interviews with businesspeople and a variety of scripted recordings. You will develop listening skills such as listening for information and note-taking. You can also watch the interviews and find further practice exercises on the DVD-ROM.

LANGUAGE FOCUS

This section focuses on common problem areas at elementary level. You will become more accurate in your use of language. Each unit contains a Language focus box which provides an overview of key grammar items. A Grammar reference section can be found at the back of the book and on the DVD-ROM. The DVD-ROM also provides extra grammar practice.

SKILLS

You will develop essential business communication skills, such as making presentations, taking part in meetings, negotiating, telephoning, and using English in social situations. Each Skills section contains a Useful language box, which provides you with the language you need to carry out the realistic business tasks in the book. The dialogues from the Skills sections appear on the DVD-ROM, which also supplements the Course Book with additional activities.

CASE STUDY

Case studies are linked to the business topics of each unit. They are based on realistic business problems or situations and allow you to use the language and communication skills you have developed while working through the unit. They give you the opportunity to practise your speaking skills in realistic business situations. Each Case study ends with a writing task.

WORKING ACROSS CULTURES

These four units focus on different aspects of international communication. They help to raise your awareness of potential problems or misunderstandings that may arise when doing business with people from different cultures.

REVISION UNITS

Market Leader Elementary third edition also contains four revision units, each based on material covered in the preceding three Course Book units. Each revision unit is designed so that it can be completed in one session or on a unit-by-unit basis.h people from different cultures.

EXTRA BUSINESS SKILLS

The new Business Skills lessons offer the learner a task-based, integrated skills approach to the development of core business skills such as Presentations, Negotiations, Meetings, and Small Talk. These lessons appear at the end of every three units and incorporate performance review, suggestions for professional development and goal setting. They are based on the Global Scale of English Learning Objectives for Professional English. These objectives are signposted at the top of each new lesson in the Student's book and the carefully scaffolded activities are crafted around each objective, creating a clear sense of direction and progression in a learning environment where learners can reflect on their achievement at the end of the lesson.

UNIT 1 Introductions

'James Bond, Universal Exports.'
Sean Connery, British actor, in From Russia With Love

OVERVIEW

VOCABULARY
Nationalities

LISTENING
Meeting business contacts

READING
Angela Ahrendts

LANGUAGE FOCUS 1
to be

LANGUAGE FOCUS 2
a/an with jobs, *wh-* questions

SKILLS
Introducing yourself and others

CASE STUDY
A job fair in Singapore

STARTING UP

A Work in pairs. Complete the sentences below with words from the box. There are two words you do not need.

| from   I'm   my   name's   she   you |

1 .... Emma. Emma Schneider, from Habermos in Hamburg.
2 Good morning. .... name's Shi Jiabao.
3 My .... Akim, by the way. Akim Anyukov.
4 How do you do. I'm Nuria Sosa, ... RTA Seguros.

B ◆ CD1.1–1.4 Now listen to the four businesspeople (1–4) introducing themselves. Check your answers to Exercise A. Match the speakers to their business cards (A–D) on page 7.

C ◆ CD1.1–1.4 Listen again. Where is each speaker? Choose from the following places.

a) on the phone   b) in a hotel   c) at a conference   d) at the airport

D Talk about yourself.

Hello. My name's .... I'm from ....

UNIT 1 ▸▸ INTRODUCTIONS

A ☐
ASTENA Consulting Group
Akim Anyukov
Accountant
PO Box 103
St Petersburg
193015 RUSSIA
Tel: +7 (812) 275-5626
Cell: +7 (812) 101-4046
E-mail: akim@accounts.ru

B ☐
Habermos GmbH
Emma Schneider
Product Manager
Steintwiete 47
20459 Hamburg Germany
Tel: +49 (0) 40-56 91 65 56
Mobile: +49 (0) 177-7 46 94 36
Skype: emmaschneider
E-mail: eschneider@habermos.de

C ☐
RTA Seguros S.A.
Nuria Sosa
Senior Manager
Ayacucho 3813
(B1765ETL) Recoleta
Buenos Aires, Argentina
+(54 11) 4625-1796
E-mail: sosa@rtas.com.ar

D ☐
Shi Jiabao
88 Xue Yuan Road, Hangzhou,
Zhejiang Province, P.R. China 310012
Tel: (0086-571) 2152433
E-mail: jia@mail.zjzs.edu.cn

E 🔊 **CD1.5** Listen to these letters and practise saying them.

| A H J K | F L M N S X Z | O | R |
| B C D E G P T V | I Y | Q U W | |

F 🔊 **CD1.6** Listen and write the words that are spelled.

1 ....   2 ....   3 ....   4 ....

G Work in pairs. Spell the names of some people.

Student A: Turn to page 130.   Student B: Turn to page 136.

VOCABULARY
Nationalities

A Complete the chart of countries and nationalities below using the words from the box. Add other countries and nationalities.

~~Brazilian~~ Polish ~~Germany~~ Kuwaiti French Oman
Italian Spain Russia Turkey Japanese Swedish
China Greece British American Indian Mexican Korean

Country	Nationality	Country	Nationality
	-an		*-ish*
Brazil	*Brazilian*	Poland	....
Germany	German	....	Spanish
India	....	Sweden	....
Mexico	....	....	Turkish
Italy	....		*others*
....	Russian	France	....
Korea	....	....	Greek
	-ese	the UK	....
Japan	....	the USA	....
....	Chinese		
	-i		
Kuwait	....		
....	Omani		

B 🔊 **CD1.7** Listen and check your answers to Exercise A.

UNIT 1 ▸▸ INTRODUCTIONS

C **Work in pairs. Ask and answer questions about the nationality of the companies from the box below.**

Student A: Turn to page 132.

Student B: Turn to page 138.

A: *Is Sony Japanese?*

B: *Yes, it is. Is Chanel Swedish?*

A: *No, it isn't. It's French.*

| Sony | Chanel | Ikea | Zara | Prada | Gazprom | Michelin | Mercedes |
| McDonald's | Samsung | Petrobras | Tesco | Tata Group | Telcel |

 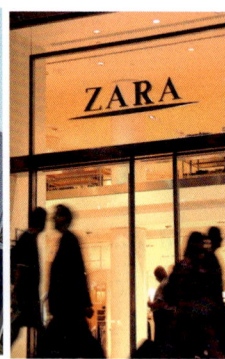  

*See the **DVD-ROM** for the i-Glossary.*

D **What are the most famous companies in the world, in your opinion? What is their nationality?**

LISTENING
Meeting business contacts

Jeremy Keeley

A 🔊 **CD1.8** **Jeremy Keeley is a consultant. Listen to him introducing himself in the first part of the interview and decide whether these statements are true (T) or false (F). Correct the false ones.**

1. He lives in London.
2. He has three very young children.
3. He runs his own business.
4. His business works for organisations across the USA and Asia.
5. He helps leaders become better leaders.
6. He always shakes hands when he meets people.

B 🔊 **CD1.9** **Listen to the second part. Complete what Jeremy says about meeting new business contacts and exchanging business cards.**

I usually say, 'Hello, ...¹ are you?', '............² do you come from?', '............³ do you do?'. I usually find out ....⁴'s important to them, ...⁵ they're there. I usually wait until they've asked me a question before I talk too much about myself.

I usually ....⁶ until the person I'm meeting ....⁷ me a business card before I offer them mine, so we'll ....⁸ them at that point.

*Watch the interview on the **DVD-ROM**.*

C **In business, when do you:**

- shake hands?
- kiss?
- bow?
- exchange business cards?

8

READING

Angela Ahrendts

A Read this article. Then complete the chart below.

From small town to global leader

Angela Ahrendts is the American CEO* of Burberry, the $2.2 billion fashion company. Burberry is one of the biggest luxury brands in the world. The headquarters of this British company are in London, and it has more than 270 stores in 80 countries.

Fifty-year-old Ahrendts is from a small town in Indiana. She is married to Greg, her high-school sweetheart. They have a son (15) and two daughters (14 and 11). Their son, Jennings, dreams of being a rock star. The children are at an American international school in London.

Ahrendts is always elegant. Most days she wears Burberry – usually something from its Prorsum range.

She usually gets up around 4.30. 'I need a quiet time in the morning to answer e-mails,' she explains. On days when Ahrendts is in London, she often has back-to-back meetings for 10 hours. She keeps going by drinking six Diet Cokes a day. She travels on business one week a month, but tries to get home for weekends.

Family is important for Ahrendts. 'I'm at work or with my family. I don't have time for other things.' When she is not working, she likes to eat a takeaway pizza with her children or play basketball with them. Ahrendts and the family go back to Indiana for holidays several times a year. 'We want our children to stay in contact with their cousins,' she says.

* A CEO (chief executive officer) is the person with most authority in a company.

Angela Ahrendts

Age	50
Job	
Nationality	
Family	
Interests outside work	

B Decide whether these statements are true (T) or false (F). Correct the false ones.

1. Burberry is an American company.   F (It's a British company.)
2. Burberry is a global fashion company.
3. All Ahrendts's children are teenagers.
4. They are at school in America.
5. Most mornings, Ahrendts is up before 5 a.m.
6. She is away on business most weeks.
7. She has a lot of interests outside work.
8. For Ahrendts, keeping in contact with relatives is important.

C Work in pairs. Write five questions about Angela Ahrendts and Burberry.

Is Angela married?
Where is she from?

D Now work with a different partner. Close your books and ask each other your questions from Exercise C. See who can remember the most answers!

UNIT 1 ▸▸ INTRODUCTIONS

LANGUAGE FOCUS 1
to be

We often use the verb *to be* to describe people.

*Angela Ahrendts **is** CEO of Burberry. She **is** American. She **is** married.*

I	am	(I'**m**)	
You		(You'**re**)	
We	are	(We'**re**)	
They		(They'**re**)	Spanish.
He		(He'**s**)	
She	is	(She'**s**)	
It		(It'**s**)	

I	am not	(I'**m not**)	
You		(You **aren't**)	
We	are not	(We **aren't**)	
They		(They **aren't**)	Italian.
He		(He **isn't**)	
She	is not	(She **isn't**)	
It		(It **isn't**)	

➡ page 145

A Complete this information about Maristella with short forms of the verb *to be*.

My name'*s*¹ Maristella. I........² Brazilian and I........³ from São Paulo. I........⁴ a research analyst for an investment bank in New York. I........⁵ married with two children, a boy and a girl. They........⁶ at high school in Scarsdale. My husband........⁷ American and he........⁸ a doctor. My sister........⁹ in New York, too. She........¹⁰ a student at Columbia University. We........¹¹ all interested in sports and movies. My son........¹² a good tennis player.

B 🔊 CD1.10 Listen and check your answers.

C Complete this chart about yourself. Then introduce yourself to a partner.

1	Name	....	4	Nationality	....
2	Job	I'm a(n)	5	Interests	....
3	City	I'm from	6	Favourite sports	....

D Now write a paragraph about your partner. Use the text in Exercise A as a model.

My partner's name is ...

E Complete these sentences with negative forms of *to be*.

1 She's Russian, but *she isn't* from Moscow.
2 They're Japanese, but .... from Tokyo.
3 He's German, but .... from Munich.
4 I'm in sales, but .... the manager.
5 The office is in Paris, but .... in the centre.
6 Her name is Sophia, but .... Italian.

UNIT 1 ▸▸ INTRODUCTIONS

F **Match the questions and answers about Sergio.**

1 Are you Spanish?
2 Are you a sales manager?
3 Are you married?
4 Is your wife a manager?
5 Is she Italian?

a) No, I'm a marketing manager.
b) No, she's Mexican.
c) No, I'm Italian.
d) No, she's a lawyer.
e) Yes, I am. That's a picture of my wife.

G **Work in pairs. Ask and answer questions about Maristella in Exercise A.**

A: *Is Maristella American?*
B: *No, she isn't. She's Brazilian.*

LANGUAGE FOCUS 2
a/an **with jobs;**
wh- **questions**

- We use *a* before words beginning with a consonant sound (e.g. *b, c,* etc.):
  a receptionist
- We use *an* before words beginning with a vowel sound (e.g. *a, e,* etc.):
  an architect
- We do not use *a* or *an* with plural nouns:
  They are architects.
- We use question words such as *what, who* and *where* to ask for information:
  '***What**'s your job?*' '*I'm **a** lawyer.*' (NOT *I'm lawyer.*)
  '***What**'s your wife's job?*' '*She's **an** engineer.*'
  '***Where**'s your office?*' '*It's in New York.*'
  '***Who**'s your boss?*' '*Julio Cordón.*'
  '***Where** are you from?*' '*I'm Russian.*' / '***Where**'s he from?*' '*He's Spanish.*'

➡ page 145

A **Write the correct article (*a*/*an*) for each job.**

accountant   architect   artist   cashier   consultant   director   doctor
engineer   executive   journalist   lawyer   manager   office worker
optician   personal assistant (PA)   pilot   receptionist   research analyst
sales assistant   technician   telephone operator   trainee

B **Work in pairs. Talk about your job and the jobs of your family and friends.**

I'm a sales manager. My husband/wife/partner is a doctor. My brother is an engineer. My sister is a housewife. My friend is an architect.

C 🔊 **CD1.11 –1.13 Listen to three people talking about their jobs and complete this chart.**

	Pierre	Gustavo	Silvia
1 What is his/her job?		a lawyer	
2 Where is he/she from?	Switzerland		
3 Where is his/her office?	Singapore		Rome
4 What does his/her partner do?		a journalist	a househusband

D **Work in pairs. Ask and answer questions about the three people in Exercise C.**

UNIT 1 ▸▸ INTRODUCTIONS

SKILLS
Introducing yourself and others

Watch the conversations on the DVD-ROM.

A 🔊 **CD1.14 –1.16** Listen to three conversations. Decide whether these statements are true (T) or false (F). Correct the false ones.

CD 1.14
1 Jim Davis works in the advertising department.
2 Paula will be an intern in the company for three weeks.

CD 1.15
3 Lucy Collins works in finance.
4 Jonathan Ross is Jenny Bradshaw's assistant.

CD 1.16
5 Jeff and Susan work for different companies.
6 Jeff's boss is Richard Mason.

B 🔊 **CD1.14 –1.16** Listen again and complete these extracts. Use the Useful language box below to help you.

CD 1.14
Bob: Hello, Jim. ....^{1} is our new intern, Paula Atkins.
Jim: ....^{2} to meet you, Paula.

CD 1.15
Lucy: Good morning. My ....^{3} Lucy Collins. I'm a finance director. I work for a supermarket group.
Jenny: Hello, I'm Jenny Bradshaw. I'm a ....^{4} of public relations. I work for a big media company.
Lucy: How do you ....^{5}?
Jenny: Nice to meet you.
Lucy: Let me ....^{6} you to my ....^{7}, Jonathan Ross. He's my assistant.
Jonathan: ....^{8} to meet you, Jenny.

CD 1.16
Jeff: Hi, I'm Jeff. I'm ....^{9} Sales.
Susan: Hi, Jeff, I'm Susan. I ....^{10} in Human Resources.
Jeff: How are things ....^{11} in your department?
Susan: Pretty good. I enjoy my work. My ....^{12} are really nice, and I like my boss.

C Work in pairs or groups of three. Look at the audio scripts of the conversations on pages 158–159. Choose a conversation and practise it.

D Work in pairs. You meet over breakfast in a hotel where a business conference is being held. You do not know each other. Role-play the situation. Use phrases from the Useful language box to help you.

Student A: Turn to page 134.
Student B: Turn to page 140.

USEFUL LANGUAGE

INTRODUCING PEOPLE
I'm … / My name's …
I work for …
This is …
He's/She's in sales / with Nokia.

ASKING QUESTIONS
Where are you from?
What's the reason for your visit?
How's your business doing?
What's the weather like in your country?
Where are you staying?
What's your hotel like?

OFFERING A DRINK
Would you like a drink?
How about a cup of tea / a coffee?
Another drink?

REPLYING
I'm from …
The weather's (quite) good/hot/cold in my country.
I'm staying at [name of hotel].
I'm here to [reason for visit].
The room is [describe the room].
We're doing OK / quite well / very well.

Thanks very much. I'd love one.
Yes, please. / No, thanks.

GREETINGS
How do you do?
Pleased to meet you.
Nice to meet you.
Good to see you again.

SAYING GOODBYE
See you later.
Nice talking to you.
Have a good day.

A job fair in Singapore

A film company is looking for a sales assistant

Background

You and a colleague work for the Treadlight Film Company, a television production company. You are both at a job fair in Singapore. You want to find an assistant for your sales manager in Singapore. On a website, you read information about three young people at the fair looking for a job in sales. Read about them, then do the task below.

Jenny Wong
- **Age:** 20 **Born:** Taiwan
- **Education:** high-school certificate
- **Work experience:** sales assistant in bookshop
- **Languages:** fluent Chinese, basic knowledge of English
- **Personality/appearance:** elegant, friendly
- **Interests:** music, international cinema

Cindy Tan
- **Age:** 21
- **Born:** Hong Kong
- **Education:** university graduate (geography)
- **Work experience:** –
- **Languages:** fluent Chinese, good standard of English
- **Personality/appearance:** well-dressed, confident
- **Interests:** conversation, people

David Chong
- **Age:** 24
- **Born:** Singapore
- **Education:** university graduate (computing)
- **Work experience:** website designer
- **Languages:** fluent Chinese and English
- **Personality/appearance:** serious, hard-working
- **Interests:** computer games, karate

Task

Work in pairs.

1. **Talk about the people in the profiles.**

   Jenny Wong is from Taiwan.
   She isn't a university graduate.
   Cindy Tan has no work experience.
   David Chong is interested in computer games.

2. **Imagine you have time to talk to only one of the candidates. Decide which person you want to meet.**

   A: I'd like to talk to .... because ....
   B: I agree / don't agree. I think ....

3. **You meet at the job fair and talk about the sales position.**

   Student A
   You are a director of Treadlight Film Company. Ask the job seeker questions based on these prompts:
   - Where / you come / from?
   - Why / you want / job?
   - What / your best quality?
   - What / your favourite film or television programme?
   - Why / you like the film / television programme?

   Student B
   You are a job seeker. Think of answers to Student A's questions.

Writing

Write an e-mail to your boss about the person you talked to at the conference.

→ *Writing file* page 126

Hi Bob,

I met an interesting person at a conference in Singapore. Here is some information about him/her …

UNIT 2 Work and leisure

'If you like what you do, it's not work.'
Maria Fiorini Ramirez, US business executive

OVERVIEW

VOCABULARY 1
Days, months, dates

READING
Describing your routine

LANGUAGE FOCUS 1
Present simple

VOCABULARY 2
Leisure activities

LISTENING
Working and relaxing

LANGUAGE FOCUS 2
Adverbs and expressions of frequency

SKILLS
Talking about work and leisure

CASE STUDY
Hudson Design Inc.

STARTING UP

A What do people want from work? Discuss in pairs.

a large office, nice colleagues, …

B Work in pairs. Make three word partnerships in each section to find out what four people want from work.

1	high	colleagues	2	company	phone	3	friendly	security	4	fast	facilities
	long	salary		mobile	facilities		travel	opportunities		flexible	promotion
	helpful	holidays		parking	car		job	boss		sports	hours

🔊 CD1.17–1.20 Now listen and check the word partnerships they use.

C Match six of the word partnerships in Exercise B to their meanings (1–6).

1 a lot of money — *high salary*
2 a lot of time away from work
3 good people to work with
4 the chance to go to different places on business
5 move quickly to a higher position at work
6 you can change the times when you start and finish work

D What do *you* want from work? Use the word partnerships from Exercise B and make a list. Work in pairs. Compare your lists and choose the five most important things.

UNIT 2 ▸▸ WORK AND LEISURE

VOCABULARY 1
Days, months, dates

A Put the days of the week in order. Which days are 'the weekend'?

Friday ☐   Monday ☑1   Saturday ☐   Tuesday ☐
Sunday ☐   Thursday ☐   Wednesday ☐

B Write the months of the year under the correct seasons.

June   April   January   August   December   February
May   October   March   September   November   July

Spring	Summer	Autumn	Winter

C Complete these time phrases with *in*, *at* or *on*. Then write the phrases under the correct preposition in the table below.

1 ...*at*... night   4 .... Thursday   7 .... June
2 .... the autumn   5 .... the afternoon   8 .... New Year
3 .... 15th February 6 .... Tuesday evening 9 .... the weekend

in (x3)   **at** (x3)   **on** (x3)
                   at night

D 🔊 CD1.21 Listen and check your answers to Exercise C.

E Complete these sentences with *in*, *at* or *on*.

1 We have a lot of big orders ...*in*... March.
2 The office closes for three days .... New Year.
3 There is an important meeting .... 15th June.
4 The CEO visits our branch .... the summer.
5 We deliver large goods .... Monday afternoons.

F Work in pairs. When are you busy during the day, week and year? What are the quiet times?

A: *When are you busy during the day?*
B: *I'm very busy in the morning. When are the quiet times for you?*
A: *Business is quiet in the summer. Which days are you busy during the week?*
B: *I'm always busy on Mondays.*

G Write about yourself, your company or your school.

- When are the busy times?
- When are the quiet times?
- Which moments in the year do you particularly enjoy? Why?

See the DVD-ROM for the i-Glossary.

UNIT 2 ▸▸ WORK AND LEISURE

READING
Describing your routine

A Before you read the article, discuss these questions.

1 What do you think is a typical day in the life of the CEO of a big company?
2 How much time do CEOs spend travelling?
3 Do CEOs need holidays?

B Look through this article. Can you find any of the ideas you discussed in Exercise A?

FT

Business diary: Eugene Kaspersky
by Mary Watkins

Eugene Kaspersky is CEO of Kaspersky Lab, the Russian security software company. The company is based in Moscow and has offices in 29 countries. Its main competitor is Symantec. Most of the company's sales are outside Russia.

Kaspersky spends 50% of his time in Moscow, but the other 50% he travels. He is often away for more than three weeks at a time. When he is away, he attends meetings, goes to trade shows and sometimes gives presentations. When he is in the office, he spends time talking informally to colleagues – at their desks or in the company restaurant.

The Moscow office is like a big family. Many people in the office are friends. Some go on holiday together. Everyone dresses informally. Kaspersky normally wears shirts and jeans, but he has a suit for important meetings with presidents and prime ministers.

In Moscow, he does not get up early, especially after a business trip. "On some business trips, I only get three or four hours' sleep a night, so I need to relax," says Kaspersky. At the end of a busy Moscow office day, he goes to the gym with his personal trainer. "It's a great way to relax after a busy day in the office." If he can, he also takes two days off a month.

Holidays are important too. "In winter, I go skiing. In the summer, I often go to the mountains, where I can't use the Internet or my mobile phone. But I can get a satellite connection."

C Answer these questions.

1 Is Kaspersky a formal or informal CEO?
2 Is most of his business in Russia or in other countries?
3 Does he work 24/7 (24 hours a day, seven days a week)?

D Decide whether these statements are true (T) or false (F). Correct the false ones.

1 Kaspersky travels a lot. T
2 He wears formal business clothes in the office.
3 He gets up early every day.
4 He goes to the gym after work.
5 He likes to have time to relax when he's in Moscow.
6 He only has holidays in summer.

E In each box, match the words that go together.

1	trade	a)	trip	5	attend	e)	presentations
2	business	b)	show	6	give	f)	skiing
3	personal	c)	day	7	spend	g)	meetings
4	office	d)	trainer	8	go	h)	time

F Work in pairs. Tell your partner about your day and your holidays.

I get up ...

I arrive at work/school at ...

For my holidays, I ...

LANGUAGE FOCUS 1
Present simple

- We use the present simple to talk about habits and work routines.
  *I **travel** on business.*   *We **work** long hours.*

- We add an **-s** to the verb for *he/she/it*.
  *He **attends** meetings.*   *She **works** in Tokyo.*

- We use *do* and *does* in negatives and in questions.
  *They **don't** work late.*   *She **doesn't** leave work until 8 p.m.*
  ***Do** you drive to work?*   ***Does** he travel in his job?*

➡ page 146

A Darren Throop works for Entertainment One, a media company in Toronto, Canada. Complete the article below about his working day using the verbs from the box.

| checks | does | drives | finishes | ~~gets~~ | has | likes | makes | spends | travels |

Darren Throop ...gets...¹ up at 6 a.m. and ....² some exercise in the gym in his house. At about 6.30, he ....³ breakfast for his two daughters. Then he ....⁴ his e-mails in his home office. He ....⁵ to work. At lunch time, he ....⁶ a salad at his desk. At work, he ....⁷ a lot of time in meetings and on conference calls. He ....⁸ his office day at about 5 p.m. He ....⁹ on business a lot, so he ....¹⁰ to spend all his free time with his family.

B Complete this information about Masami Kimura. Use the correct form of the verbs in brackets.

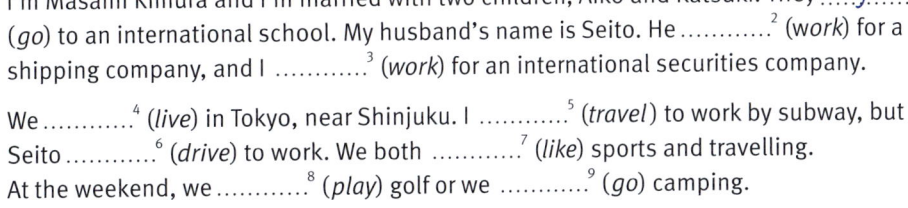

I'm Masami Kimura and I'm married with two children, Aiko and Katsuki. They ...go...¹ (*go*) to an international school. My husband's name is Seito. He ....² (*work*) for a shipping company, and I ....³ (*work*) for an international securities company.

We ....⁴ (*live*) in Tokyo, near Shinjuku. I ....⁵ (*travel*) to work by subway, but Seito ....⁶ (*drive*) to work. We both ....⁷ (*like*) sports and travelling. At the weekend, we ....⁸ (*play*) golf or we ....⁹ (*go*) camping.

C Write a paragraph like the one in Exercise B about yourself.

UNIT 2 ▸▸ WORK AND LEISURE

VOCABULARY 2
Leisure activities

A Complete the leisure activities below using words from the box. Sometimes more than one answer is possible.

| going to   listening to   playing   watching |

1 *playing* golf
2 .... TV
3 .... restaurants
4 .... music (on my iPod)
5 .... tennis
6 .... the cinema
7 .... football
8 .... the gym
9 .... concerts
10 .... the guitar
11 .... DVDs
12 .... computer games

B Talk about your leisure activities. Use the verbs in box 1 and the time phrases in box 2.

I love running at the weekend.
I like going to the cinema on Friday night.

1	love like quite like don't like	2	at the weekend on Friday/Saturday night in the summer/winter in August/December in the morning/afternoon/evening

See the **DVD-ROM** for the i-Glossary.

LISTENING
Working and relaxing

Ros Pomeroy

A ◉ CD1.22 Listen to the first part of an interview with Ros Pomeroy. What does she like most about her job?

B ◉ CD1.22 Listen again and complete these notes.

Ros can be:
- in ....¹
- ....² a workshop or a ....³
- in her own ....⁴ in front of a ....⁵ screen
- on the ....⁶

C ◉ CD1.23 Listen to the second part of the interview and answer these questions.
1 What two things sometimes make it difficult to find enough time for leisure?
2 Overall, does Ros have enough time for leisure?

Watch the interview on the **DVD-ROM**.

D In pairs, predict what Ros likes doing to relax.

E ◉ CD1.24 Listen to the final part and check your answers.

F In pairs, discuss what you like doing to relax.

UNIT 2 ▸▸ WORK AND LEISURE

LANGUAGE FOCUS 2
Adverbs and expressions of frequency

- We use adverbs of frequency with the present simple to say how often we do things.
  never   sometimes   often   usually   always
- They often go:
  - before the main verb: *Karla **sometimes works** from home.*
  - after the verb *to be*: *I **am never** at work before 9 a.m.*
- Expressions of frequency can go at the beginning or the end of a sentence.
  ***Two nights a week**, he works late at the office.*
  *He works from home **once a month**.*

→ page 146

A Write the words in brackets in the correct place in these sentences.

1 She gets up early. (*usually*) — *usually*
2 They start their first meeting at nine o'clock. (*always*)
3 We are late for meetings. (*never*)
4 I am busy in the afternoon. (*often*)
5 The office closes at 3 p.m. (*sometimes*)

B Read these pairs of sentences. Cross out the incorrect word in sentence b) of each pair.

1 a) He reads the papers every day.
   b) He *always / sometimes* reads the papers.
2 a) We eat in the company cafeteria four times a week.
   b) We *usually / sometimes* eat in the company cafeteria.
3 a) I work late once a month.
   b) I *usually / sometimes* work late.
4 a) The managers don't go to business dinners at the weekend.
   b) The managers *never / sometimes* go to business dinners at the weekend.
5 a) The Company Director travels on business twice a week.
   b) The Company Director *always / often* travels on business.

C 🔊 CD1.25–1.27 An interviewer asks three people about their typical day. Listen and complete this table.

	Mark	Isabelle	Dan
1 What do you do when you get to work?	Say hello to colleagues, check e-mail		
2 Where do you have lunch?			
3 How often do you travel on business?			
4 What do you do at the weekend?			

D Work in pairs. Ask and answer the questions in Exercise C.

E Work in pairs. Ask and answer these questions. Add your own questions.

How often do you ...

1 play sports?
2 use a mobile phone?
3 drive to work/college/university?
4 go to a gym / fitness centre?
5 entertain at home?
6 go on business trips?
7 go abroad on holiday?
8 buy a newspaper/magazine?

UNIT 2 ▶▶ WORK AND LEISURE

SKILLS
Talking about work and leisure

A Match the questions (1–6) to the answers (a–f).

1. What do you do in your job?
2. What do you like best about your job?
3. How many hours a week do you work/study?
4. When do you finish work?
5. Do you meet your colleagues after work?
6. What do you do in your free time?

a) Usually about six o'clock.
b) I manage a web team at an IT company.
c) From time to time. We sometimes go for a meal.
d) I play golf.
e) I work flexible hours, which is great.
f) Between 30 and 35 hours.

B Work in pairs. Ask and answer the questions in Exercise A.

C 🔊 CD1.28 Listen to a conversation between Pat and Tim. Tick (✓) the questions and answers from Exercise A that you hear.

D 🔊 CD1.28 Complete the extract below from the conversation using the words from the box. Then listen again to check.

| enjoy | interested | into | ~~love~~ | love | playing | really | watching |

Pat: What do you do in your free time?

Tim: I ...love...¹ sports. I ....² like karate and I ....³ playing golf. But I'm not really ....⁴ in watching sports on TV. I don't ....⁵ watching professional golf, for example. What about you?

Pat: I like golf too, but I'm also ....⁶ French cinema and jazz music. I like ....⁷ DVDs and I really enjoy going to concerts. I also like ....⁸ the guitar. I'm interested in computer games, but I'm not very good at them.

Watch the conversation on the DVD-ROM.

E Work in pairs. Tell your partner how you feel about your work or studies. Use phrases from the Useful language box below.

I really enjoy having flexible hours. *I don't enjoy doing overtime.*
I like my boss/colleagues. *I don't like long meetings.*

F Work in pairs. Ask and answer questions about what you do in your free time. Use phrases from the Useful language box.

A: *What do you do at the weekend?* B: *I usually visit friends.*

G Change partners. Tell your new partner about your first partner's likes and dislikes.

John likes playing football on Saturdays. He doesn't like writing e-mails.

USEFUL LANGUAGE

ASKING QUESTIONS

What do you do {
- at work / in your studies?
- during the day?
- in your free time?
- at the weekend?
- after work?
- in the evening?
}

Do you like …?
How often do you …?

Yes, I do. / No, I don't.

EXPRESSING FEELINGS

I like/love …	I don't like …
I'm really into …	I'm not into …
I'm keen on …	He isn't really keen on …
I really enjoy …	She doesn't enjoy …
I'm interested in …	We aren't interested in …

HUDSON DESIGN INC.

Why are staff unhappy at a design business?

Background

Hudson Design is based in New York. It designs websites for companies. Hudson's head office is in an expensive area of the city. It is on the 20th floor, and staff have a beautiful view of New York. The company is making a lot of money. However, many employees are unhappy, and the owners are worried that some will leave. A team from Human Resources is interviewing people in different departments: a receptionist, a website developer, a writer and a graphic designer.

🔊 **CD1.29** Listen to a member of Human Resources interviewing one of the company's employees. Discuss what the employee likes and dislikes about his work.
In your opinion, how should he solve his problem?

Task

1. Work in pairs.
   Student A: See right.
   Student B: Turn to page 135 and choose one role.
   Read your role card and prepare for the interview.
2. Do the interview.
3. Meet as two groups: interviewers and employees. Make a list of the problems and decide which ones are important.
4. Meet as one group and choose three working conditions to change at Hudson Design.

Student A

Interviewer (Human Resources)

Interview a staff member and ask questions. Note down the answers.

- Position: (What / job?)
- Routine: (What / do / each day?)
- Hours: (What / hours / work?)
- Breaks: (How often / breaks?)
- Lunch: (When and where / have lunch?)
- Feelings about job: (What / like / not like about job?)

Writing

Imagine that you work for Hudson Design. Write an e-mail to Human Resources. Tell them what you:

- like about your job
- don't like about your job
- want to change in the company.

➡ *Writing file* page 126

Case study 2

UNIT 3 Problems

'A problem is a chance for you to do your best.'
Duke Ellington (1899–1974), US composer and musician

OVERVIEW

VOCABULARY
Adjectives
too/enough

LISTENING
Typical work problems

READING
Workplace problems

LANGUAGE FOCUS 1
Present simple: negatives and questions

LANGUAGE FOCUS 2
have
some and *any*

SKILLS
Telephoning: solving problems

CASE STUDY
High-Style Business Rentals

STARTING UP

1 always being busy
2 difficult customers
3 changes to orders
4 computer crashes
5 rude people
6 missing documents
7 delivery delays
8 machinery not working

A What sort of problems might these people have at work?

a) an office worker
b) a factory worker
c) a shop/sales assistant
d) a call-centre worker

Look at the problems on the left. Which do you think go with which person?

B 🔊 CD1.30–1.33 Listen to four people. Look back at Exercise A. Where does each of them work (a–d), and which problems do they mention (1–8)?

1 *Person c, problems 7, ...*

C What problems do you have at work / in your studies?

VOCABULARY
Adjectives; *too/enough*

A Complete the sentences below using adjectives from the box.

| broken | clean | confusing | fast | ~~flexible~~ | noisy |

1 Our employees enjoy having *flexible* hours.
2 The new sales assistant got a .... promotion.
3 We want a .... and well-furnished apartment.
4 Their old printer is .... , so they want a new one.
5 The instructions are not clear. They are very ....
6 When the machinery in the factory starts, it is very ....

22

UNIT 3 ▸▸ PROBLEMS

B **Work in pairs. Ask and answer questions about adjectives and their opposites.**

Student A: Turn to page 130.
Student B: Turn to page 137.

C **Look at these sentences.**

The <u>bed</u> is **too** hard. It **isn't** soft **enough**.

The <u>seats</u> **aren't** wide **enough**. They're **too** narrow.

Write sentences using *too* or *enough* and adjectives from Exercise B relating to the underlined words.

1 The <u>report</u> doesn't give much information. (*too/enough*)

   It's too short. / It isn't long enough.

2 I can't carry these <u>suitcases</u>. (*too*)
3 I can't meet you at six o'clock <u>in the morning</u>. (*too*)
4 I don't want this <u>car</u>. Its top speed is only 100 kilometres per hour. (*too/enough*)
5 Don't take any visitors to those <u>areas</u> late at night. (*too/enough*)
6 That <u>camera</u> doesn't fit in my pocket. (*too/enough*)
7 The <u>hotel room</u> is $1,000 dollars a night. (*too/enough*)
8 I can't sleep because of the <u>music</u> from the party. (*too/enough*)

See the **DVD-ROM** for the i-Glossary.

D **Work in pairs. Tell each other about some of the problems you have where you work or study.**

My office is too small. My office isn't big enough.

LISTENING
Typical work problems

Jeremy Keeley

A 🔊 **CD1.34** Jeremy Keeley, a specialist in change leadership, talks about problems he has at work. Listen to the first part of the interview and decide whether these statements are true (T) or false (F). Correct the false ones.

1 Jeremy often works with a large number of people.
2 His clients have quite complicated problems.
3 Jeremy's biggest problem is having enough time to do a good job.
4 He also faces urgent requests for help when he is already very busy.

B 🔊 **CD1.35** Listen to the second part, in which Jeremy talks about the biggest problems in companies, and complete these notes.

- Biggest problem – amount of ....¹ they have to go through at speed.
- Second problem – difficult to plan their needs and resources (staff, ...², ...³, money they need to satisfy their customers).
- Another problem – customers expect them to reduce ....⁴ at the same time as companies have increasing ....⁵.

Watch the interview on the **DVD-ROM**.

C 🔊 **CD1.36** Listen to the third part of the interview and answer these questions.

1 What sorts of problem is Jeremy asked to solve?
2 What was the problem Jeremy had to solve?
3 Which different groups did he bring together to solve the problem?

UNIT 3 ▸▸ PROBLEMS

READING
Workplace problems

A Which of these adjectives describe work in a call centre?

> badly paid   boring   interesting   noisy   quiet   relaxing   stressful   well paid

B Three call-centre workers answer the question 'What are the biggest problems for you at work?'. Read their replies.

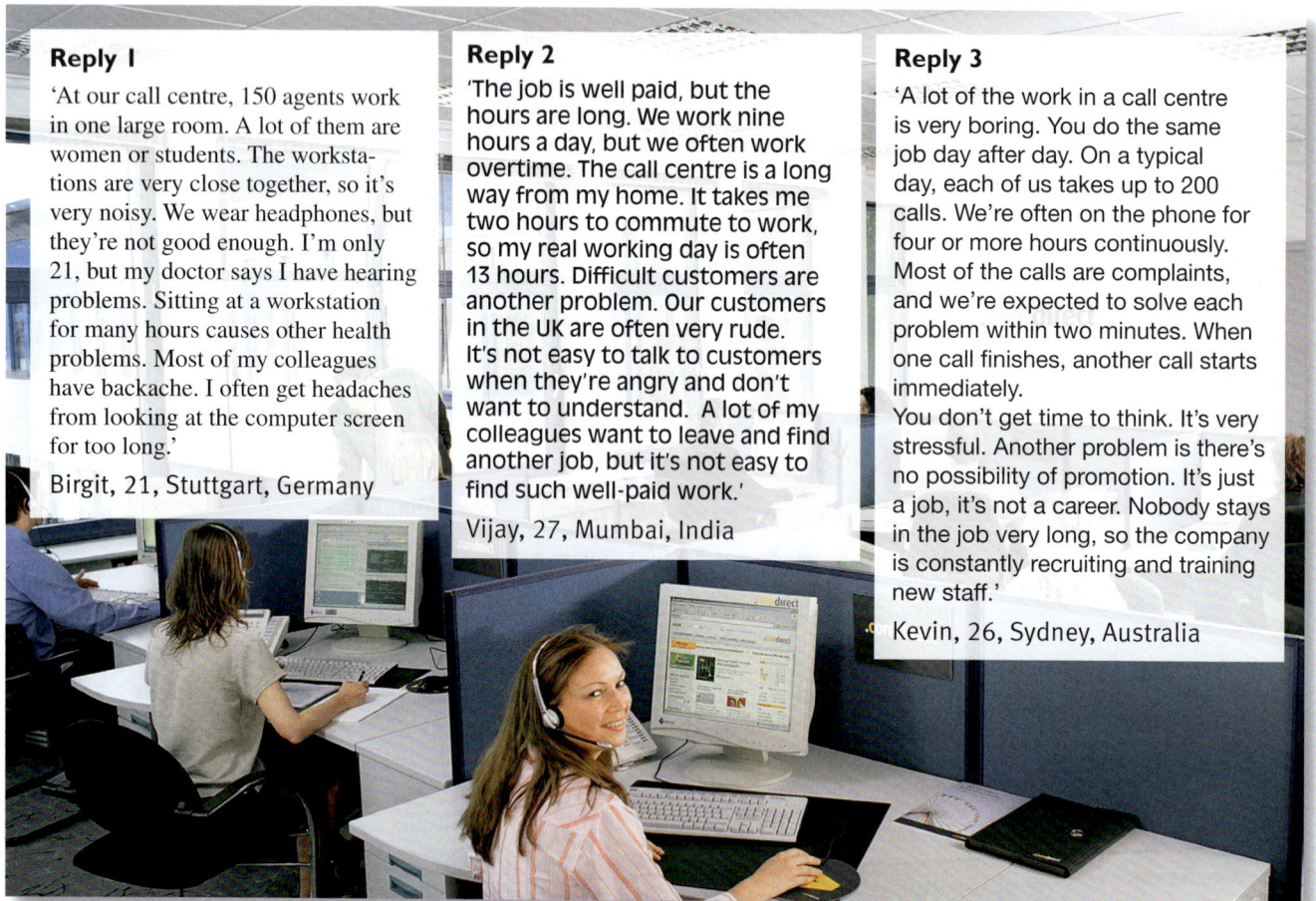

Reply 1

'At our call centre, 150 agents work in one large room. A lot of them are women or students. The workstations are very close together, so it's very noisy. We wear headphones, but they're not good enough. I'm only 21, but my doctor says I have hearing problems. Sitting at a workstation for many hours causes other health problems. Most of my colleagues have backache. I often get headaches from looking at the computer screen for too long.'

Birgit, 21, Stuttgart, Germany

Reply 2

'The job is well paid, but the hours are long. We work nine hours a day, but we often work overtime. The call centre is a long way from my home. It takes me two hours to commute to work, so my real working day is often 13 hours. Difficult customers are another problem. Our customers in the UK are often very rude. It's not easy to talk to customers when they're angry and don't want to understand. A lot of my colleagues want to leave and find another job, but it's not easy to find such well-paid work.'

Vijay, 27, Mumbai, India

Reply 3

'A lot of the work in a call centre is very boring. You do the same job day after day. On a typical day, each of us takes up to 200 calls. We're often on the phone for four or more hours continuously. Most of the calls are complaints, and we're expected to solve each problem within two minutes. When one call finishes, another call starts immediately.
You don't get time to think. It's very stressful. Another problem is there's no possibility of promotion. It's just a job, it's not a career. Nobody stays in the job very long, so the company is constantly recruiting and training new staff.'

Kevin, 26, Sydney, Australia

C Look at the chart and tick (✓) the problems the call-centre workers talk about in the replies. Who talks about each problem? Write Birgit (B), Vijay (V) or Kevin (K).

Problems		Name	Problems		Name
long working day	✓	V	angry customers		
breaks too short			low pay		
long hours at workstation			no time between calls		
boring work			high staff turnover		
no promotion			a lot of noise		

D Which three physical problems are mentioned in Birgit's reply?

E Underline the adjectives from Exercise A in the replies.

F Work in pairs. Ask and answer questions about problems in your place of study or workplace.

A: *What are the biggest problems for you at work/college?*
B: *One problem is … Another problem is …*

UNIT 3 ▸▸ PROBLEMS

LANGUAGE FOCUS 1
Present simple: negatives and questions

- To form the present simple negative of most verbs, we use *don't/doesn't* + verb.
- In present simple questions, we use *do/does*.

Negatives
They **don't** come to work on time.
He **doesn't** go to meetings.

Questions
Does he work well with colleagues?
Where do you work?

➡ page 147

A Work in pairs. Match the questions (1–6) to the answers (a–f).

1 What do you think about the new boss?
2 What time does the meeting start?
3 Where does she live?
4 Why does he need the money?
5 Who do I report to?
6 When do I finish work?

a) Peter. He's your line manager.
b) He has to pay for the office party.
c) You can leave at five o'clock.
d) She's very efficient.
e) In the city centre.
f) It starts at two o'clock.

B Put these words in the correct order to make questions.

1 weekend / work / they / Do / at / the / ?   *Do they work at the weekend?*
2 Pierre / in / sales / Does / work / ?
3 you / do / travel / abroad / How / often / ?
4 you / spell / How / *business* / do / ?
5 finish / does / the / meeting / When / ?

C Ask and answer these questions.

Student A: Turn to page 132.   Student B: Turn to page 144.

1 What time / start work?   *What time do you start work?*
2 When / finish work?
3 Where / work?
4 Who / report to?
5 How often / work at the weekend?

D Make negative sentences. Use *don't* (*do not*) or *doesn't* (*does not*).

1 I like meetings. (*presentations*)
   I like meetings, but I don't like presentations.
2 We waste a lot of paper. (*electricity*)
3 They agree about most things. (*money*)
4 Susan sends a lot of e-mails. (*faxes*)
5 Our management team discusses business strategy. (*employee problems*)

E Tick (✓) the sentences that are true for you. Change the other ones to make them true. Then compare and discuss your sentences in pairs.

1 I agree with my manager about everything.
2 I don't work in teams very often.
3 I always come to work/college on time.
4 I don't like giving presentations.
5 I never take work home in the evening or at the weekend.

25

UNIT 3 ▸▸ PROBLEMS

LANGUAGE FOCUS 2
have;
some and *any*

- We use *have* to talk about possession.
  I **have** a new printer, but it doesn't work very well.
  The office **doesn't have** a lift.
  '**Do** you **have** a problem with training?' 'Yes, we **do**.' / 'No, we **don't**.'

- We use *some* with plurals in positive sentences.
  We have **some** problems with deliveries.

- We use *any* with plurals in questions and negative sentences.
  Do you have **any** meetings today?

- In British English, we often use *have got*.
  The office **hasn't got** a lift.
  We **haven't got** any large boxes.

  ➡ page 147

A Make sentences about what Marco has and doesn't have.

1 *Marco has a company car. He doesn't have a sat-nav.*

1 a company car ✓   a sat-nav ✗
2 an iPhone ✗   an iPad ✓
3 an interesting job ✓   a high salary ✗
4 a nice boss ✗   some great colleagues ✓
5 a desktop computer at work ✗   a laptop ✓

B Complete these questions with *does have* and *do have*.

1 *Do* you *have* a new mobile phone?
2 What kind of car .... she .... ?
3 .... the company .... a restaurant?
4 .... all the rooms .... air conditioning?
5 .... I .... time to finish this?

C Work in pairs. Look at the list in Exercise A. Tell each other what you have and what you don't have.

D Work in pairs. Do a survey to find out what your colleagues/friends have.

1 Prepare five questions, e.g. *Do you have an iPod?*
2 Ask three people your survey questions.
3 Give the results to the class, e.g. *Two people have iPods*.

SKILLS
Telephoning:
solving
problems

A ◉ CD1.37 Listen to the conversation between Marcia and Harry. Answer these questions.

1 Why is Marcia phoning Harry?
2 How do you spell the name of the new marketing assistant?

B ◉ CD1.37 Listen again. What does Marcia say to:

1 introduce herself?
2 ask Harry to spell the man's name?
3 ask Harry to give the information again?
4 end the conversation?

Check your answers by looking at the audio script on page 160.

UNIT 3 ▸▸ PROBLEMS

C 🔊 CD1.38–1.41 **Listen to four phone calls. Match the calls (1–4) to these problems (a–d).**

a) There is a problem with the invoice. ☐
b) The date of the meeting is not suitable. ☐
c) The quantity is not correct. ☐
d) There are no instructions. ☐

D 🔊 CD1.38–1.41 **Listen again and complete these sentences.**

1 I can't meet your ...., Vanessa Gordon, next Wednesday.
2 I'm sure we can .... another time.
3 It's about the .... of mobile phones.
4 Sorry about that. I'll .... with it immediately.
5 There are no .... in the package.
6 Sorry, I didn't .... that. Could you .... it, please?
7 Also, I think the .... are wrong.
8 I'll .... the matter and send you another ....

Watch the phone calls on the DVD-ROM.

E 🔊 CD1.38–1.41 **Look at the Useful language box below. Listen again and tick (✓) the expressions you hear.**

F **Work in pairs. Use these role cards to role-play a conversation. Use some of the expressions from the Useful language box.**

Student A	Student B
Sales Representative	**Customer**
• Answer the phone. • Ask for details. • Apologise for the first problem. • Apologise again and offer solutions. • Say goodbye.	• Introduce yourself. Say you have some problems with an order. • Give details of first problem (ordered grapefruit juice, not orange juice). • Give details of second problem (want 1,000 bottles, not 100 cans, as soon as possible). • Thank the sales representative. • Say goodbye.

USEFUL LANGUAGE

GETTING THROUGH
Can I speak to (Jane Porter), please?
Call me back later, please.

ANSWERING
Hello, this is (Carl Fisher).
Good morning, (David Seymour) speaking.

INTRODUCING YOURSELF
Hello, this is David Patterson, Hudson Motors.
Hello, David Patterson here, Hudson Motors.

STATING THE PROBLEM
I have a problem (with …)
There are some problems with …

APOLOGISING
(Oh dear! I'm) sorry to hear that.
(I'm very) sorry about that.

GETTING DETAILS
Can you give me some more information?
Which model is it?

GIVING DETAILS
The invoice is incorrect.
It's the wrong part/model/item.
There's a piece missing.

FINDING SOLUTIONS
We can give you a refund.
We can send you new ones.
I can talk to the manager.

FINISHING THE CONVERSATION
Thank you.
Thanks for your help. Bye.

Case study 3

High-Style Business Rentals

Are the apartments as good as the adverts say?

Background

High-Style Business Rentals provides apartments for businesspeople who are working abroad. Guests usually want to stay in high-quality apartments which are well furnished and equipped.

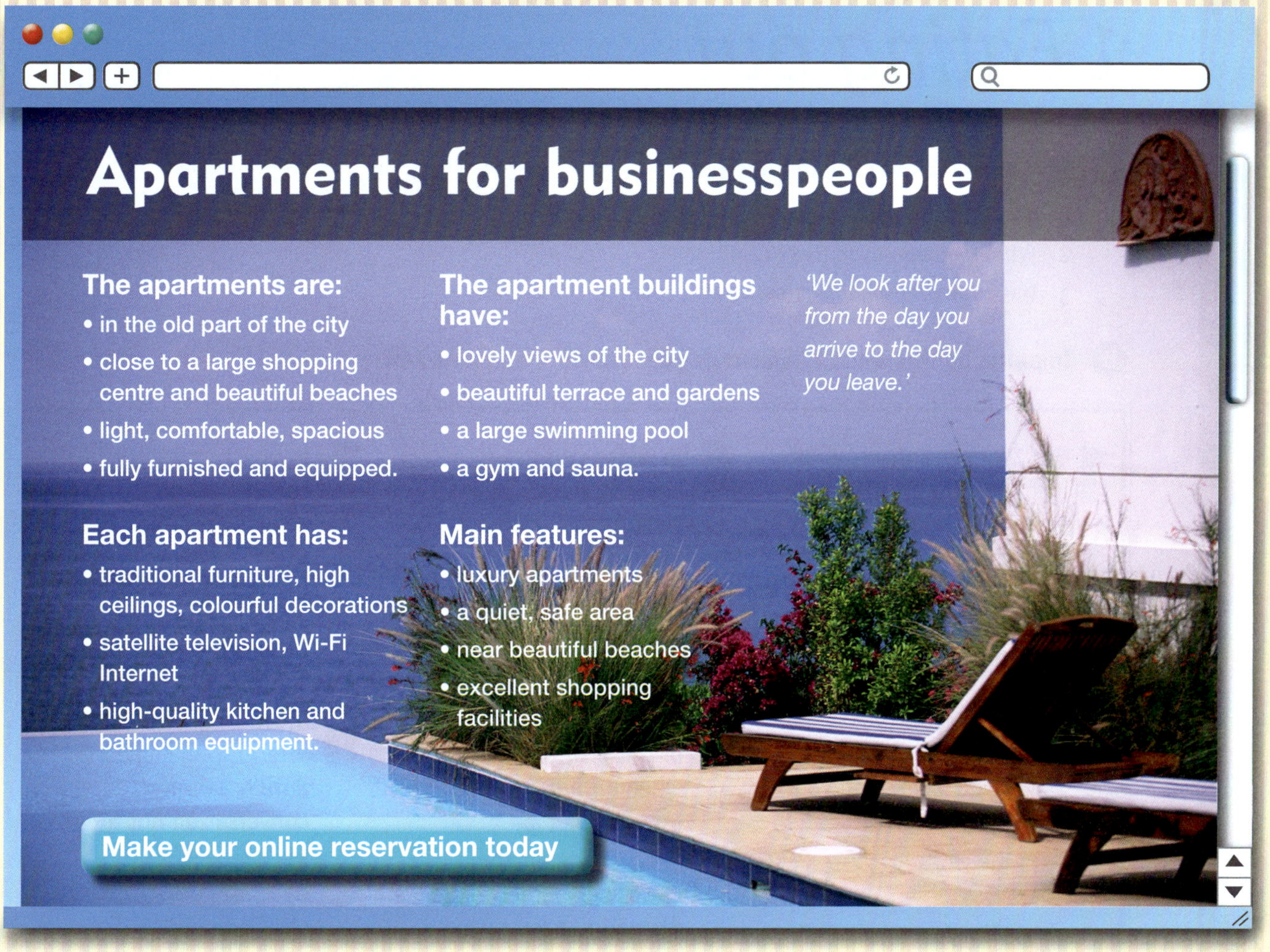

UNIT 3 •• PROBLEMS

Apartments for businesspeople

The apartments are:
- in the old part of the city
- close to a large shopping centre and beautiful beaches
- light, comfortable, spacious
- fully furnished and equipped.

Each apartment has:
- traditional furniture, high ceilings, colourful decorations
- satellite television, Wi-Fi Internet
- high-quality kitchen and bathroom equipment.

The apartment buildings have:
- lovely views of the city
- beautiful terrace and gardens
- a large swimming pool
- a gym and sauna.

Main features:
- luxury apartments
- a quiet, safe area
- near beautiful beaches
- excellent shopping facilities

'We look after you from the day you arrive to the day you leave.'

Make your online reservation today

🔊 CD1.42–1.45 Listen to comments from four High-Style guests and make notes.

Task

Work in pairs. You are guests at High-Style Business Rentals.

1 Compare what the online advertisement promises with the guests' experience of the apartments. Say what is different.

The apartments don't have lovely views. The rooms aren't colourful.

2 Student A: See below.   Student B: Turn to page 138.

Read your role cards. Then make the telephone call.

Student A

Guest at High-Style Business Rentals

Telephone the company's manager. You are very unhappy with your apartment.
Tell the manager that you want a:
- bigger apartment
- cheaper Internet price ($3 an hour)
- desk and more chairs in the sitting room
- new television with satellite programmes.

Writing

You are Diana Nolan, Manager at High-Style Business Rentals. Write an e-mail to Jason Parker at Head Office.

- Explain the problems you have with High-Style guests.
- Say that you want a meeting with the Director of Marketing.
- Say that you want to discuss High-Style's future advertising policy.

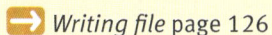 *Writing file page 126*

WORKING ACROSS CULTURES

1 Eating out

A In groups, answer these questions.

1. What is your favourite dish?
2. What food don't you like to eat?
3. Have you ever made a mistake when dining? If so, what?

B In pairs, do this quiz. Then check your answers on page 144.

1 In which country is it OK to arrive up to 30 minutes late for dinner?
 a) Germany
 b) China
 c) Italy
 d) Denmark

2 In which country is it OK to fill your own glass after you have filled your guest's?
 a) the UK
 b) Korea
 c) Russia
 d) Japan

3 In which country is it a good idea to leave some food on your plate?
 a) Norway
 b) Malaysia
 c) Singapore
 d) Egypt

4 In which country is chewing gum *not* rude?
 a) Luxembourg
 b) the USA
 c) Singapore
 d) Switzerland

5 In Arab cultures, which of these should you avoid when eating?
 a) standing up
 b) drinking anything
 c) using your left hand
 d) eating a lot

6 Who usually pays for a business meal in France?
 a) the oldest person
 b) the host
 c) the guest
 d) Everyone shares it.

7 In which country is it common to go out to eat after 10 p.m.?
 a) Sweden
 b) Denmark
 c) Austria
 d) Spain

8 In which country is interrupting someone during a dinner conversation not rude?
 a) Canada
 b) Brazil
 c) Germany
 d) Japan

9 In which country is a strong handshake not good?
 a) the USA
 b) the UK
 c) Germany
 d) the Philippines

C 🔊 CD1.46 Listen to the introduction at a workshop on dining. In the first column of this chart, complete the seven topics that the speaker wants to look at.

	Topics	Examples
1		
2		Germany: wait until you are shown where to sit
3		
4	What you use to eat	
5		
6	Body language	Germany: bad to rest your elbows on the table
7		

D 🔊 CD1.46 Listen again and complete the examples in the second column.

WORKING ACROSS CULTURES ›› EATING OUT

Task

1 The Chinese prefer to entertain in public places rather than at home. Look at the notes for guests on the right.

2 Make notes for a short talk giving advice on dining habits for some foreign businesspeople coming to your country or a country you know well. You can use the notes on the right or the headings in the Topics column of the chart in Exercise C to help you.

3 In pairs, give your talks to each other.

- Arrive on time.
- Dress well.
- Greet the eldest person first.
- Learn how to use chopsticks.
- Do not point with your chopsticks.
- Wait to be told where to sit.
- Wait for the host to begin eating first.
- Try everything that is offered to you.

UNIT A Revision

1 Introductions

VOCABULARY

Choose the best word to complete each sentence.

1 Mr Dubois lives in Germany, but he comes from *French / France*.
2 Both Aslan and Zeynep are *Turkish / Turkey*.
3 Is JVC a *Japanese / Japan* company?
4 The new accountant is from *Kuwaiti / Kuwait*.
5 What's the capital of *Omani / Oman*?
6 Lloyds isn't *a USA / an American* bank.
7 The company's CEO is *the UK / British*.
8 We manufacture our products at a factory in *China / Chinese*.
9 The company closed its office in *Greece / Greek*.
10 Nokia isn't *a Sweden / Swedish* company!

TO BE

Complete the conversations below using the words from the box.

'm 'm not are are aren't is isn't

A: Where ………¹ you from?

B: I ………² from Poland – Warsaw. How about you? Are you Chinese?

A: No, I ………³. I come from Japan.

A: ………⁴ your co-workers American?

B: My boss ………⁵ American. He's from New York City. But my other co-workers ………⁶ American. They're French and German.

A: Excuse me. May I use this office for a few minutes?

B: I don't know. It ………⁷ my office. I don't work here. I'm visiting today!

A: Oh, sorry.

WH- QUESTIONS

Complete these questions with *What*, *Where* or *Who*.

1 ……… is Mr Santos from?   He's from Cuenca, Ecuador.
2 ……… is Lenore's job?   She's a manager.
3 ……… are you doing?   I'm writing an e-mail.
4 ……… is waiting outside?   Mr Jones and three colleagues.
5 ……… is the receptionist?   She's in the conference room.
6 ……… are you working with?   Ursula and Piet.

2 Work and leisure

VOCABULARY

Complete these sentences with *in*, *at* or *on*.

1 The new office opens .... 30th March.
2 All of our shops are open .... night.
3 Can we have a meeting .... Friday?
4 We always have our sales conference .... July.
5 We don't schedule meetings .... Monday mornings.
6 I sometimes work .... the weekend.
7 I usually visit my clients .... the afternoon.
8 I often start new projects .... the spring.
9 We always have a big office celebration .... New Year.

ADVERBS AND EXPRESSIONS OF FREQUENCY

Match the pairs of sentences.

1 He never wakes up before six.
2 He sometimes wakes up before six.
3 He often wakes up before six.
4 He usually wakes up before six.
5 He always wakes up before six.

a) On Mondays and Tuesdays, he wakes up at 5.45. Other days, he wakes up at 6.15.
b) Every day, he wakes up at 5.45.
c) On Mondays, he wakes up at 6.15. Other days, he wakes up at 5.45.
d) On Mondays, Tuesdays and Wednesdays, he wakes up at 5.45. Other days, he wakes up at 6.15.
e) Every day, he wakes up at 6.15.

SKILLS

Put the words in the correct order to make questions.

1 time / What / free / you / in / do / your / do / ?
2 do / finish / you / work / When / ?
3 about / What / like / do / best / you / job / your / ?
4 your / you / in / do / do / job / What / ?
5 Do / colleagues / your / you / after / meet / work / ?
6 work / How / you / hours / many / a / do / week / ?

WRITING

Write an e-mail (40–60 words) to a new colleague telling them about yourself. Use these topics to help you.

- company/college
- live
- nationality
- enjoy/don't enjoy
- married/single
- work
- hobbies/job
- name

UNIT A ›› REVISION

3 Problems

VOCABULARY

Write sentences with the opposite meaning. Use the words from the box and *too* or *enough*.

big confusing fast late noisy short ~~soft~~ wide

1 My chair is too hard. *My chair isn't soft enough.*
2 His hotel room is too small.
3 The office isn't quiet enough.
4 The report isn't clear enough.
5 Her laptop is too slow.
6 We weren't early enough to get seats on the train.
7 The spaces in the car park are too narrow.
8 The electrical cable isn't long enough.

PRESENT SIMPLE: NEGATIVES AND QUESTIONS

Complete this conversation with *does*, *doesn't*, *do* and *don't*.

A: ....^{1} you know where Mr Sato is?
B: He ....^{2} work in this office on Wednesdays.
A: Where ....^{3} he work?
B: At the factory. You can call him there on his mobile.
A: I ....^{4} have his mobile number. ....^{5} you have it?
B: Yes. It's 8477-3991.
A: Thanks. So what ....^{6} he do at the factory on Wednesdays?
B: He talks with the engineers.
A: ....^{7} he have an office at the factory?
B: No, he ....^{8}.

HAVE; SOME AND *ANY*

Complete the sentences below using the words from the box.

any do doesn't doesn't have don't have has have some

1 I .... a car, so I take the bus to work.
2 Do you have .... money?
3 Luke .... a pen. Can he borrow yours?
4 Lorraine .... a new computer.
5 The new office .... have a car park.
6 .... you have any time this afternoon?
7 We .... a staff meeting every Monday morning, and everyone hates it.
8 I have .... questions for you. Can we have a meeting?

UNIT A ▸▸ REVISION

SKILLS

Match the sentence halves.

1 Can I speak
2 Call me
3 Hello, this is
4 Hello, Michel Dupont
5 I have a
6 I'm sorry
7 Can you give me
8 I can talk

a) back later, please.
b) here.
c) to Ahmed Al Harbi, please?
d) Sheila Smith, Castle Electrics.
e) to hear that.
f) to the manager.
g) some more information?
h) problem with an invoice.

WRITING

Write a description (40–50 words) of your office or a room at home. Write about the things that it has and doesn't have.

Cultures 1: Eating out

A Match the expressions with the same meaning.

1 be punctual
2 be late
3 have good manners
4 show bad behaviour
5 guest
6 stay
7 greet
8 dining habits

a) be rude
b) behaviour while eating
c) don't leave
d) arrive on time
e) say hello to
f) visitor
g) be polite
h) arrive after the meeting time

B For each of the statements below (1–12), choose the cultural topic area (a–f) that each person is speaking about.

a) Leaving
b) Drinking
c) What you use to eat
d) How much you eat
e) Seating
f) Arrival

1 In my country, the position furthest from the door is for the most important person.
2 It's best to try any food that your host offers, and to finish it if possible.
3 Here, we rarely use chopsticks.
4 No one notices if you come 15 minutes after the appointment time.
5 We usually kiss the cheek of everyone in the group at the end of the evening.
6 We always wait for the organiser to show us which chair to take.
7 We never have alcohol at business meals.
8 Here, people go home when they are ready to go.
9 It's very strange to arrive early. We never do that.
10 Wait for someone to fill your glass.
11 We never touch food with our left hand.
12 If you leave some food on your plate, it shows you are full.

1.1 Small talk

Objectives

Speaking
- Can make an introduction and use basic greeting and leave-taking expressions.
- Can ask and answer questions about what they do at work and in their free time.

Lesson deliverable
To participate in an activity to practise small talk in a business context.

Performance review
To review your own progress and performance against the lesson objectives at the end of the lesson.

A SPEAKING 1

1 What is small talk? Do you use it? Work in two groups, A and B, and discuss the questions below.

Group A
- Why do we use small talk?
- Is it easy to start a conversation in English?
- How do you greet someone in English?
- How do you introduce a colleague to someone?

Group B
- When do we use small talk?
- Why can it be difficult?
- How do you introduce yourself to someone?
- What do you say if you don't understand something?

2 Now work in pairs with someone from another group. Take turns to read out the questions you discussed and share your ideas. When your partner tells you their ideas add more suggestions where possible.

3 Work in new pairs and discuss what topics you can talk about when you meet someone for the first time. Share your ideas with the class.

B LISTENING

1 Look at the list below and discuss which are good topics when you meet someone for the first time.

weather ☐   traffic ☐   jobs ☐   home and family ☐
company information ☐   salary ☐   hours of work ☐
likes and dislikes ☐   free-time activities ☐
business travel ☐   politics ☐   accommodation ☐
drink or food ☐

2 🔊 BSA1.1.1 Listen to the first conversation. Tick the topics mentioned in question 1.

3 Which topics on the list are not good to talk about when you meet someone for the first time?

4 🔊 BSA1.1.2 Listen to the second conversation. Wesley Moore makes two social mistakes when he's talking to Emi Fujimori. What are they?

5 🔊 BSA1.1.3 Listen to the third conversation. What phrases can you hear for the following?

getting attention	....
introducing someone	....
greeting and response	....
saying goodbye	....

6 🔊 BSA1.1.1– BSA1.1.3 Listen to the three conversations again and complete the phrases.

Talking about general topics

1 W............ the weather l............ in Italy at the moment?
2 W............ do you l............ in Italy?
3 Is t............ your first v............ to the UK?
4 What do you l............ doing in your f............ time?

Talking about work

5 What c............ do you w............ for?
6 Is t............ a J............ company?
7 Do you travel m............ for your w............?

BUSINESS SKILLS: SMALL TALK

Dealing with problems

8 Let's n............ talk a............ politics now

9 I'd l............ you to m............ someone else

Offering

10 Would y............ like t............ come to a concert this evening?

C SPEAKING 2

1 Work in groups of four (Students A, B, C and D). You each have a *find someone who* card.

Student A: Turn to page v.

Student B: Turn to page v.

Student C: Turn to page v.

Student D: Turn to page v.

Do not show each other your cards. Introduce yourself, then ask and answer questions to find a match for the person described on your card.

2 When you have talked to everyone in your own group, move to other groups and repeat the exercise until the teacher asks you to stop. Use as many of the phrases you noted down as possible.

Task

Part 1: Preparation

Context: You and some of your colleagues are going to an international network meeting for business people. This is the first time for some of them. You need to help them prepare things to say when they meet people. The meeting is at Group A's offices.

In two groups, A and B, decide:
- the name of your company and what it does
- each person's position in the company
- what you are going to say about your company

Turn to page v for role cards (choose from A, B, C or D if required).

Then prepare:
- how to introduce yourself
- how to ask the other person for information about themselves and their company
- what personal details you can give

Part 2: Small talk

Now talk to the people from the other group. Find out as much as you can about each other and the companies you work for. Talk to people for one or two minutes and then move on.

Part 3: Introduction

Introduce someone from your group to someone in the other group and tell them what you know about them.

◉ EXTRA PRACTICE: DVD CLIP AND WORKSHEET 1

D PEER REVIEW

1 Look at the objectives again at the beginning of the lesson and think about your small talk exercises. Talk together about the good and bad things in the meeting.

2 Then answer the questions below to see how well your small talk language meets these objectives.

- What was the best part of the conversation for you and your partner(s)?
- Why do you think it was good?
- What can you do better?

E SELF-ASSESSMENT

To assess your own performance complete the following sentences.

I can ....

I can't ....

F PROFESSIONAL DEVELOPMENT AND PERFORMANCE GOALS

Write two sentences about ways you can improve your small talk.

I can ....

I need to ....

1.2 Telephoning

Objectives

Speaking
- Can introduce themselves on the phone and close a simple call.
- Can use brief, everyday expressions to describe wants and needs, and request information.
- Can ask for repetition or clarification on the phone in a simple way.

Lesson deliverable
To plan, prepare and participate in a telephone conversation in a business context and write a short follow-up document.

Performance review
To review your own progress and performance against the lesson objectives at the end of the lesson.

A SPEAKING 1

Look at what these people say about telephoning and answer the questions.

1 Do you agree with the speakers?
2 What do you like or not like about telephoning?
3 What is easy or difficult for you about telephoning in English?

A I'm Rob. I'm an office manager. I like telephoning because it's fast. You can get and give information quickly.

B I'm Sofia. I'm a secretary. Telephoning in English is difficult for me. Sometimes I don't understand the words the other person uses.

C I'm Guy. I'm a sales manager. I don't like telephoning. I like seeing the person I'm talking to.

B LISTENING

1 🔊 **BSA1.2.4** Listen to a telephone call to the Dunedin Language School in Edinburgh, Scotland, and complete the office manager's form, below.

2 **Work in pairs. Put the words in the correct order to make phrases from the beginning and end of the call.**

1 to / speak / Rob Walker, / I / Can / please / ?
....
2 for / help / you / Thank /your
....
3 welcome, / You're / goodbye
....
4 you / How / I / help / can / ?
....
5 Language School, / Dunedin / afternoon / good
....
6 Sofia Marquez / This / from / ELC / is / in Malaga, Spain
....

3 🔊 **BSA1.2.5** Listen again to the beginning and end of the call and check your answers, above.

4 🔊 **BSA1.2.6** Listen to the middle of the call again and complete sentences 7–11 below.

7 Can .... give .... some .... about Mr Dupont?
8 What .... by pets?
9 Can you .... something about them?
10 Sorry, ... that.
11 Can .... , please?

Host family request

Student's name: Luc Dupont
Company: ELC, Malaga, Spain
Course dates: 3–23 September

Family with pets: Yes No[1]
Family with children: Yes No[2]

Meals
Eats everything: Yes No[3]
Vegetarian: Yes No[4]

Possible family:
Mr and Mrs ....[5]

Action points:
1 Check if family are free in ....[6].
2 Find out about ....[7].
3 E-mail Sofia Marquez.

A3

5 Match sentences 1–11 from Exercises B2 and 4 with the headings in the table below.

Getting through	
Answering	Speaking.
Introducing yourself	
Asking what the call is about	
Finishing the conversation	
Asking for information	
Explaining a communication problem	Sorry, I don't understand.
Asking for repetition	
Asking for clarification	

C SPEAKING 2

Work in pairs. Role-play the conversation between Rob Walker (RW) and Sofia Marquez (SM). Use this plan and the phrases from Exercise B5.

RW: Answer the phone.

SM: Identify yourself.

RW: Ask what the call is about.

SM: Explain: Luc Dupont wants to stay in a family.

RW: Ask for information about Mr Dupont.

SM: Tell him about *pets / children / food*.
(Both: Ask for clarification/repetition if necessary.)

RW: Tell Sofia about the Ross family.
(Both: Ask for clarification/repetition if necessary.)

SM: Ask about tennis clubs.

Both: Finish the conversation.

Task

Part 1: Preparation

Context: A manager from your company is going to the Dunedin Language School. He/She has got a booking, but he/she wants you to get more information for him/her.

Group work
Work in small groups to plan the telephone call. Complete these notes to prepare for the call.

Your name:
Your company:
The name of the person who is going to the language school:
His/Her position:
The dates he/she will be there:
You need more information about:

Part 2: Making and receiving calls

1 Work in pairs. Role-play the telephone conversation.

Student A:
Make the call. Use your notes from Part 1.

Student B:
You work for the Dunedin Language School. Answer the call. After the call, write down your action points.

2 Now swap roles and role-play another conversation.

D PEER REVIEW

1 Look at the action points your partner wrote after the call. Are the details correct? Is all the important information there? Give your partner some feedback.

2 Now talk about your telephone conversations with another pair. Think about the lesson objectives and discuss these questions.

- What was good about the calls?
- What was not so good?
- Did you manage to get all the information you needed?
- Did you ask for repetition and clarification? If so, did it help you to understand?

E SELF-ASSESSMENT

Think about the calls you made, the lesson objectives and the feedback from your colleagues. Complete these sentences.

- When I was the caller, I performed *well / badly* because ....
- When I answered the call, I performed *well / badly* because ....
- The action points I wrote afterwards *were / were not* correct.

F PROFESSIONAL DEVELOPMENT AND PERFORMANCE GOALS

Write two sentences about ways you can improve your telephone skills.

Next time I make a call in English, I will .... before I make the call.

Next time I receive a call in English, I will ....

UNIT 4 | Travel

'He who lives sees much. He who travels sees more.'
Arab proverb

OVERVIEW

VOCABULARY
Travel details

LISTENING
A business traveller

LANGUAGE FOCUS 1
can/can't

READING
Business hotels

LANGUAGE FOCUS 2
there is / there are

SKILLS
Making bookings and checking arrangements

CASE STUDY
The Gustav Conference Centre

STARTING UP

A How often do you travel? Where do you like to go? Do you ever travel on business?

B When you travel, which of the following do you like or not like? Write sentences.

I love meeting new people.
I like eating new food.
I don't mind packing a case.
I don't like flying.
I hate checking in.

- checking in
- waiting for luggage
- going through security checks
- speaking a foreign language
- packing a case
- being away from home
- travelling to the airport/station
- meeting new people
- flying
- eating new food

Can you add any others?

C 🔊 CD1.47–1.54 Listen to extracts 1–8. Where (a–e) can travellers hear or say these things?

a) in a taxi   b) at an airport   c) at a railway station   d) at a hotel   e) on a plane

1 ..b.. 2 ..... 3 ..... 4 ..... 5 ..... 6 ..... 7 ..... 8 .....

36

UNIT 4 ▸▸ TRAVEL

VOCABULARY
Travel details

A 🔊 CD1.55–1.58 **Listen to each part of the recording. Then answer these questions.**

Part 1

1 What time is the next train to Manchester?

Part 2

2 Which flight is boarding at gate 23?

Part 3

3 What time does the train leave?

4 Which platform does it leave from?

Part 4

5 The passenger chooses a flight. What time does it leave?

6 When does the flight arrive?

7 What is the flight number?

8 Which terminal does it leave from?

B **People often do these things when they travel. Match the verbs (1–5, 6–10) with the correct phrases (a–e, f–j).**

1 buy	a) security	6 watch	f) a hotel room
2 confirm	b) a ticket	7 take	g) some shopping
3 collect	c) at the check-in	8 book	h) at the hotel
4 go through	d) their flight	9 do	i) an in-flight movie
5 queue	e) their luggage	10 check in	j) a bus or taxi

C **Work in pairs. Put actions 1–10 from Exercise B in order.**

1 buy a ticket, 2 book a hotel room, …

D **Complete the sentences below using the nouns from the box.**

> bill ~~booking~~ call centre flight luggage
> passport password receipt reservation seat

At the ticket office

1 I need to change my *booking*.

2 Is there a direct …………?

At the check-in desk

3 Can I take this as hand …………?

4 Can I have an aisle …………?

5 Which way is control?

In a taxi

6 Please take me to the city ………….

7 Can I have a …………, please?

At the hotel

8 I have a ………… for two nights. My name's Burkhard.

9 Can I have an alarm ………… at 6.45, please?

10 I'm checking out today. Can I have the …………, please?

11 Can I have the ………… for the Wi-Fi, please?

E **You are expecting a visitor to your company. You need to check your information. Work in pairs.**

Student A: Turn to page 131.
Student B: Turn to page 138.

See the **DVD-ROM** for the *i-Glossary*.

UNIT 4 ▸▸ TRAVEL

LISTENING
A business traveller

Liz Credé

Watch the interview on the DVD-ROM.

A 🔊 **CD1.59 Listen to the first part of an interview with Liz Credé and answer these questions.**

1 Why does she travel to a) Amsterdam? b) Singapore and Chicago?
2 How often does she travel to a) Amsterdam? b) Singapore and Chicago?
3 What is Liz's favourite business location, and why?

B **Liz says she likes flying business class and she likes staying in the same hotel. In pairs, predict why she likes doing those two things.**

C 🔊 **CD1.60 Listen to the second part of the interview and check your answers to Exercise B.**

D **In pairs, discuss this question.**

Where would you most like to go for a business conference, and why?

LANGUAGE FOCUS 1
can/can't

- We use *can* to say we are able to do something.
  He **can** program a computer.
  I **can't** speak French.

- We also use *can* to talk about what is possible.
  '**Can** I get a snack in the bar?' 'Yes, you **can**. It serves food until 11.'

  '**Can** I fly direct from Baltimore to Moscow?' 'No, you **can't**. You need to go via New York or Atlanta.'

➡ page 148

A **Ask people in your class about the languages they can speak.**

A: *Can you speak Japanese?*
B: *No, I can't.*

Work in pairs. Try to remember the languages people can and can't speak.

John can speak English and German, but he can't speak Chinese.

B **Put this dialogue into the correct order.**

Paul:	Hi, Judith.	☐
Judith:	Well, I can't do Thursday, but Friday is OK.	☐
Paul:	Paul Robinson speaking.	1
Judith:	Oh, hello, Paul. This is Judith Preiss here.	2
Paul:	I'm sorry, Judith, I can't. But I can make Thursday or Friday.	☐
Judith:	Paul, I'm calling about that meeting. Can you make next Wednesday?	☐
Paul:	Of course. I can pick you up from the station if you like.	☐
Judith:	Ten o'clock's fine. Oh, and can I bring my colleague, Sabrina? You met her at the conference.	☐
Paul:	OK. Friday it is. Can we meet in the morning – say 10 o'clock?	☐
Judith:	Great. See you on Friday. Bye.	☐

C 🔊 **CD1.61 Listen and check your answers.**

UNIT 4 ▸▸ TRAVEL

D **Look at the dialogue in Exercise B. Write questions beginning with *can*.**

Can Judith and Paul meet on Friday?

Work in pairs. Ask each other your questions. How much can you remember?

A: *Can Paul meet Judith on Wednesday?*
B: *No, he can't.*

E 🔊 **CD1.61 Listen to the dialogue again. Then practise it with a partner.**

F **Complete the e-mail that Judith writes to Sabrina about the arrangements.**

To:	Sabrina Monti
From:	Judith Preiss
Subject:	Meeting with Paul Robinson

Sabrina

I called Paul Robinson about the meeting. He says he ....[1] make it on Wednesday, but he ....[2] do ....[3] at 10 o'clock. He says of course you ....[4] come with me! And he ....[5] pick us up from the ....[6]. ....[7] you text me today and let me know if Friday is still OK for you? I don't think we need to meet before Friday. We ....[8] go through my notes for the meeting on the train.

See you then,
Judith

G **Work in pairs. Role-play this situation.**

Student A: See below.
Student B: Turn to page 137.

Student A

Part 1

You plan to visit one of your company's overseas offices for a week. Student B works there. Ask him/her for this information:
- rent a car at the airport?
  Can I rent a car at the airport?
- change money at the airport?
- walk from the hotel to the office?
- use the Internet at the office?

Part 2

A visitor from head office (Student B) contacts you about a visit. Use these notes to answer his/her questions.
B: *Can I use a computer?*
A: *Yes, you can. You can use the computer in my office.*
- No, ... It's better on Wednesday.
- No, ... The office isn't open until 9 a.m.
- Yes, ... , but it's very busy at lunchtime.
- Yes, ... You can use the computer in my office.

UNIT 4 ▸▸ TRAVEL

READING
Business hotels

A What kind of hotel do you like to stay in when you are on holiday or on business?

B Tick (✓) the facilities you expect to find in a business hotel.

beauty salon	gift shop	business centre
health club	childcare service	tennis courts
concierge desk	restaurants	coffee shop

C Underline the words from Exercise B in the text below.

D Take turns to ask and answer questions about the Hilton Tokyo.

1 check your e-mail in your room?
   A: *Can you check your e-mail in your room?*   B: *Yes, you can.*
2 swim outside at the hotel?
   B: *Can you swim outside at the hotel?*   A: *No, you can't.*
3 play tennis at the hotel?
4 eat Chinese food in the Musashino?
5 host a dinner for 1,500 people?
6 use the health club at night?
7 get from Narita Airport direct to the hotel?

Hilton Tokyo

About the hotel

The Hilton Tokyo is in the centre of Tokyo's Shinjuku skyscraper business district. This luxury hotel has 808 guest rooms and a choice of seven inviting bars and restaurants.

Guests can swim in the hotel's indoor pool, play tennis on one of the two rooftop tennis courts, or relax in the jacuzzi and sauna in the hotel's 24-hour health club.

Guests can visit nearby Tokyo attractions, including Yoyogi Park, the Meiji Shrine and the Imperial Palace. For guests with children, the Tokyo Disney resort is about 20 kilometres from the hotel. The hotel's 24-hour reception team offers advice on places to visit. Guests can also book sightseeing tours and theatre tickets. Shinjuku's busy shops are a 10-minute walk from the hotel.

Guests feel at home in the spacious rooms, with large windows and city views. In each room, there is a desk, air conditioning and voicemail. Rooms have high-speed internet access, a flat-screen TV and on-demand videos.

The Musashino serves Japanese specialities. Le Pergolese offers French cuisine. Guests can try Chinese food at the Dynasty and order a midnight snack at the Marble Lounge.

The Hilton Tokyo is the perfect place for meetings. There are 16 meeting rooms. The largest room has space for 1,200 people. There is also a 24-hour business centre.

From Narita International Airport, the easiest way to arrive is to take the airport limousine. It takes about two hours. Getting around is easy. There is a free shuttle service from the hotel to Shinjuku station. The hotel is also directly connected to the Tokyo Metro subway.

UNIT 4 ▸▸ TRAVEL

E **Answer these questions.**
1. How far is the hotel from the Shinjuku shopping area?
2. How long is the business centre open?
3. How long does it take to travel from Narita Airport to the hotel?

F **Match the words on the left (1–6) to the words on the right (a–f) to make word partnerships from the text.**

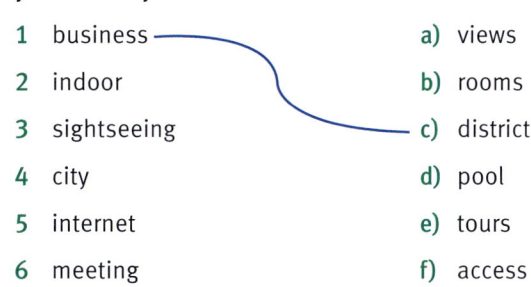

1. business
2. indoor
3. sightseeing
4. city
5. internet
6. meeting

a) views
b) rooms
c) district
d) pool
e) tours
f) access

LANGUAGE FOCUS 2

there is / there are

- We often use *there is / there are* before *a/an* or *some/any*.
There is an indoor swimming pool.
There are three restaurants.
There aren't any shops in the area.
'**Are there any** meeting rooms in the hotel?' 'Yes, **there are**.' / 'No, **there aren't**.

➡ page 148

A **Complete these sentences with the correct form of *there is* or *there are*.**
1. It's a very small airport. *There aren't* any shops in the terminal.
2. .... a problem with my ticket?
3. .... any aisle seats available.
4. .... a stopover in Frankfurt.
5. .... any flights to Zurich tonight?
6. I'm afraid .... a flight to Warsaw this afternoon.
7. .... two cafés in the terminal.
8. .... any buses from the airport to the city centre?

B **In pairs, ask and answer questions about the facilities at the Hilton Tokyo.**

A: *Is there a health club?* B: *Yes, there is.*
B: *How many guest rooms are there?* A: *There are 808.*

C **Work in pairs. Role-play this situation.**

Student A: See below. Student B: Turn to page 139.

Student A

Part 1

You have a new job abroad. Student B lives there. Ask him/her about these points.
- international school?
  Is there an international school?
- good local transport?
- big supermarkets?
- houses to rent with gardens?

Part 2

Student B has a new job abroad. You live in that country. Use these notes to answer his/her questions.
B: *Are there any good restaurants?*
A: *Yes, there are lots of good local restaurants.*
- No, ... any cinemas.
- Yes, ... lots of good local restaurants.
- No, ... , but you can swim in one of the hotels.
- Yes, ... tennis club with five courts.

41

UNIT 4 ▸▸ TRAVEL

SKILLS
Making bookings and checking arrangements

A 🔊 CD1.62 Simon is flying to Rome on business. Listen to the phone call and choose the correct answers to these questions.

1	When is Simon arriving?	(Monday) / Wednesday
2	When is he leaving?	Tuesday / Wednesday
3	What kind of room does he want?	single / double
4	How much does the room cost per night?	€120 / €150
5	How many nights is he staying at the hotel?	one night / two nights
6	What time will he arrive?	seven o'clock / six o'clock

B Work in pairs. Study the Useful language box below. Then role-play the telephone call.

Student A: You work for the Delta Hotel in Frankfurt, Germany.
Student B: You are a business traveller. You want to book rooms for yourself and a colleague.

A: Answer phone. Give name of hotel.

B: Give your name. Ask for two single rooms with baths from 16th to 20th July.

A: Check booking is for four nights from 16th to 20th July.

B: Price?

A: €150 per night for a single room.

B: Restaurant? Car park?

A: Restaurant: yes
Car park: no
Ask for credit-card details.

B: Visa number: 4921 4456 3714 1009
Expiry date: 12/16

Watch the phone call on the DVD-ROM.

C Work in the same pairs. Study the Useful language box.

Student A: Turn to page 132.
Student B: Turn to page 136.

Role-play the telephone call.

USEFUL LANGUAGE

RECEPTIONIST / SALES EXECUTIVE

Hello, Capri Hotel / Big Bird Airways. How can I help you?
I can give you a single/double on the first floor.
Is that single (BrE) / one way (AmE) or return (BrE) / round trip (AmE)?
So, that's a single room for two nights, the 4th and 5th.
So, that's a round-trip business-class ticket from London Gatwick to New York?
Can I have your credit-card details, please?
And what are the last three digits of the security number on the back of the card?
What time do you expect to arrive?
Could you repeat that, please?

CALLER

I'd like to book a room from Tuesday the 4th to Thursday the 6th.
I'd like to book two tickets to New York, please.
How much is it per night?
Is there a restaurant in the hotel?
Is there a car park?
Is there a pick-up service?
Can I pay with American Express / MasterCard / Visa?
It's a Visa card. The number is …
The expiry date is …
What time does the flight arrive?

42

THE GUSTAV CONFERENCE CENTRE

Meeting the needs of different clients

Background

The Gustav Conference Centre is just outside the city centre of Vienna, Austria. Three companies want to stay at the conference centre during the period Friday July 7th to Sunday July 9th.

Read the information about the companies and their needs. Then read the information on the Conference Centre's meeting rooms on page 140.

Company	Number of staff	How long at conference?	Meeting rooms	Seminar rooms
Minnesota Chemicals	80	3 days	1	2 (every day)
Elegant Ways Beauty Products	90	3 days	1	2 (every day)
JooC Designs	35	2 days	1	1 (every day)

Notes
- Minnesota Chemicals is a large international company. It is a new customer for the Conference Centre.
- Elegant Ways Beauty Products and JooC Designs had conferences at the Centre last year.

Other requirements
- Minnesota Chemicals wants: video-conferencing; projector + large screen (5m x 4m), direct access to the terrace and garden
- Elegant Ways Beauty Products wants: video-conferencing; projector + large screen (5m x 4m), direct access to the terrace and garden, technical support
- JooC Designs wants: large screen (5m x 4m), 10 laptops, technical support

🔊 **CD1.63** Listen to the conversation. The conference organiser from JooC Designs makes a request to the Conference Centre. Note down what she wants.

Task

1 Work in pairs. You are the Manager and Assistant Manager of the Conference Centre. Discuss these questions.
   1 Which meeting room do you want to offer company?
   2 What will you say to the conference organiser at JooC Designs?
   3 Is there a problem with the seminar rooms? If so, how can you solve it?

2 The Manager of the Conference Centre telephones the conference organiser of each company. The Manager offers each organiser a meeting and seminar room, and discusses any problems. Role-play the telephone calls. Take turns playing the role of the Manager and conference organiser.

We can offer you the ...... Room. It has a seating capacity of 100. There is a large screen, but ...

Writing

You are a receptionist at the Conference Centre. Choose one of the companies and write an e-mail to their conference organiser. Confirm the details of their stay. Include the date of arrival, the date of leaving, the type of meeting room, the number of seminar rooms and some of the room's best features.

→ *Writing file* page 126

UNIT 5 **Food and entertaining**

'*Conversation is food for the soul.*'
Mexican proverb

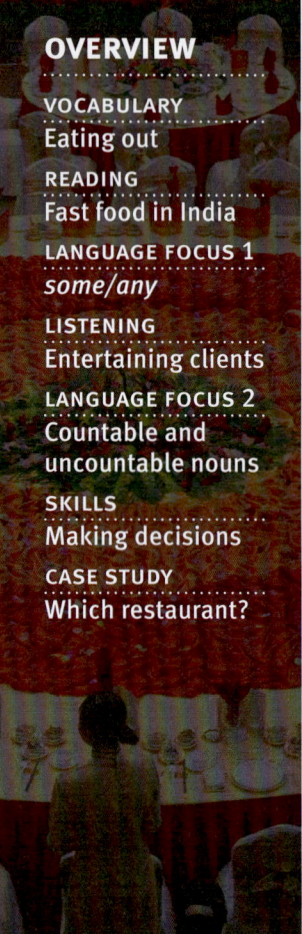

OVERVIEW

VOCABULARY
Eating out

READING
Fast food in India

LANGUAGE FOCUS 1
some/any

LISTENING
Entertaining clients

LANGUAGE FOCUS 2
Countable and uncountable nouns

SKILLS
Making decisions

CASE STUDY
Which restaurant?

STARTING UP

A What kind of food do/don't you like? Make adjectives from these countries.

| China   Japan   Thailand   India   Turkey   Greece   Italy |
| France   Germany   Russia   Sweden   the UK   Spain   Mexico |

I like Chinese food. I love Italian food.

B Match the typical dishes to the adjectives. Then make sentences.

Curry is an Indian dish.

curry snails sushi spaghetti	American Italian Indian
goulash burger paella	French Mexican Chinese
sweet-and-sour chicken fajitas	Japanese Spanish Hungarian

What other typical dishes do you know?

C In your country, do businesspeople usually:

1. have business breakfasts?
2. entertain businesspeople at home?
3. entertain businesspeople at the weekend?

44

UNIT 5 ▸▸ FOOD AND ENTERTAINING

VOCABULARY
Eating out

A Choose the odd one out in each group of food words below. Use the words from the box to explain your answers.

| fish | fruit | meat | vegetable | seafood |

1	salmon	tuna	cod	onion	*onion: It's a kind of vegetable.*
2	beef	apple	lamb	chicken	
3	carrots	peas	trout	broccoli	
4	veal	grapes	cherries	peaches	
5	cabbage	prawns	cauliflower	aubergine	

~~soup~~   steak   pâté
salad   ice cream
grilled fish   fruit
chocolate mousse
spring rolls   tiramisu
cheesecake   pork
roast duck   mutton
prawn cocktail
beef stew   apple pie
stuffed mushrooms

B Look at these words for parts of a menu. Write the dishes from the box on the left under the correct headings.

Starter	Main course	Dessert
soup		

C Think of some unusual food from your country or a country you have visited. How can you describe it?

It's a kind of ... You have it as a starter / main course / dessert.
You eat it with (potatoes/rice).

D Choose the correct word to complete each of these sentences.

1. You ask for the *receipt / menu* at the start of a meal.
2. You ask for the *check / bill* at the end of a meal in London.
3. You ask for the *check / bill* at the end of a meal in New York.
4. You ask for the *tip / receipt* after you pay.

E 🔊 CD1.64 A man and a woman are ordering a meal in a restaurant. Listen and write *M* for man and *W* for woman.

1	**Starter**	salad ☐	snails ☐	soup W
2	**Main course**	spaghetti ☐	paella ☐	sushi ☐
3	**Dessert**	ice cream ☐	fruit ☐	apple pie ☐

F Put these sentences into the order you would hear them during a meal.

a) You should try the roast duck. It's delicious. ☐
b) No, thanks. I'm full. ☐
c) Would you like a starter? 1
d) Right. I'll get the bill. ☐
e) I'd like the soup, please. ☐
f) Would you like a dessert? ☐
g) What do you recommend for the main course? ☐
h) Thanks very much. That was a lovely meal. I really enjoyed it. ☐

G 🔊 CD1.65 Listen and check your answers.

H You are in a restaurant.

Student A: Turn to page 130.
Student B: Turn to page 140.

*See the **DVD-ROM** for the i-Glossary.*

45

UNIT 5 ▸▸ FOOD AND ENTERTAINING

READING
Fast food in India

A Discuss these questions in pairs.

1 How often do you eat in fast-food chains?
2 How popular are they in your country? Who is a typical customer?
3 How do they change their menus for the local market? Give some examples.

B Do international fast-food companies need to change their menus to be successful in India? Read this article to find out.

FT

India likes fast-food chains
by Amy Kazmin

Busy lives, higher salaries and an increasing number of women at work all mean there is a lot of demand in India for fast food.

In India, McDonald's has a lot of fans because of its low prices and vegetarian dishes. At lunchtime, the McDonald's at Mumbai's Phoenix Mills – a big shopping centre – is full of college students, mothers and office workers.

Akshaya Batta, 30, has a quick lunch at McDonald's at least once a week, rather than carry a lunch box from home, as a lot of Indians still do. Sahal Amlani, 30, a store manager, spends Rs50 ($1.10) on an afternoon snack at McDonald's twice a week and takes his family for a McDonald's meal, spending about Rs300 ($6.60) every weekend.

International fast-food companies like McDonald's know how important it is to adapt their food for Indian tastes. They make the menus more spicy and they offer more vegetarian dishes, all at a low price.

In its restaurants, McDonald's does not offer any beef dishes because the mainly Hindu population does not eat beef. Instead, it offers mutton and chicken Maharaja Mac.

Kentucky Fried Chicken (KFC) adapts its chicken dishes for local tastes with the use of Indian spices and cooking techniques. The Pizza Hut menu has a mix of Indian and international dishes. Anup Jain, Director of Marketing for Pizza Hut India, says, "We adapt 20% of our menu for Indian tastes. About 60% of people are vegetarian, so we have a lot more vegetarian toppings on our pizzas."

C Match the words (1–5) to their meanings (a–e).

1 salaries
2 demand
3 adapt
4 tastes
5 spicy

a) with a strong and hot flavour
b) the kind of things that someone likes
c) the money people earn for their jobs
d) the need people have for a service
e) change something

D Read the article again and answer these questions.

1 What type of customer goes to the Phoenix Mills McDonald's at lunchtime?
2 How many times a week does Akshaya Batta go to McDonald's?
3 How much does Sahal Amlani typically spend in McDonald's at weekends?
4 How do these fast-food companies adapt their menus for Indian customers? Complete these sentences:

   a) McDonald's offers …   b) In its chicken dishes, KFC uses …   c) Pizza Hut has …

5 Why is it necessary to make these changes?

E Work in pairs. Choose a fast-food chain in your country and decide on two ways to improve it. Think about the design of the restaurant or its menu.

Share your ideas with another pair.

One idea is to … Another idea is to …

UNIT 5 ▸▸ FOOD AND ENTERTAINING

LANGUAGE FOCUS 1
some/any

- We use *some* in positive statements.
  There are **some** very good restaurants in the city centre.
- We also use *some* when we offer things and ask for things.
  Would you like **some** more coffee? Can I have **some** tea, please?
- We use *any* in most questions.
  Do you have **any** beef?
- We also use *any* in negative statements.
  We haven't got **any** beef today.

➡ page 149

A Tick (✓) the correct sentences. Correct the mistakes in the other sentences.

1 I'd like any water.
   I'd like some water.
2 Could I have any more coffee, please?
3 Are there any restaurants near here?
4 There isn't some wine left.
5 I'd like some cheese, please.
6 Do you have any soft drinks?

B Choose the correct words to complete this dialogue.

Mina: There are *some / any* ¹ good restaurants in the centre.

Ivan: Yes, but there isn't *some / any* ² parking. We could go to the Texas Steakhouse near the airport.

Mina: Do they serve *some / any* ³ vegetarian dishes?

Ivan: I don't think so. How about the Marina? They do *some / any* ⁴ great fish dishes, and they have *some / any* ⁵ vegetarian starters, too.

Mina: Good idea. I'll see if they've got a table for nine o'clock.

LISTENING
Entertaining clients

A 🔊 CD1.66 Jeremy Keeley is a specialist in change leadership. Listen to the first part of an interview with him. He is talking about how he entertains business contacts and his favourite entertainment. Complete these notes.

- I like to get to ....¹ my contacts.
- I give them a chance to ....² me about themselves.
- I take them places that we can ....³.
- We walked across a ....⁴ together.
- While we walked, we ....⁵.
- We spent the time talking about what was really ....⁶.

Jeremy Keeley

B 🔊 CD1.67 Listen to the second part of the interview and decide whether these statements are true (T) or false (F). Correct the false ones.

1 In restaurants, you should consider noise levels.
2 Sometimes you need to take out clients you don't like.
3 Do not take vegetarians to steak restaurants.
4 You should spend a lot of money entertaining clients.

C Work in pairs. How would you plan a meal for a mixed group of nationalities?

Watch the interview on the DVD-ROM.

D 🔊 CD1.68 Listen to the third part of the interview. Compare your answer in Exercise C to what Jeremy says.

UNIT 5 ▸▸ FOOD AND ENTERTAINING

LANGUAGE FOCUS 2
Countable and uncountable nouns

- Most nouns in English are countable.
  a table, two tables; an apple, two apples

- Some nouns are usually uncountable.
  water, tea, sugar, milk, bread

many, much and a lot of

- We use *many* with countable nouns in questions and negatives.
  How **many** hours do you work a week?
  I don't go to **many** meetings.

- We use *much* with uncountable nouns in questions and negatives.
  How **much** money does she earn?
  I don't get **much** time for holidays.

- We use *a lot of* in all types of sentence.
  The company has **a lot of** employees.
  He doesn't earn **a lot of** money.
  Does the company have **a lot of** products?

➡ page 149

A Tick (✓) the countable nouns.

1 reservation ✓	7 equipment	13 menu	19 transport
2 food	8 hotel	14 money	20 soup
3 air conditioning	9 information	15 overtime	21 work
4 bathroom	10 seat	16 receipt	22 shopping
5 bill	11 luggage	17 dish	23 suitcase
6 employee	12 flight	18 tip	24 leisure

B Correct the mistakes in these sentences. Use *a lot of*, *many* or *much*.

1 They don't have ~~much~~ vegetarian dishes here. *a lot of / many*
2 How many does it cost?
3 The restaurant hasn't got much tables left.
4 I don't have many time at the moment.
5 I drink much coffee.
6 There aren't much hotels in the city centre.
7 It costs much money.
8 I don't want many spaghetti. There's ice cream for dessert.

C Work in pairs. Complete these questions with *many* or *much*. Then ask and answer the questions with a partner.

1 A: How *much* cash do you have in your wallet?
  B: *About 20 euros.*

2 How .... phone calls do you make a day?
3 How .... people are there in your company?
4 How .... time do you have for lunch?
5 How .... holiday do you get a year?
6 How .... languages do you speak?
7 How .... fast-food restaurants are there where you live?
8 How .... water do you drink a day?

UNIT 5 ▸▸ FOOD AND ENTERTAINING

SKILLS
Making decisions

A What can businesspeople do to entertain a group of visitors? Which of these do you think are a good idea?

- eating local food
- watching a sports match
- eating international food
- going on a tour of the area
- seeing a show (e.g. at the theatre)
- visiting a local sight (e.g. a museum or art gallery)

B 🔊 CD1.69 Two managers are discussing how to entertain a group of important foreign visitors. Listen and decide whether these statements are true (T) or false (F). Correct the false ones.

1 They both like the idea of visiting the castle.
2 They talk about three different restaurants.
3 They decide to go to an Italian restaurant.
4 The table is for 10 people on Tuesday.

C 🔊 CD1.69 Listen again and complete these extracts.

1 I don't .... about that. I think we .... something more interesting for them to do.
2 Yes, I .... I also .... it's too far away. Why .... we invite them for dinner?
3 Good .... Which restaurant do you recommend?
4 We .... try the new restaurant at the Grand Hotel. It's very popular.
5 Yes, that's right, ... it's very expensive!
6 How .... a restaurant by the river?
7 Yes, that's a .... idea.

Watch the discussion on the DVD-ROM.

D Find examples in Exercise C of these functions.

a) giving opinions
b) agreeing
c) disagreeing
d) making suggestions

E Role play. Work in groups of three. You are managers in a company. You meet to discuss how to entertain a group of six foreign visitors.

Student A: Turn to page 134.
Student B: Turn to page 136.
Student C: Turn to page 143.

F Meet together and discuss your ideas. Decide on the best way to entertain the visitors.

USEFUL LANGUAGE

SUGGESTING
Why don't we visit an art gallery?
How about (trying) the Mexican restaurant?
My suggestion is to go for a cocktail.
Let's go to the new French restaurant.

GIVING OPINIONS
I think Lucio's is the best restaurant. The food is delicious.
We need to go to the Chinese restaurant. It's close to the office.
In my opinion, an Indian curry is the best idea.
For me, a typical Spanish evening is a great idea.

AGREEING
Yes, exactly, because it's easy to get a large table.
Yes, I agree. It's very easy to find.
That's true. There's a nice view of the lake.
Yes, that's a great idea.
You're right. The food is great.

DISAGREEING
I see what you mean, but I don't think we have time.
I don't know about that.
I think it's too far away.
That's right, but it's not cheap.
That's a good point, but you need to book/reserve.

49

Case study 5

Which restaurant?

Choosing the right place for guests

Background

You work for a food company, Organic 3000, in Sydney, Australia. Four important overseas customers are visiting your head office. You want to take them to a good restaurant. Each customer prefers a different type of food. You have three restaurants to choose from.

PACO AND ROSITA
MEXICAN RESTAURANT

A popular place. High-quality food, good value for money. No reservations, so you often wait a long time for a table.

Location:	In the city-centre restaurant area, close to office and hotels
Access:	By bus or car; difficult to find parking spaces
Atmosphere:	Lively, noisy, loud music
Average cost:	$40 per person

ON THE MENU
- Hot, spicy Mexican dishes
- Grilled steak, pork and chicken
- Not many vegetarian dishes
- No desserts

WHAT PEOPLE SAY
- Delicious meals at low prices
- Very friendly but slow service

KERALA SANDS
SOUTH INDIAN RESTAURANT

Delicious food. Many Indian customers. It isn't near the centre and is expensive.

Location:	5 miles from the city centre
Access:	By car; lots of parking spaces
Atmosphere:	Very quiet; no music
Average cost:	$70 per person

On the menu
- A variety of South Indian dishes
- Vegetable curries
- Well-known dish: prawns with garlic and cabbage
- Many desserts

what people say
- High-quality food and service
- Not much atmosphere
- Food portions rather small

UNIT 5 •• FOOD AND ENTERTAINING

THE Happy Lobster

*Top-class food. Varied fish and seafood dishes.
The restaurant is mentioned in all the guide books.*

Location:
2 miles from city centre; on the shore; wonderful view of the bay and city at night

Access:
About half an hour by boat, 20 minutes by car; parking available

Atmosphere:
Quiet; classical music playing all the time

Average cost:
$120 per person

On the menu
- Prawns, crab and oysters. It is famous for its giant crab with spring onions
- Vegetarian dishes
- A few beef and pork dishes
- Delicious desserts

What people say
- Good food, but very expensive
- Usually a long wait for service and the bill
- Very quiet atmosphere

Task

1 **Work in groups of four. Choose a role card. Each of you has information about one of the customers.**

   Student A: Turn to page 132. Student C: Turn to page 141.
   Student B: Turn to page 139. Student D: Turn to page 142.

2 **Read your role cards. Then exchange information about the customers. Take notes on their preferences and the things they dislike.**

3 **Choose *one* of the restaurants to take the four customers for a meal. Compare your choice with the other groups.**

Writing

Write an e-mail to one of the customers. Invite him or her to dinner and give details of the restaurant. Include the date and time, and the name, location and type of restaurant.

Dear …
I would like to invite you for a meal on …

→ *Writing file* page 126

UNIT 6 | **Buying and selling**

'*I buy when other people are selling.*'
J. Paul Getty (1892–1976), US entrepreneur, oil-industry executive and financier

OVERVIEW

VOCABULARY 1
Choosing a product

READING
A success story

LANGUAGE FOCUS 1
Past simple

VOCABULARY 2
Choosing a service

LISTENING
How to sell

LANGUAGE FOCUS 2
Past time references

SKILLS
Describing a product

CASE STUDY
NP Innovations

STARTING UP

A What was the last thing you bought? Where did you buy it? What do you buy online?

B 🔊 CD1.70–1.72 Listen to three people talking about the products they buy. Where and when do they buy them? Complete this chart.

Speaker	Product	Place	How often
1		on the Internet	
2			once a year
3			

C Where do you buy the products in Exercise B? How often do you buy them? Use the words from the box.

I buy clothes in high-street stores. I usually buy something every month.

| usually   once a week   at the weekend   sometimes   every day |

D Work in pairs. Choose two other products you buy. Talk about where and how often you buy them.

E Is there a product you prefer *not* to buy online? Why?

52

UNIT 6 ▶▶ BUYING AND SELLING

VOCABULARY 1
Choosing a product

A Read the Elise sales advert below and find expressions which mean the following.

1 There are some good offers.   *great deals*
2 The buyer pays only a small amount of money at the beginning.
3 The buyer pays some money every four weeks for a year.
4 There is no cost for transporting the goods to the buyer.
5 It doesn't cost extra to pay over 12 months.

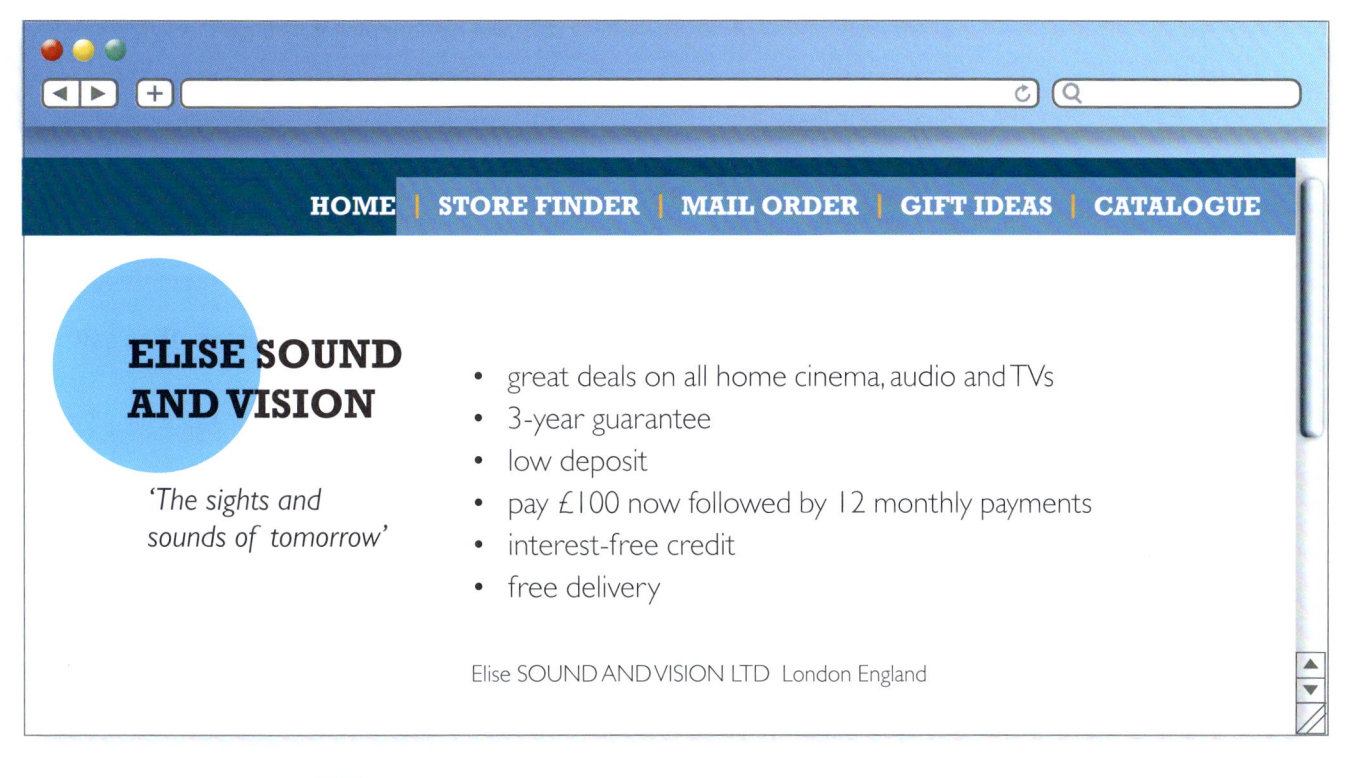

HOME | STORE FINDER | MAIL ORDER | GIFT IDEAS | CATALOGUE

ELISE SOUND AND VISION

'The sights and sounds of tomorrow'

- great deals on all home cinema, audio and TVs
- 3-year guarantee
- low deposit
- pay £100 now followed by 12 monthly payments
- interest-free credit
- free delivery

Elise SOUND AND VISION LTD London England

B Read these sentences. Does a buyer (B) or a seller (S) say them?

1 We offer great deals. [S]
2 I'd like to place an order. [ ]
3 Do you give a guarantee? [ ]
4 I'd like to compare prices. [ ]
5 Are the goods in stock? [ ]
6 Can you pay a deposit? [ ]
7 We always deliver on time. [ ]
8 Can I make monthly payments? [ ]

C 🔊 CD1.73 Listen to a conversation between a buyer and a seller. Underline the correct answers to these questions.

1 Which model does Karl want? PS7 / TX7
2 How long is the guarantee? three years / two years
3 How much deposit is needed for large orders? 15% / 10%
4 What does the seller say is a large order? over 50 units / over 25 units
5 Does the seller always have goods in stock? yes / no

D What is important for you when you buy a product like a computer, TV or car? Put these items in order of importance.

- a three-year guarantee
- interest-free credit
- a low deposit
- free delivery
- a big discount
- great after-sales service

See the **DVD-ROM** for the i-Glossary.

UNIT 6 ▸▸ BUYING AND SELLING

READING
A success story

A Before you read the article below, discuss these questions.

1 What global fashion companies do you know?
2 Which are the most successful in your country?
3 What do you know about Uniqlo, the global fashion retailer?

B Match these words (1–6) to their meanings (a–f).

1 expansion   a) employ someone to do a job
2 strategy   b) when something gets bigger in size
3 relaunch   c) clothes produced by a designer for the season
4 flagship store   d) introduce something new again
5 hire   e) a detailed plan for achieving something
6 collection   f) a company's main store, often big and in an important shopping area

C Read the article quickly and underline these numbers and dates. Then say what they refer to.

1 1984   2 2003   3 2005   4 November 2006   5 April 2009   6 ¥49.8 bn   7 64

Uniqlo: a global success story

Tadashoi Yani, the founder of Uniqlo, is Japan's richest man. That's not bad for someone who started with a single store in Hiroshima in 1984 and now has a global retail business. The company sells high-quality casual clothes at low prices.

Uniqlo grew quickly in Japan during the 1990s. In 1998, it had over 300 stores. Following the good results in Japan, Yani decided on global expansion. It started with stores in the UK in 2001. It didn't work. Most of the stores were too small and in the suburbs of cities. In 2003, Uniqlo closed most of them. In 2005, Yani changed strategy. The new strategy was to open large stores in major cities around the world. The relaunch of Uniqlo began in November 2006 with the opening of a flagship store in New York. Over the next two years, the number of international stores went up from 54 to 92, including flagship stores in London and Paris.

Yani also hired the German designer Jil Sander in April 2009. Her role was to design a collection for Uniqlo and to be the creative consultant for the company. The collection went on sale in selected stores in March 2010. In 2010, Uniqlo made profits of ¥49.8 bn.

Yani sees Asia as a key market for Uniqlo. In 2007, the company had 26 stores across Asia. The number increased to 64 at the end of 2010, including a flagship store in Shanghai. Yani's plan is for another 500 stores over the next five years, mainly in China. Yani also aims to introduce Uniqlo stores in the fast-growing Indian and Brazilian markets.

D Decide whether these statements are true (T) or false (F). Correct the false ones.

1 In the 1990s, Japan was Uniqlo's main market.
2 Uniqlo had a lot of success when it entered the UK market in 2001.
3 Yani's new global strategy was to open big stores in important cities.
4 At the end of 2008, Uniqlo had 92 international stores.
5 Yani hired Jil Sander to design all Uniqlo's clothes.
6 Uniqlo opened 64 stores in Asia between 2007 and 2010.

UNIT 6 ▸▸ BUYING AND SELLING

E Look through the article and find the missing verbs.

1 Uniqlo .... quickly in Japan during the 1990s.
2 Over the next two years, the number of international stores .... from 54 to 92.
3 The number (of stores) .... to 64 at the end of 2010.

What do the verbs have in common?

F What makes a business successful? Put these points in order for you. Add other points to the list.

- ability to learn from mistakes
- hard work
- luck
- money
- personal contacts
- having clear strategy and plan

LANGUAGE FOCUS 1
Past simple

- We use the past simple to talk about completed actions in the past.
  *Last year, we **increased** our sales by 15 per cent.*

- We usually form the past simple by adding *-d* or *-ed* to the verb.
  save – saved   launch – launched   export – exported

- About 150 irregular verbs form the past simple differently.
  cost – cost   be – was – were   grow – grew
  spend – spent   give – gave   go – went

For a list of the most common irregular verbs, see page 157.   ➡ page 150

A 🔊 CD1.74 Listen to how the *-ed* endings of these verbs are pronounced.

1 saved; delivered /d/   2 launched; worked /t/   3 decided; visited /ɪd/

B 🔊 CD1.75 Listen and put these verbs into the correct group from Exercise A (1, 2 or 3).

| started   finished   advised   lived   wanted   opened   missed   booked   invited |

🔊 CD1.75 Listen again and practise saying the verbs.

C Complete this sales report. Use the past simple of the verbs in brackets.

Report on sales trip – South Korea

Last December, I visited¹ (*visit*) our major customers from big department stores in South Korea.

I ....² (*arrive*) in Seoul on Monday 5th December. The next day, I ....³ (*meet*) Mrs Kyoung Ai Lee in Seoul. On 7th December, I ....⁴ (*make*) a presentation to Mrs Lee's sales staff on our products and ....⁵ (*advise*) them how to display them.

The following day, I ....⁶ (*go*) to Busan, and our agent ....⁷ (*introduce*) me to Mrs Ha, the chief buyer of a new department store in the city. She ....⁸ (*ask*) me to send her 500 brochures. I ....⁹ (*give*) her some samples of our products.

I ....¹⁰ (*fly*) back to head office in Paris on 9th December.

D Work in pairs. Take turns to describe a trip you made for business or pleasure.

UNIT 6 ▸▸ BUYING AND SELLING

VOCABULARY 2
Choosing a service

A Use words from the box to complete the Dart leaflet below.

| discount | free | period | price | ~~save~~ |

Dart Car Hire

Dart Car Hire Gold Club
The best the business traveller can get

Join our Dart Car Hire Gold Club today
- Save [1] up to 50% on selected models
- Three days for the ....[2] of two
- ....[3] insurance and unlimited mileage
- Extra 10% ....[4] until the end of July
- For a limited ....[5] only

As a Gold Club member, you …
- get free hire days or airline miles as your reward
- can use our express service, available at all international airports in the country
- don't wait for a piece of paper when you return the car – we e-mail you a detailed receipt.

B Decide whether these sentences about the Dart leaflet are true (T) or false (F).

1 There is an extra cost for insurance. *F*
2 The customer can get some deals for half price.
3 The price is cheaper if the customer is quick.
4 The offer is for the whole year.
5 Gold Club members have a choice of reward.
6 Gold Club members get their receipt by express post.

See the DVD-ROM for the i-Glossary.

C Rewrite the false statements in Exercise B to make them true.

1 *There is no extra cost for insurance.*

LISTENING
How to sell

A In pairs, discuss these questions.

1 What advice would you give to new sales staff?
2 What mistakes do salespeople often make?

Ros Pomeroy

B 🔊 CD1.76 Listen to Ros Pomeroy, a management consultant, answering the questions in Exercise A and complete each gap with a word.

- Be ....[1].
- Take time to build ....[2].
- Make sure you fully ....[3] the product or service you are selling.
- Do not try to sell something to a customer that they do not actually ....[4] or ....[5].
- Take ....[6] to understand what the customer ....[7].
- Customers like to be ....[8] to.

C 🔊 CD1.77 Listen to Ros talking about what being a successful buyer involves. Number her points in the order in which she mentions them.

a) Asking for a written quotation ☐
b) Being prepared to walk away from the purchase if you are not happy ☐
c) Working out the maximum price you are prepared to pay ☐
d) Looking at ways of getting additional extras or discounts ☐
e) Contacting several different suppliers ☐
f) Doing a lot of preparation [1]

UNIT 6 ▸▸ BUYING AND SELLING

Watch the interview on the DVD-ROM.

D 🔊 CD1.78 **Listen to the third part of the interview in pairs and take notes about the best thing Ros bought. Retell her story to each other.**

E **In pairs, tell each other about the best thing you have bought.**

LANGUAGE FOCUS 2
Past time references

Some time references refer only to the past.
*The special deals ended two months **ago**.*
***Last week**, we sold 500 units – a record!*

The prepositions *in, on, from, to, for* and *during* often refer to periods of time in the past.

in	months years	*I went on a business trip **in** August.* *He moved to Germany **in** 1999.*
on	dates days	*The goods left the warehouse **on** 9th April.* *The offer finished **on** Monday.*
from ... **to**	beginning and end of a period	*They worked on the sales campaign **from** February **to** March.*
for	a period of time	*He lived in France **for** five years.*
during	at some point in a period	***During** October, we reached our sales target for the year.*

➡ page 150

A **Underline the correct words to complete this article.**

PROFILE

Christian Sanchez graduated from Tufts University *at / on / in* ¹ 2001, with a degree in chemistry. As part of his course, he did an internship at Merck *for / during / in* ² eight months. After his degree, Merck offered him a permanent job as a chemical analyst at the company's research centre in New Jersey. He worked there *in / from / for* ³ 2001 to 2003. *During / For / On* ⁴ his time at Merck, Christian realised he wanted to change career, so he decided to do an MBA. *In / On / For* ⁵ May 2004, he started a two-year MBA at Stanford University. Following his MBA, he joined the sales team at Johnson and Johnson *in / on / for* ⁶ 15th September 2006. Two years *since / ago / last* ⁷, he became the Regional Sales Manager for the Americas. *Last / First / Next* ⁸ month, he accepted an exciting new job as Country Manager in Argentina.

B 🔊 CD1.79 **Mikael Ohlsson is the CEO of furniture retailer IKEA. Listen to an interview about his career and complete the missing information in these notes.**

Profile

Born:	27th December¹, 1957	1984–1988	Did management jobs in training and ....⁵	
Education:	Studied ....² at Linköping University	1988	Got a job in Belgium as ....⁶	
Career in IKEA		...... –......⁷	Worked as Country Manager, Canada	
............³	Worked as carpet salesman, Linköping store, Sweden	............⁸	Became Managing Director, Sweden	
............⁴	Became Store Manager, Sundsvall, Sweden	2000–2009	Was Regional Manager for ....⁹	
		............¹⁰	Named CEO	

UNIT 6 ›› BUYING AND SELLING

C Make notes about your career or studies. Use the notes in Exercise B to help you.

D Work in pairs. Take turns to describe your career/studies. While your partner is speaking, make brief notes about important dates and events.

E Use your notes from Exercise D to write a short profile about your partner's career/studies. Include these prepositions.

in   on   from ... to   for   during

Helena did a course in business administration from 2006 to 2009. During her holidays, she worked part-time in a sports shop. In September 2010, she got a job with Tesco as a management trainee. ...

SKILLS
Describing a product

A 🔊 CD1.80 Listen to an advertisement for a new women's bag and complete the details.

Model: *Kachet*

Target market: smart, ...[1] women

Material: It's made of soft ....[2].

Features: It's got lots of ....[3] and a special ....[4] to keep things safely.

Colours: ....[5], blue and ....[6]

Price: ....[7]

Delivery: within a ....[8]

B 🔊 CD1.80 Look at the Useful language box below. Listen to the advertisement again and tick the expressions you hear.

Watch the advertisement on the DVD-ROM.

C Work in pairs. Role-play this situation. You are at a trade fair.

Student A: Turn to page 131.
Student B: Turn to page 136.

USEFUL LANGUAGE

DESCRIBING A PRODUCT
It's stylish and fashionable.
It's a very popular model.
It's our best-selling product.
It's made of leather/wood/plastic/steel/aluminium.

TARGET MARKET
It's aimed at stylish women.
The target market is young women who want to look good.

COLOURS
It comes in three colours.
We offer it in four colours.

WEIGHT
It weighs about half a kilo.
It's lightweight.
It's quite heavy.

MEASUREMENTS
It's just 35 centimetres long.
It's 25 centimetres high.
It's 15 centimetres wide.

FEATURES
It has a unique design.
You can close it easily.

PRICE
The trade price is 50 euros.
It costs 65 euros.
It's just 75 euros.

DELIVERY
We can deliver within three days.
We'll deliver within a week.
The price includes postage and packaging.

NP INNOVATIONS

6 Case study

Which gift will be the next best-seller?

Background

NP Innovations (NPI) is a group of stores in Seattle, US, selling gifts for the home, office and travel. At present, the company is looking for an exciting product to add to its toy or sports goods sections.

🔊 **CD1.81** Listen to a conversation between a general manager and Jim, a buyer at NPI's main store. Discuss these questions. If necessary, listen again.

1. Why was the electronic tennis game so successful?
2. What products does Jim mention?
3. What are Jim's reasons for suggesting each product?

Task

1. Work in groups of three. Read the description of your product and note down key points on the table below.

    Student A: Turn to page 132.   Student B: Turn to page 138.   Student C: Turn to page 143.

2. Tell each other about your products and complete the chart below for the other two products.
3. In groups, discuss the products. Decide which one the company should buy for its stores, with your reasons.
4. Present your group's decision to the rest of the class. Give reasons for your choice.

PRODUCT INFORMATION			
Product name	RC1 spaceship	Mememe	Inside track
Product description			
Price			
Target market			
Colours			
Selling points			
Discounts			

Writing

You work in the buying department of NPI. Write an e-mail to the manufacturer of one of the products. Ask them to send you a catalogue, price list and sample of the product you are interested in. Find out also about their delivery date if you place an order.

➡ *Writing file* page 126

2 Communication styles

WORKING ACROSS CULTURES

A Business cultures: China, Germany, the US

1 Match each country (China, Germany, the US) to the description of its business culture (1–3). Then check your answers on page 136.

2 In groups, discuss which business culture is closest to the one in your own country, or in a country you know well. Give reasons for your answer.

Business culture 1

'We have a direct, formal style of communication, which may seem rude to people from other cultures.'

'We generally use surnames when talking to each other at work.'

'We do not have an open-door policy. We often work with our office doors closed.'

Business culture 2

'We believe that "time is money", so we like to get down to business quickly.'

'We are direct and open in our business relationships, and are open about our personal lives, too.'

'We generally use first names or nicknames when talking to each other at work.'

Business culture 3

'We believe in consensus, so everyone should agree about an opinion or idea.'

'In our country, staff obey their managers and respect their instructions.'

'It is very important to know the title and status of people we communicate with.'

B Business culture in the US

1 Decide whether these statements are true (T) or false (F).

1 A light handshake is best when you meet American businesspeople.
2 When you talk to Americans, do not look directly at them.
3 Americans do not stand very close to people when talking to them.
4 Americans have a formal style of speaking.
5 Agendas are not usually changed during meetings in the US.
6 You should hold your business card in both hands when presenting it.

2 ◁)) CD1.82 Listen to an expert on international communication. He is talking to a group of executives about business culture in the US. Check your answers to the statements in Exercise 1.

3 What is your impression of the business culture in the US? Are there any features of its culture that you like/dislike?

C Business culture in Germany

1. Read these extracts about German business culture from an online guide.
2. In pairs, discuss the similarities and differences to your own country's business culture.

Greetings
When German people greet each other, they shake hands briefly but firmly, keeping direct eye contact.

Personal space
Personal space is important for Germans. They like to keep someone at arm's length when talking to them, unless they know the other person well.

Communication style
Germans have an open and direct way of communicating. People from other cultures can sometimes be surprised or upset by this.

Punctuality
Punctuality is important in German business. They expect you to be on time for meetings and appointments.

Names and titles
Titles are important when you first meet German businesspeople. When you talk to them, use *Herr* (Mr) or *Frau* (Mrs/Ms), followed by their title and surname. For example, if the person has an academic degree, such as *Doktor*, you should address them as *Herr* (or *Frau*) *Doktor Müller*.

Meetings
Agendas are followed strictly and there are usually definite beginning and ending times.

D Business culture in China

🔊 CD1.83 Gayle Bradley, an American business executive, has just returned to the US after working for a year in the company's subsidiary in Shanghai, China. She talks to a colleague, Don Sanders, about the Chinese business culture. Listen and answer these questions.

1. When do you usually shake hands in a Chinese company?
2. Why do the Chinese try not to say *no* to you?
3. What is the difference between the Chinese and American way of communicating?
4. What is a good way of finding out what a Chinese person really means?
5. What is the best way of addressing a Chinese business contact?
   a) by surname only   b) by title and surname   c) by title only
6. How should you present your business card?
7. Why is it not good to interrupt a Chinese person in a meeting?

Task

Work in groups. You work for a multinational company. You have the opportunity of a one-year posting to a subsidiary in either China, the US or Germany. You will work with a departmental manager and local staff.

Discuss these questions.

1. Which subsidiary do you want to go to? Give reasons for your answer.
2. How will you prepare for your posting?
3. What do you hope to learn from your one-year visit?

UNIT B Revision

4 Travel

VOCABULARY

Complete the text below using the words from the box.

book   buy   check in   do   go through   queue   take   watch

I often travel from England to South Africa for business. It's always the same. First, I go on the Internet and ....¹ a plane ticket. I also ....² a hotel room for my stay.

When I get to the airport, I never ....³ at the check-in desk. I use electronic check-in and I carry my luggage onto the plane with me. Of course, I always ....⁴ security. Sometimes they look inside my suitcase.

On the plane, I usually have lunch and ....⁵ an in-flight movie.

When I arrive, I ....⁶ a taxi to my hotel. I ....⁷ at the hotel, have a shower and eat. Then it's time for bed.

When I return home, I ....⁸ some shopping at the airport. I always buy souvenirs.

THERE IS / THERE ARE

Complete this conversation with the correct form (positive, negative or question) of *there is* or *there are*.

A: Excuse me, ...¹ a bank near here?

B: I'm afraid ....² a bank near here, but ....³ two cash machines.

A: Oh, that's fine. Where are the cash machines?

B: ....⁴ a cash machine in the supermarket. Do you know where that is?

A: No, I don't.

B: OK, do you know where the Tourist Information Office is?

A: Yes, I do. ....⁵ a cash machine there?

B: Yes, very near there.

A: OK, I can find that. One more question.

B: Yes?

A: ....⁶ any bookshops near the hotel?

B: Sorry, ...⁷ any. But ....⁸ a lot of bookshops in the town centre.

A: OK. Thank you.

SKILLS

A Who asks the question? Write R (receptionist) or C (customer).

1 Hello, City Hotel. How can I help you?

2 So, that's a single room for two nights, the 4th and 5th?

3 Is there a car park?

4 How much is it per night?

5 Can I have your credit-card details, please?

6 Can I pay with Visa?

7 What time do you expect to arrive?

8 Is there a pick-up service?

UNIT B ▸▸ REVISION

B Match each reply (a–h) with a question from Exercise A (1–8).

a) It's a Visa card. The number is 4409 …

b) Yes, that's right.

c) I'd like to book a room from Monday 9th to Thursday 12th.

d) Yes, Visa is no problem.

e) At about six o'clock.

f) It's 80 euros.

g) Yes, there is. Our driver can meet you at the airport.

h) No, I'm afraid there isn't. But there's a public car park near the hotel.

5 Food and entertaining

VOCABULARY

Put these food items in the correct column of the table below.

| apple apple pie aubergine beef cheesecake chocolate mousse |
| cod grapes lamb onion peach peas trout tuna veal |

| meat | fish | fruit | dessert | vegetable |

SOME/ANY; MANY, MUCH AND A LOT OF

Choose the best words to complete this conversation.

Ian: How *many / much*^{1} time do you have for lunch?

Ben: I have an hour. Are there *any / much*^{2} restaurants near here?

Ian: Yes, there are *any / some*^{3} restaurants about five minutes from here. What kind of food would you like?

Ben: How about *some / a lot of*^{4} hot, spicy food?

Ian: There are *a lot of / much*^{5} restaurants with spicy food: Thai, Indian, Mexican …

Ben: There aren't *many / some*^{6} Mexican restaurants in my town, so let's try Mexican.

SKILLS

A Match the sentence halves.

1 Let's go

2 My suggestion is

3 How about

4 Why don't we

5 In my opinion,

6 I see what you mean,

a) to go for a coffee.

b) visit the museum?

c) but I don't think we have time.

d) to the new Italian restaurant.

e) trying the Indian restaurant?

f) an Indian curry is the best idea.

B Complete the sentences below using the words from the box.

| agree exactly know point right true |

1 Yes, …………, because it's easy to reserve a private room.

2 I don't ………… about that. I think it's too far away.

3 You're …………. The food is great.

4 That's a good …………, but you need to book.

5 That's …………. There 's a nice view of the mountains.

6 Yes, I …………. The prices are reasonable.

63

6 Buying and selling

VOCABULARY

Read this advertisement. Choose the best word to complete each sentence below.

> ### The Bristol Chair and Sofa Company
> This weekend, we're offering great deals on sofas:
> - 20% discount on everything in our shop
> - 66% discount on selected sofas
> - two for the price of one on selected chairs
> - free delivery in the Bristol area
> - interest-free credit for one year
> - low deposit

1 *Some / All* of the shop's products have special lower prices this weekend.
2 Some sofas are *half / a third* of the usual price.
3 The price for *two chairs / one chair* is half of the usual price.
4 There is *a small price / no charge* for bringing a sofa to your house in Bristol.
5 It *costs / doesn't cost* extra to pay for the sofa over one year.
6 There is *a small amount of / no* money to pay at the beginning.

PAST SIMPLE

Complete the text below using the past tense of the verbs from the box.

| become   decide   do   graduate   join   offer   start   work |

Emily Sykes ....[1] from London University in 2005 with a degree in accountancy. As part of her course, she ....[2] an internship in the accounts department of an advertising agency. After her degree, the firm ....[3] her a permanent job as an accountant. She ....[4] there from 2005 to 2007. During this time, she ....[5] to do a Master's degree in accountancy. In 2007, she ....[6] a one-year course at the London School of Economics. Following her Master's course, she ....[7] an import–export firm in London. Two years ago, she ....[8] the head of the accounting department.

WRITING

Write a paragraph (75–100 words) about Lars Karlsson.

2003–2006	studies at Stockholm University; does internship with marketing firm as part of his course; graduates with a degree in marketing
2006	graduates with a degree in marketing; after graduation, JKKL Market Research offers him a job as a researcher
2006 to 2009	works for JKKL; decides to start his own small market-research company
2009	leaves JKKL; opens a small research company, called Lars Karlsson Marketing
two years ago	hires three researchers
now	business very successful

Cultures 2 : Communication styles

A Choose the correct words to complete these tips for Germans doing business in China.

Greetings

When you *meet / notice* ¹ Chinese colleagues at work, you shake hands. You also shake hands at the end of the day, too. It's common to *listen / nod* ² as well. This sort of greeting is very familiar to Germans and will come naturally.

Directness

Words such as 'maybe', 'we'll see' and 'perhaps' often *mean / understand* ³ 'no'. This is because simply saying 'no' feels too direct and impolite in Chinese culture. *Notice / Listen* ⁴ carefully to everything people say in a business meeting. You may not hear the word 'no', but the meaning of what you do hear could be 'no'.

This also means that the usual direct German way of communicating may be surprising or upsetting. You may need to learn to *understand / use* ⁵ indirectness, and to be more indirect in your own communication.

One way to understand the meaning of indirect words is to *notice / present* ⁶ the speaker's body language, facial expressions and gestures. This is part of understanding the whole message.

Names and titles

Chinese businesspeople generally *understand / use* ⁷ a title such as Mr, Mrs and Miss followed by their surname. For example, you might say, 'Good morning, Chief Engineer Tung'. As with greetings, this aspect of Chinese culture will seem very familiar to Germans.

Business cards

You should *meet / present* ⁸ your business card with both hands. One side must be in Chinese, and that's the side you *use / show* ⁹ to your Chinese contact.

B Match each of these statements about doing business in the US with one of the four headings in Exercise A.

1 'We prefer first names.'
2 'There are no special rules about this. Sometimes we fold them up or write on them.'
3 'We really like to get to the point.'
4 'Look us in the eye and shake hands firmly.'

2.1 Meetings

Objectives

Speaking
- Can ask someone to repeat a specific point or idea.
- Can ask simple questions to find out about a subject.

Listening
Can generally identify the topic of discussion around them when conducted slowly and clearly.

Lesson deliverable
To plan and participate in meetings where you have to reach a decision.

Performance review
To review your own progress and performance against the lesson objectives at the end of the lesson.

A SPEAKING

Discuss these questions in pairs. Then compare your ideas with the class.

1 What is a *trade fair*?
2 Do you know any famous ones?
3 What products are on show at the trade fair in the photo?

B LISTENING 1

1 🔊 **BSA2.1.7** Louise is Head Buyer of gifts and stationery for a UK retail chain. She has called a team meeting. Listen and circle the correct answer. What are they discussing?

which trade fair to visit / which products to buy

2 🔊 **BSA2.1.7** Listen again and circle the correct sentences.

1 There are *two / three* people in the meeting.
2 It's *June / July* now.
3 They *don't have much time / have a lot of time* to choose a trade fair.
4 They *didn't visit / visited* Birmingham last year.
5 The fair at the NEC has *29,000 / 2,900* visitors.
6 It has *400 / 1,400* exhibitors.
7 It lasts *four / five* days.
8 Louise *agrees / doesn't agree* that they can visit two fairs this year.

C LISTENING 2

1 🔊 **BSA2.1.7** Listen to the recording again and complete the gaps.

1 Jurgen: Sorry, Louise ………… ………… visitors did you say?
2 Jurgen: And how many exhibitors ………… ………… ………… ?
3 Emily: ………… Louise, ………… ………… 400 exhibitors?
4 Emily: How much ………… ………… we spend there?
5 Emily: Can we go to ………… ………… ………… fair this year?

2 Match sentences 1–5 in Exercise C1 above with the correct description below.

A Asking someone to repeat a specific point.
B Asking a simple question to find out about a subject.

1 ……… 2 ……… 3 ………
4 ……… 5 ………

BUSINESS SKILLS: MEETINGS

Task

Pre-task: Preparation

Work in teams of three, A, B and C. You all work for the same gift company. You are going to hold a meeting to decide which trade fair to visit this year.

Student A: Turn to page vi and read the information on your card.

Student B: Turn to page viii and read the information on your card.

Student C: Turn to page x and read the information on your card.

Use the information on your card to:

- prepare questions about your partners' trade fairs
- get ready to answer questions about your trade fair

Part 1: Meeting 1

1 In your groups, hold your meeting. The aim of the meeting is to agree which trade fair to visit.

2 After the meeting, report back to the class on which trade fair your group wants to go to.

Turn to page 49 for useful meetings and discussions language.

Part 2: Meeting 2

1 You know which trade fair and which city you are going to visit. In your groups, hold another meeting to discuss the type of hotel you want to stay in. Think about the city you are going to and discuss the following points:

- **Location** – how far do you want to be from the centre, the airport, the train station, local restaurants?
- **Rooms and room rates** – do you want a 5-star luxury hotel, or a budget hotel?
- **Facilities** – what is important to you? Do you want a good hotel restaurant, a gym or a pool?

2 After the meeting, report back to the class the on which kind of hotel your group wants to go to.

EXTRA PRACTICE: DVD CLIP AND WORKSHEET 2

D PEER REVIEW

In your groups, discuss your meetings. Were they successful? Did everyone speak and ask questions? Think about the good points. Think about the points you can work on.

E SELF-ASSESSMENT

Look at the lesson objectives. Write sentences about you.

I can ....

I can't ....

F PROFESSIONAL DEVELOPMENT AND PERFORMANCE GOALS

List three situations where you can practise your meetings skills in your organisation.

1 ....
....

2 ....
....

3 ....
....

A6

2.2 Presentations

Objectives

Speaking
- Can say what they like and dislike.
- Can ask someone to repeat a specific point or idea.

Listening
Can extract key factual information such as prices, times, and dates from short, clear, simple announcements.

Lesson deliverable
To plan, prepare and give a presentation about the venue for a conference: location and facilities.

Performance review
To review your own progress and performance against the lesson objectives at the end of the lesson.

A SPEAKING 1

Look at the advice for giving presentations. In pairs, agree on the two most important points for you.

a To speak slowly and clearly. ....
b To have good visuals ready. ....
c To be ready to answer questions. ....
d To practise before you start. ....
e To look at the audience. ....

B PRE-LISTENING

Teresa Kent, events coordinator for computer company Darby Tech, is giving a presentation about the venue for their next conference. Which points, a–f, are mentioned on the slide below?

a location   b size   c food
d travel   e conference facilities   d cost

Orange County Convention Center

Always working towards better meetings.

- 2,643 seat theater
- 74 meeting rooms
- 3 full-service restaurants

C LISTENING 1

1 Look at points a–e from an introduction to a presentation. In pairs, put them in a logical order.

a Say your job.
b Thank the audience for coming.
c Introduce the topic of your presentation.
d Explain if you want questions at the end or in the middle of your presentation.
e Give your name.

2 🔊 BSA2.2.8 Listen to the first part of Teresa's introduction to the presentation and check your ideas from question 1.

3 🔊 BSA2.2.9 Listen to the main part of the presentation and complete the key information.

Location: ....^{1}, USA.

Travel: ....^{2} from airport.

Facilities: Total number of rooms: ....^{3}

All sessions in ....^{4} building.

Food: Three restaurants – seat ....^{5} people.

Entertainment: Near ....^{6}.

Dates: ....^{7} to ....^{8} June.

4 🔊 BSA2.2.9 Listen again and put the phrases in the order you hear them in the presentation.

a So, Teresa's going to talk now about …
b Now, let's look at …
c To start, …
d Finally, …
e So, turning to …

D LISTENING 2

🔊 BSA2.2.10 Listen to the two endings to the presentation. Which ending is better? Why?

BUSINESS SKILLS: PRESENTATIONS

E SPEAKING 2

Work in pairs. Take turn to present information about another conference centre. Listen to your partner, take notes and give feedback.

Student A: Turn to page vi.

Student B: Turn to page viii.

F LISTENING 3

🔊 **BSA2.2.11** Listen to the question and answer session at the end of the presentation. Complete the sentences with the words you hear.

1 A: What about parking?

   B: James, ………… you ………… this?

2 A: ………… restaurants?

   B: Do you ………… in Orlando?

3 A: ………… the cost of entertainment be included?

Task

Pre-task: Research

Context: You work for an international company looking for a suitable conference centre for a training meeting.

Work in two groups, A and B. You are going to give a group presentation about one of the conference centres on page vii. Read the information and make notes.

Part 1: Preparation

1 In your groups, prepare a 3–4 minute presentation. Decide who will speak in each section of the presentation. Think about the presentation structure, techniques and language.

2 Complete the gaps using phrases from Exercises A and C4.

Structure:

- **Introducing the presentation:** Who are you? Why are you giving the presentation? What are you going to talk about?
- **Main part of the presentation:** Give the main factual information about the centre: location, travel, facilities, food and entertainment.
- **Ending:** What main points do you need to repeat?

Techniques and language:

- Speak …………^{1} and …………^{2} at the audience.
- Use this phrase to introduce another speaker and explain what they are going to talk about …………………………………^{3}.
- Use these phrases to introduce a new point. …………^{4}, …………^{5}, …………^{6}, …………^{7}.

Part 2: Presentation

Take turns to give your presentations in groups.

Presenters: Use the structure in Part 1. Give your presentation.

Audience: Make notes on the key information while you listen. Think of one question to ask.

G PEER REVIEW

Complete the sentences about another presentation. Give feedback.

You covered these things in the main part of your presentation:

………………………………………………………………………

………………………………………………………………………

You used these techniques / this language when presenting:

………………………………………………………………………

………………………………………………………………………

One thing you did very well was ………….

One suggestion to improve your presentation is ………….

H SELF-ASSESSMENT

Look back at the lesson objectives. Complete the sentences.

I can ………….

I can't ………….

I PROFESSIONAL DEVELOPMENT AND PERFORMANCE GOALS

What information do you need to present in your job? Write three sentences about how you could use the skills in this lesson.

1 ………………………………………………………………………

2 ………………………………………………………………………

3 ………………………………………………………………………

A8

UNIT 7 People

'A company is only as good as the people it keeps.'
Mary Kay Ash (1918–2001), US businesswoman (founder of Mary Kay Cosmetics)

OVERVIEW

VOCABULARY
Describing people

LISTENING
Managing people

LANGUAGE FOCUS 1
Past simple: negatives and questions

READING
Andrea Jung

LANGUAGE FOCUS 2
Question forms

SKILLS
Dealing with problems

CASE STUDY
Tell us about it

STARTING UP

Me	My partner
1	1 ....
2	2 ....
3	3 ....
4	4 ....
5	5 ....
6	6 ....
7	7 ....
8	8 ....

A Work in pairs. Take it in turns to ask each other these questions, then write the answers in the chart on the left.

1 Do you like to work ...
   a) alone?   b) in a team?   c) with a partner?

2 For appointments, do you like to be ...
   a) early?   b) on time?   c) five minutes late?

3 Do you prefer to work ...
   a) at home?   b) in an office?   c) outside?

4 Do you like to travel ...
   a) to new places?   b) to places you know well?   c) only when you need to?

5 In meetings, do you prefer ...
   a) not to speak much?   b) to speak a lot?   c) to be the chairperson?

6 When do you work best?
   a) In the morning   b) In the afternoon   c) In the evening or at night

7 Do you think a lot about the ...
   a) future?   b) past?   c) present?

8 Do you like your friends or colleagues to be ...
   a) intelligent?   b) good-looking?   c) funny?

B Work in new pairs. Tell each other about your own and your first partner's answers.

I like to work in a team. Selim likes to work in a team, too. Selim likes to be on time for appointments, but I like to be early.

UNIT 7 ▸▸ PEOPLE

VOCABULARY
Describing people

A Match the statements (1–10) to the adjectives (a–j).

They ...
1 like to spend time with other people.
2 want to reach the top in their career.
3 have a lot of new ideas.
4 do what they promise to do.
5 are usually calm.
6 spend a lot of time doing a good job.
7 like to be on time.
8 encourage other people to work well.
9 are good at making things work.
10 like to do things for other people.

They are ...
a) ambitious.
b) creative.
c) hard-working.
d) motivating.
e) helpful.
f) punctual.
g) relaxed.
h) sociable.
i) practical.
j) reliable.

B Use adjectives from Exercise A to complete this human-resources report.

Maria Karlsson

Maria is good in a team and she gets on well with her colleagues. She is extremely _sociable_¹. She is never late for meetings – she is always ....² . She is very ....³; she always meets deadlines. She is in the office at 8.00 a.m. every day and usually stays late, so she is very ....⁴. Her boss says this is very ....⁵ to others. Her colleagues have a lot of respect for her work and attitude.

She is also a very ....⁶ person with a lot of good ideas for the future of the company.

C Look again at the adjectives in Exercise A. Which do you think are the three most important for a) a boss; b) a colleague in a team? Discuss your answers with a partner.

I think a hard-working boss is important.
I like to work with ambitious people. They give me energy.

See the **DVD-ROM** for the i-Glossary.

LISTENING
Managing people

A 🔊 CD2.1 Ros Pomeroy, a management consultant, talks about the people she likes to work with. Listen to the first part of the interview. Which adjectives from Vocabulary Exercise A does she mention?

B 🔊 CD2.2 Listen to the second part of the interview and answer these questions.
1 Why did team members hide information from one bad manager?
2 Why were the team members not prepared to take any risks?

C 🔊 CD2.3 Listen and complete the final part of the interview.

Well, luckily, I have met and worked with several good managers, and these are people who are willing to delegate; that is, they will give a ....¹ to a team member to get on and ....². They are less ....³ in how a task is done, but they are clear about setting the ....⁴ and being clear about what ....⁵ they expect.

And a good manager will also give ....⁶ and ....⁷ to a team member when they do a good job.

Ros Pomeroy

Watch the interview on the **DVD-ROM**.

D Answer these questions in pairs.
1 What kind of people do you like working with?
2 What kind of people do you not like working with?

67

UNIT 7 ▸▸ PEOPLE

LANGUAGE FOCUS 1
Past simple: negatives and questions

- For negatives and questions in the past simple, we use the auxiliary *did* (*didn't*) and the infinitive form of the verb.
  You **didn't like** your colleague.
  Did he **leave** the company?
  Why **did** he **leave** the company?

- Note the form with the verb *to be*.
  He **wasn't** good at his job.
  They **weren't** happy at work.
  Was Dan efficient?
  When **were** they in France?

➡ page 151

A Put these words in the right order to make sentences about problems at work.

1 the deadlines / the projects / weren't / for / realistic
  The deadlines for the projects weren't realistic.

2 most people / the office / didn't / leave / until 8 p.m.

3 a / manager / good / wasn't / she

4 on time / start / meetings / didn't

5 didn't / she / to motivate / know / the staff / how

B 🔊 CD2.4 Listen to a conversation to check your answers.

C Correct one mistake in each line of this message.

Maris, I'm sorry. I'm having a bad day. I didn't ~~sent~~ the report   1 ...*send*...
out, and I not check the figures. I didn't get to the bank   2 ....
on time, and I didn't phoned the suppliers. I tried to call you   3 ....
this morning, but you not answer. I think I need to go home.   4 ....

D Complete these questions with *did*, *was* or *were*.

1 ...*Was*... he an efficient manger?
2 When .... you born?
3 When .... Ania start to work for IBM?
4 Why .... Marcus change jobs?
5 Where .... your next job?

E Read the extract below. Then write questions using each of the words from the box.

Where did Danielle grow up?

| Why   How long   What   When   Where |

Danielle grew up in Geneva. She studied engineering at university in Paris. Then she worked for Renault for four years, from 2004 until 2008. She left Renault because she wanted to do an MBA. She did an MBA at the Harvard Business School in 2009. Her next job was with GE.

F Work in pairs. Ask your partner questions about his/her past studies and/or jobs.

READING
Andrea Jung

A Before you read the article below, discuss these questions.
1 What famous businesswomen do you know?
2 What qualities do you need to be a successful business executive?

Andrea Jung
- Born in:
  ....
- Grew up in:
  ....
- Education:
  ....
- Appearance:
  ....
- Company:
  ....
- Professional achievements:
  ....

B As you read the article, make quick notes to complete the profile of Andrea Jung on the left.

C Decide whether these statements are true (T) or false (F). Correct the false ones.
1 Avon sells cosmetics through shops.
2 Andrea Jung speaks English and Chinese.
3 Around 50 per cent of managers at Avon are women.
4 Avon has an all-female board.
5 Jung thinks all-women management teams make the best decisions.
6 She is on the boards of two other companies.

D Find words or phrases in the article with these meanings.
1 people who sell a company's products (paragraph 1)
2 when you decide to do something and do not let anything stop you (paragraph 3)
3 leave a job without finishing it (paragraph 3)
4 all the money that a company receives regularly (paragraph 4)
5 a very strong liking for something (paragraph 6)

E Work in pairs. Imagine you are going to interview Andrea Jung. Write five questions that you would like to ask her.

FT

Women at the top: Andrea Jung

1 In 2011, Andrea Jung celebrated 12 years as Chief Executive of Avon Products. It is a big job. Avon sells cosmetics door to door in more than 120 countries. It has 6.2m sales representatives and a billion customers. It sells four lipsticks and 190 mascaras every second.

2 Jung was born in Toronto to Chinese immigrant parents. Her parents moved to the US when she was two, to get a better education for their children. She grew up in Massachusetts and graduated from Princeton. She speaks fluent Mandarin.

3 "My parents were important in forming my views about leadership," she says. Determination is a strong quality in Chinese culture. In her early career, she had a job that wasn't interesting. She told her parents she didn't like the job and wanted to quit. "'Quit?' they said. 'The Chinese don't quit. You learn more from bad than good experiences – that's how you grow.'"

4 Jung joined Avon in 1994. Four years later, she became Avon's first female CEO. At that time, the company had revenues of $4bn. Today, its revenues are more than $10bn.

5 Avon is known as "the company for women". Most of Avon's representatives are women. About half the managers and four out of the nine members of Avon's board are women. Jung says there are good business reasons for management teams with a mix of men and women. "In mixed teams, communication and decision-making are better."

6 Famous for her long black hair, pearl necklaces and her passion for Avon, Jung is one of the world's top business leaders. She is also on the board of GE and Apple.

UNIT 7 ▸▸ PEOPLE

LANGUAGE FOCUS 2
Question forms

- We form questions which can be answered with *yes* or *no* in two ways.

With *be* or a modal verb (e.g. *can*)	Form of *be* / modal verb	Subject	
He is ambitious.	**Is**	he	ambitious?
She can see us now.	**Can**	she	**see** us now?

With all other verbs	Form of *do* (or other auxiliary)	Subject	
Ana likes Madrid.	**Does**	Ana	**like** Madrid?
Joe left the company.	**Did**	Joe	**leave** the company?

- We begin other types of question with a question word such as *why, where, when, how,* etc.

	Question word	Form of *do, be*, modal or auxiliary	Subject	
She works hard.	Why	**does**	she	**work** hard?
He went away.	When	**did**	he	**go** away?
They were stressed.	Why	**were**	they	stressed?

➡ page 151

A **Discuss these questions in pairs.**

1 What was Steve Jobs's greatest success?
2 What made him successful?

B **Read this article (ignoring the missing information), then write the questions to complete the quiz on page 71. Use the article to help you.**

Barack Obama described Steve Jobs as 'one of the greatest American innovators'. This is his story. He was born on February 24, 1955, ...¹. In 1976, after dropping out of college, Jobs started Apple with ....². The company quickly became successful. In ....³, Apple introduced the famous Macintosh computer. The following year, in 1985, Jobs left Apple because of ....⁴.

After leaving Apple, Jobs set up a new computer company called NeXT. He also bought a company called Pixar. It specialised in ....⁵.

Jobs married his wife, ...⁶ at a Zen Buddhist ceremony in 1991. The couple had three children.

The early nineties were difficult years for Apple, and the company soon wanted Jobs back. In December 1996, Apple bought Jobs's company NeXT. Apple paid ....⁷ for it. Jobs returned to Apple and in 1997 became the CEO. Under his leadership, Jobs turned the company around, with innovative products such as the iMac, iPod, iPhone and iPad. In ....⁸, after a long period of illness, Steve Jobs resigned as Apple's CEO. He died two months later at the age of ....⁹. ....¹⁰ is Apple's new CEO.

In his time at Apple, Steve Jobs created the most valuable technology company in the world. Today, it employs more than ....¹¹ people worldwide.

UNIT 7 ▸▸ PEOPLE

1 **Where was Steve Jobs born?**
   a) In California
   b) In Portland, Oregon
   c) In Chicago

2 ………………………………………………?
   a) A manager at Hewlett Packard
   b) His father
   c) His friend Steve Wozniak.

3 ………………………………………………?
   a) In 1980
   b) In 1982
   c) In 1984

4 ………………………………………………?
   Because of …
   a) bad health.
   b) a great job offer.
   c) disagreements with the CEO, John Sculley.

5 ………………………………………………?
   a) Music
   b) Computer animation
   c) Computer software

6 ………………………………………………?
   a) Melinda
   b) Patricia
   c) Laurene

7 ………………………………………………?
   a) $400m   b) $200m   c) $600m

8 ………………………………………………?
   a) March 2011
   b) August 2011
   c) October 2011

9 ………………………………………………?
   a) 50   b) 56   c) 65

10 ………………………………………………?
   a) Tim Cook
   b) Jonathan Ive
   c) Phil Schiller

11 ………………………………………………?
   More than …
   a) 20,000.
   b) 57,000.
   c) 46,500.

C 🔊 CD2.5 **Listen and check the questions you wrote.**

D **Answer the questions in the quiz above and use your answers to complete the article on page 70.**

E 🔊 CD2.6 **Now listen and check your answers.**

F **Work in pairs. Take it in turns to choose five questions from the quiz and 'test' your partner. Help with answers if necessary.**

G **Complete these sentences. Give true information about yourself.**
   1 Last year, I bought *a new camera*.
   2 Yesterday, I was …
   3 Last summer, I …
   4 When I was a child, …

H **Work in pairs. Tell each other your true sentences. Ask as many follow-up questions as you can.**
   A: *Last year, I bought a new camera.*
   B: *Really! What make was it? / Where did you buy it? / How much did it cost?*

UNIT 7 ▸▸ PEOPLE

SKILLS
Dealing with problems

A Work in pairs. Discuss which of these suggestions you agree with.

When two people try to solve a problem, it is a good idea for them to:
1 describe the problem in detail.
2 show strong feelings.
3 give reasons if they have to say no.
4 speak quietly.
5 find a solution immediately.

B 🔊 CD2.7 Julian works for a coffee importing company. He is talking to the Office Manager, Hanna Butler. Listen and answer these questions.

1 What does Julian want the company to do?
2 What does Hanna suggest to solve the problem?
3 Does Hanna offer to give Julian any money?

C 🔊 CD2.7 Listen again and complete these extracts.

Hanna: Look, I'm really ....¹, Julian. The ....² is, we don't have enough money to pay for language courses.

Hanna: I'm sorry, Julian – it's just not ....³. Why don't you buy one of those self-study courses in Spanish? They're ....⁴, and you can improve your Spanish a lot if you study ....⁵.

Julian: OK, I'll do that. Will the company ....⁶ for a self-study course if I buy one?

Hanna: I can't ....⁷ anything, Julian. But bring the ....⁸ to me and I'll see what
I can do for you.

Watch the discussion on the DVD-ROM.

D Which of the suggestions in Exercise A do Hanna and Julian follow?

E Work in pairs. An office worker in a car-hire firm wants to start work later in the morning, but the manager does not agree. Role-play the situation.

Student A: Turn to page 131.
Student B: Turn to page 139.

USEFUL LANGUAGE

EMPLOYEE

Describing the problem ⟶
I need some training to do my job properly.
I don't have enough money to pay for classes.

Emphasising the problem ⟶
It's really important for me.
It would be really helpful to me.

MANAGER

Making suggestions ⟶
Why don't you buy a self-study course?
How about studying at home?

Giving advice
I think you should visit the shopping centre.

MANAGER

Responding
I'm sorry. It's just not possible.

Explaining the reasons
The problem is, we don't have the money for this.
You see, we have to cut costs.

EMPLOYEE

Accepting suggestions or advice
OK, I'll take a look at one.
OK, I'll think about it.

Tell us about it

Office workers share their problems and offer solutions

Background

A magazine, *Business Today*, has a message board on its website called Office Life. People who have problems at work can leave messages there, either online or by phone. Readers comment on the problems and give advice about how to solve them. Read the problems and discuss the questions below.

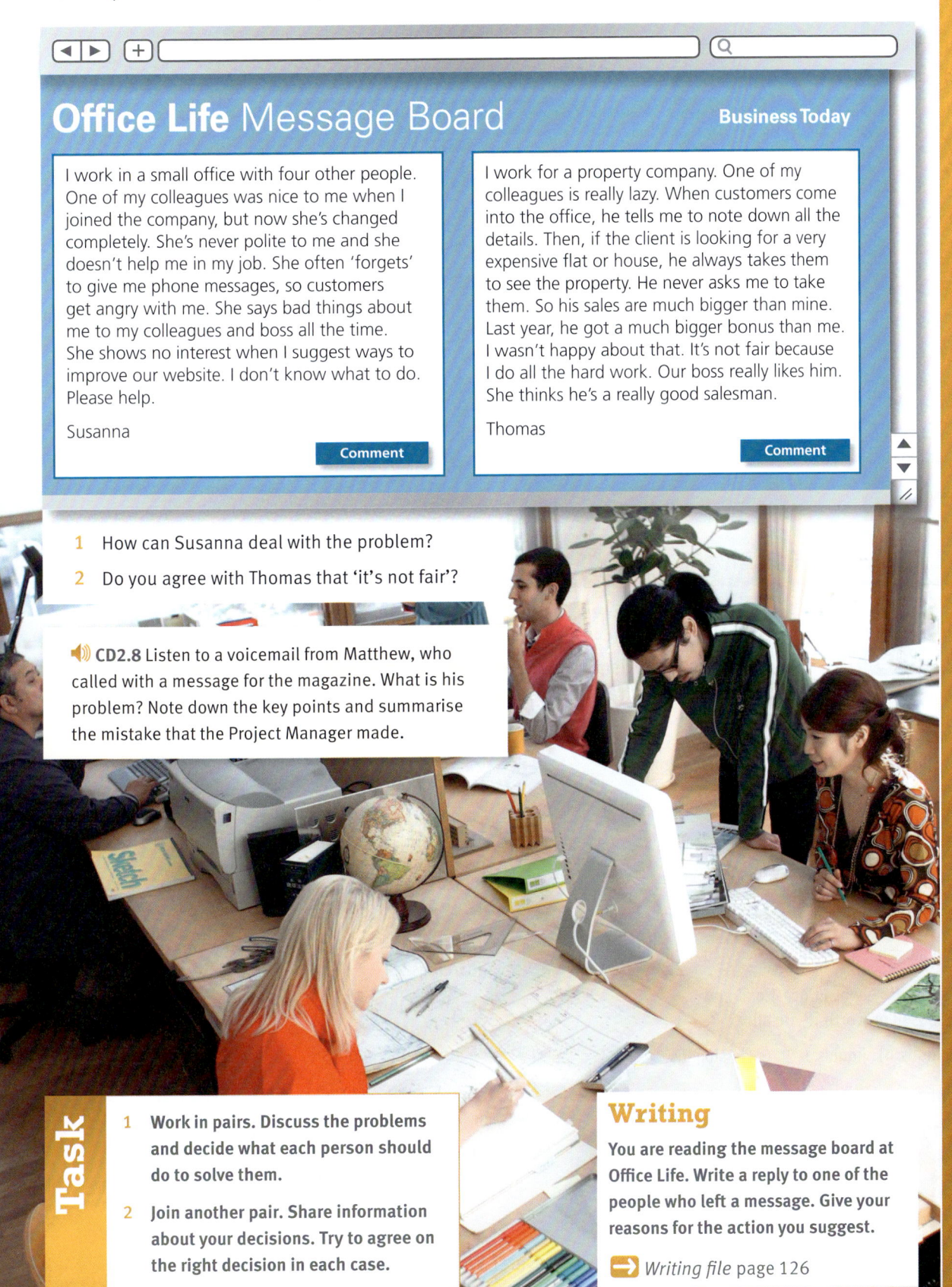

Office Life Message Board
Business Today

I work in a small office with four other people. One of my colleagues was nice to me when I joined the company, but now she's changed completely. She's never polite to me and she doesn't help me in my job. She often 'forgets' to give me phone messages, so customers get angry with me. She says bad things about me to my colleagues and boss all the time. She shows no interest when I suggest ways to improve our website. I don't know what to do. Please help.

Susanna

Comment

I work for a property company. One of my colleagues is really lazy. When customers come into the office, he tells me to note down all the details. Then, if the client is looking for a very expensive flat or house, he always takes them to see the property. He never asks me to take them. So his sales are much bigger than mine. Last year, he got a much bigger bonus than me. I wasn't happy about that. It's not fair because I do all the hard work. Our boss really likes him. She thinks he's a really good salesman.

Thomas

Comment

1. How can Susanna deal with the problem?
2. Do you agree with Thomas that 'it's not fair'?

🔊 **CD2.8** Listen to a voicemail from Matthew, who called with a message for the magazine. What is his problem? Note down the key points and summarise the mistake that the Project Manager made.

Task

1. Work in pairs. Discuss the problems and decide what each person should do to solve them.
2. Join another pair. Share information about your decisions. Try to agree on the right decision in each case.

Writing

You are reading the message board at Office Life. Write a reply to one of the people who left a message. Give your reasons for the action you suggest.

➡ *Writing file* page 126

7
Case study

UNIT 8 Advertising

'*Nobody counts the number of ads you run. They only remember the impression you make.*'
William Bernbach (1911–1982), US advertising executive

OVERVIEW

VOCABULARY
Advertising and markets

READING
TV commercials

language focus 1
Comparatives and superlatives

LISTENING
Good and bad advertising

LANGUAGE FOCUS 2
much / a lot, a little / a bit

SKILLS
Participating in discussions

CASE STUDY
Excelsior Chocolate Products

STARTING UP

A Do this advertising quiz. Compare your answers with a partner. Then turn to page 131 to check your answers.

1 The most common word in advertisements is:
   a) *world.* b) *best.* c) *you.*

2 A short song used in advertising is called a:
   a) jingle. b) pop-up. c) spot.

3 What do you call this?
   a) a slogan b) a logo c) a jingle

4 'Just do it', 'Always Coca-Cola' and 'Because I'm worth it' are all:
   a) logos. b) jingles. c) slogans.

5 In what year did internet advertising begin?
   a) 1990 b) 1994 c) 1998

6 Which company was the first to advertise on the Internet?
   a) AT&T b) McDonald's c) Sony

7 How long is a typical TV commercial?
   a) 20 seconds b) 30 seconds c) 40 seconds

8 Where do you find advertising billboards or hoardings?
   a) on the Internet
   b) in the street
   c) on mobile phones

9 Dentsu, WPP, and Ogilvy and Mather are all advertising:
   a) budgets. b) agencies. c) campaigns.

B What's your favourite advert? Why do you like it?

UNIT 8 ▸▸ ADVERTISING

VOCABULARY
Advertising and markets

A ◉ CD2.9 **Listen and repeat these numbers.**

6,300	six thousand, three hundred
75,807	seventy-five thousand, eight hundred and seven
823,120	eight hundred and twenty-three thousand, one hundred and twenty
1,255,500	one million, two hundred and fifty-five thousand, five hundred
10.5%	ten point five per cent

B ◉ CD2.10 **Listen to part of a sales presentation and underline the correct number in each sentence.**

1 Last year, the company had a market share of *10.3 / 103* per cent.
2 Last year, for the launch of Sparkle Lite, the advertising budget increased by *30 / 13* per cent.
3 Last year, the company sold more than *850,000 / 815,000* units of Sparkle.
4 The new advertising campaign cost *€90,000 / €900,000*.
5 The company wants to increase its market share to *11.5 / 11.9* per cent.
6 Next year, the company wants to sell *210,000 / 2,100,000* units of Sparkle.

C **Match the beginnings of the sentences (1–5) with their endings (a–e).**

1 Coca-Cola is a mass-market product; it
2 Selling special-interest holidays is a niche market; it
3 Rolex watches sell in a luxury market; they are
4 An export market
5 A home market

a) is a small but often profitable market.
b) is outside the producer's country.
c) is in the producer's country.
d) high-quality and expensive goods.
e) sells to large numbers of people.

D **In pairs, think of products which match the types of market in Exercise C.**

Nike shoes sell to a mass market.

Ferrari sports cars are a luxury-market product.

E **Which medium is the best way to advertise these products (or the ones you discussed in Exercise D)? Choose from the list below. Discuss your ideas with a partner.**

> a smartphone   a perfume   a health magazine
> a sports car   a new chocolate bar

- newspapers/magazines (the press)
- online/internet ads
- billboards/hoardings
- TV/radio commercials
- mobile ads
- leaflets/flyers
- free samples

See the DVD-ROM for the i-Glossary.

75

UNIT 8 ►► ADVERTISING

READING
TV commercials

A Before you read the article below, discuss these questions.

1 Which four adjectives best describe a VW Beetle?
   big   fast   feminine   fun   masculine   powerful   safe   stylish   unusual
2 In your country, how popular is the Beetle? Who typically buys it?

B As you read the article, think about these questions.

1 How is the photo in the article related to the 2012 Beetle?
2 What kind of person did VW want to see the advert?

C Choose the best option to complete these sentences.

1 *An American / A German* agency created the commercial.
2 The 2012 Beetle has a more *masculine / feminine* design than the older New Beetle.
3 The target customer for the 2012 Beetle is *male / male and female* drivers.
4 The ad *shows / doesn't show* the new car in detail.
5 VW first showed the commercial on *US / German* TV.
6 VW first showed the car to the public at an event in *Shanghai / New York*.

D In each box, match the words from the article to make word partnerships.

1	advertising	a) break	4	create	d) male drivers/customers
2	commercial	b) event	5	launch	e) the 2012 Beetle
3	launch	c) agency	6	attract	f) a commercial

E Work in pairs. Each choose a TV advertisement you like.

1 Complete these sentences about the advertisement.

   It's an advertisement for ...   *It shows ...*

   The music for the ad is ...   *I like the advertisement because ...*

2 Tell another student about your advertisement.

FT

Volkswagen's Black Beetle ad
by Bernard Simon

In spring 2011, Volkswagen asked the US advertising agency Deutsch, LA to create a TV commercial to launch its latest car, the 2012 Beetle.
5 The 2012 Beetle is bigger, more powerful and more masculine in design than the earlier model, the New Beetle, launched in 1987. Head of Design Klaus Bischoff said, "We
10 wanted to give the car a stronger and more masculine look." The idea was to attract more male drivers. More women than men bought the New Beetle. (Sales to women were
15 61 per cent in 2010.) Luca De Meo, Marketing Director, wants to see a 50–50 split between men and women for the new car.

   The 30-second advert shows a
20 beetle racing through a forest. The beetle has a racing stripe on its back and is much bigger than the other insects. It races past the other insects and cuts corners, just like a high-
25 performance car. At the end of the advertisement, the beetle changes into the outline of the car, in the shadows. The music for the advertisement is the rock song *Black*
30 *Betty*. Using an image of a beetle for the car is not the most original advertising idea, but the advert is fun to watch.
   VW first showed the advert during
35 the commercial breaks of the American football Super Bowl in April 2011. There is usually a lot of interest in the ads during these breaks, and companies can pay $3 million for
40 a 30-second commercial. Later that month, VW showed the new car to the public at launch events in three cities: first in Shanghai, then in Berlin and New York.

UNIT 8 ▸▸ ADVERTISING

LANGUAGE FOCUS 1
Comparatives and superlatives

- We compare two things with the comparative form of the adjective.
  *Sales of luxury cars were **higher** this year than last year.*
  *The Mercedes LX is **more expensive** than a Volkswagen.*

- We compare three or more things with the superlative form.
  *China is **our largest** market in Asia.*
  *What is **the most expensive** make of car?*

➡ page 152

A 🔊 CD2.11 Write the comparative forms of these adjectives. Then listen to check how they are pronounced.

1 small ....
2 fast ....
3 slow ....
4 high ....
5 bad ....
6 good ....
7 competitive ....
8 efficient ....
9 interesting ....

B Look at this chart. Decide whether the sentences below are true (T) or false (F). Correct the false ones.

	VW Passat	Mazda MX-5	Mini Hatchback
Engine size	2.0 litre	1.8 litre	1.6 litre
Maximum speed	195 kph	195 kph	203 kph
Petrol consumption	4.6 litre / 100 km	7.3 litre / 100 km	5.4 litre / 100 km
Luggage compartment	566 litres	150 litres	160 litres
Length	4,769 mm	4,020 mm	3,699 mm
Price	€19,665	€19,174	€13,410

1 The Mazda is a faster car than the Mini.
2 The Mazda has a smaller luggage compartment than the Mini.
3 The Mini has better petrol consumption than the Passat.
4 The Mazda is more expensive than the Passat.
5 The Passat is more practical for a family than the Mini.

C Complete these sentences about the cars in Exercise B. Use the comparative form of the adjectives in brackets.

1 I think the Mazda is a _more stylish_ car than the Mini. (*stylish*)
2 The Passat has a .... engine than the Mazda. (*powerful*)
3 Compared to the Passat, the Mini is .... to park in small spaces. (*easy*)
4 The Passat is .... to run .... the Mazda. (*cheap*)
5 The Passat is a .... car .... the Mini. (*spacious*)

D Complete these conversations. Use the superlative form of the adjectives.

1 A: Advertising on primetime TV is expensive.
   B: Yes, it's _the most expensive_ time of the day to show an advert.
2 A: Nike's 'Write the future' commercial was very good.
   B: Yes, I think it was .... commercial in 2010.
3 A: 2009 was a bad year for the advertising industry.
   B: Yes, it was .... year I can remember.
4 A: China has a very high number of internet users.
   B: Yes, it has .... number of users in the world.

UNIT 8 ▸▸ ADVERTISING

E Which is the best car for each of these people? Choose a car from Exercise B.

Stefan
I have a wife and three children. We drive a lot to visit relatives at weekends.

Sophie
I have a company car, but I want a fun car to drive at the weekends. I live in Paris, so parking isn't easy.

Petra
I need a car to take my six-year-old son to school and for local shopping. I don't want a car that is expensive to run.

F Work in pairs. Explain your choice to your partner.

I think the … is the best car for … It's cheaper to run than the others. It's also the smallest car, so it's easy to park in town.

LISTENING
Good and bad advertising

Liz Credé

A In pairs, discuss these questions.
1. What's your favourite advert on TV at the moment? Why do you like it?
2. Can you give an example of a bad advert?
3. Do you think there is too much advertising?

B 🔊 CD2.12 Listen to the first part of an interview with Liz Credé, an organisation development consultant. Which of the questions in Exercise A does she answer?

C 🔊 CD2.12 Listen again and answer these questions.
1. What is the product in the advert she does not like?
2. What is the advert about?
3. Why does she not like the advert? (Give two reasons.)

D 🔊 CD2.13 In the second part of the interview, Liz talks about what makes an advert really effective. Listen and complete this extract.

I think what makes it ………..¹ is for it to be very ………..², that you remember a key ………..³ or the main ………..⁴ in it. One that I particularly like at the moment is the Honda cars ………..⁵, which uses pictures of flowers in the countryside to give a very ………..⁶ message about the engine and the cars.

E In pairs, think of four ways to complete this sentence.

Adverts should not …

Watch the interview on the DVD-ROM.

F 🔊 CD2.14 Listen to the final part of the interview and complete the sentence in Exercise E for Liz. What example does she give?

UNIT 8 ▸▸ ADVERTISING

LANGUAGE FOCUS 2
much / a lot, a little / a bit

- We use *much* or *a lot* with comparative adjectives to talk about large differences. *Much* is more formal than *a lot*.
  Cars with low petrol consumption are **much** cheaper to run.
  New Zealand is a good market, but Australia is **a lot** bigger.

- We use *a little* or *a bit* to talk about small differences. *A little* is more formal than *a bit*.
  The PDX100 is **a little** more expensive than the PDX200.

➡ page 152

A Look at this chart. What does it show?

Toptek advertising spend 2010–2011

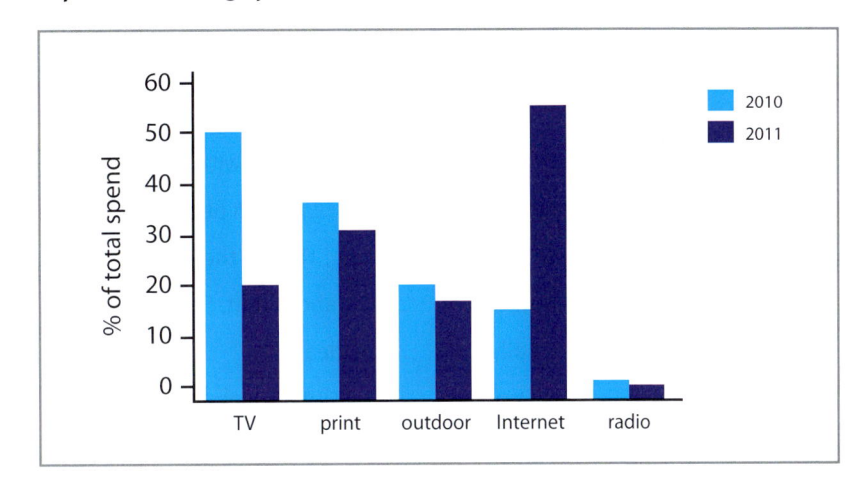

B Complete these sentences about the chart.

1 In 2010, Toptek spent most of its advertising budget on ....
2 The amount it spent on TV advertising was .... lower in 2011.
3 In 2010, the spend on outdoor advertising was a .... higher than in 2011.
4 Toptek spent most of the budget on .... advertising in 2011.

C Compare Toptek's advertising spend in 2010 and 2011. Talk about these points.

1 *In 2010, Toptek spent about 15 per cent of its budget on internet advertising. The amount it spent in 2011 was much higher.*

1 internet advertising
2 print advertising
3 radio advertising

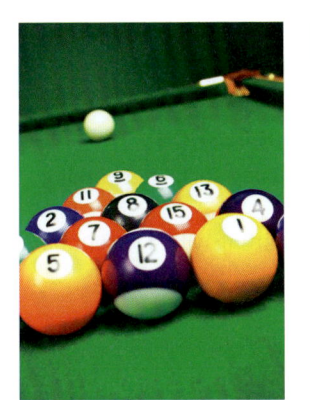

D Compare these two pool tables using *much*, *a lot*, *a little* and *a bit*.

The Classic pool table is a bit wider than the Trainer pool table.

	Trainer pool table	Classic pool table
Width	93 cm	95 cm
Length	176 cm	180 cm
Height	78 cm	80 cm
Weight	25 kg	50 kg
Price	£144	£280

UNIT 8 ›› ADVERTISING

SKILLS
Participating in discussions

A 🔊 **CD2.15** Chris, Nicky and Stephen own a chain of florists in London. They are talking about new ways of advertising their business. Listen to their conversation and choose the correct endings for these sentences.

1 Chris doesn't want a big advertising campaign because it:
   a) is too expensive.   b) is the wrong time.   c) will not be successful.
2 Chris wants to target:
   a) businesspeople.   b) wedding organisers.   c) older people.
3 Nicky suggests that they should:
   a) improve their website.   b) redesign their website.   c) try new websites.
4 They plan to start by advertising their flowers on:
   a) Facebook.   b) Twitter.   c) all the social networking sites.

B 🔊 **CD2.15** Listen to the conversation again and complete these extracts.

1 Sorry, Stephen, I don't *agree* with you.
2 I think we need to .... rich people.
3 Yeah, you're .... They're the people to aim at ...
4 How do you .... about that, Stephen?
5 I really .... the idea.
6 How about .... with a Facebook page?

C Look at the extracts in Exercise B. For each one, decide whether the speaker is:
   a) agreeing.
   b) disagreeing.   1
   c) asking for an opinion.
   d) giving an opinion.
   e) making a suggestion.

Watch the discussion on the DVD-ROM.

D Work in groups of three. Role-play this situation. You are taking part in a marketing meeting to discuss the launch of a new range of biscuits and how to promote it.

Student A: Turn to page 133.
Student B: Turn to page 139.
Student C: Turn to page 143.

USEFUL LANGUAGE

AGREEING
You're right.
I really like the idea.
I agree with you.

DISAGREEING
(Sorry,) I don't agree with you.
I'm afraid I don't agree.
I'm not sure I agree with you.

ASKING FOR AN OPINION
What do you think?
What's your opinion?
How do you feel about that?

GIVING AN OPINION
I think we need to target rich people.
In my opinion, we can use a different way of advertising.
Let's use Facebook and Twitter.

MAKING A SUGGESTION
What about using social networking sites?
How about starting with a Facebook page?

Excelsior Chocolate Products

Case study 8

What are the best ways to advertise a new chocolate bar?

Background

Excelsior Chocolate Products (ECP) is an international company based in Switzerland. It is planning to launch a high-quality dark chocolate bar early next year. The marketing department is making some decisions now concerning the advertising and promotion of the product.

The new chocolate bar

🔊 **CD2.16** Listen to a conversation between Laurence and Tracy, two members of the marketing department of ECP. They are talking about an advertising campaign **by one of their competitors, Palmer and Mason. Discuss these questions.**

1. What do they like about their competitor's advertising campaign?
2. What advantage does their competitor have when planning advertising campaigns?
3. How will this advantage affect their competitor's campaign?

Look at the options below for the new chocolate bar.

Names	Selling prices (standard bar)	Target market	Advertising agency	Advertising media	Main outlets
• High Life • Dreamland • Fantastik	• €2 • €3 • €4 or more	• Women • People in the middle-income group • Professional people with high incomes	• Butler and Jones: one of the biggest agencies in the industry • The 3T group: won an award last year for the best magazine advert • James Watson and Associates: a new, very creative agency with young staff	• Billboards • Magazines and newspapers • Internet adverts	• Specialist chocolate stores • Top department stores • Supermarkets

Task

Work in small groups. Look at the information and discuss how ECP needs to launch its new chocolate bar.

1. Discuss which option in each category is the best for the company.
2. Think of ideas for the following:
   - a good slogan for the chocolate bar
     'The best for you'
   - a famous person to advertise the product
     a film star, sports player, TV personality, etc.
   - a TV advert (for the UK, US, Australia)
     a waiter bringing the chocolate bar to customers in a restaurant
   - special events advertising
     the US 'World Series' baseball competition
3. Present your ideas to the other groups. Answer their questions.
4. Work as one group. Decide on the best idea in each category for the launch. Use language from the Useful language box on page 80 if you agree, disagree or want to make suggestions to your colleagues.

Writing

Write a short description of your plans for the launch of the new chocolate bar. Describe your ideas for the slogan, endorsements, TV adverts and special events advertising.

→ *Writing file page 127*

UNIT 9 Companies

'Companies, like people, cannot be skilful at everything.'
Dorothy Leonard, US academic and business author

OVERVIEW

VOCABULARY
Describing companies

LISTENING
A favourite company

LANGUAGE FOCUS 1
Present continuous

READING
Gamesa

LANGUAGE FOCUS 2
Present simple or present continuous

SKILLS
Starting a presentation

CASE STUDY
Presenting your company

STARTING UP

A Do this companies quiz. Discuss your answers with a partner. Then turn to page 131 to check your answers.

Which company:

1 began in 1865 as a forestry and power business?
 a) Ericsson b) Nokia c) Motorola

2 makes clothing, but is not American?
 a) Juicy Couture b) Diesel
 c) Abercrombie and Fitch

3 has its head office in San Francisco?
 a) Levi-Strauss b) Nike c) Disney

4 buys more sugar than any other company in the world?
 a) Nestlé b) Coca-Cola c) Suchard

5 employs more people than any other company?
 a) Walmart b) Siemens
 c) General Motors

6 has the largest factory in the world?
 a) Boeing b) Ford c) Sony

7 was started by Ray A. Kroc in 1955?
 a) Burger King
 b) McDonald's
 c) Kentucky Fried Chicken

8 is not based in Seattle, Washington?
 a) Starbucks
 b) Amazon
 c) Microsoft

9 produced the world's best-selling car?
 a) Ford b) Volkswagen c) Fiat

10 is the most admired in the world?
 a) FedEx
 b) Google
 c) Apple

B What famous companies come from your country? What do they do or make? What's special about them?

UNIT 9 ▸▸ COMPANIES

VOCABULARY
Describing companies

A The sentences below describe two companies, Dalotek and Green Shoots. Choose pairs of sentences which describe similar things and write them in the correct column of this chart.

Dalotek	Green Shoots
A large car-parts company	A small garden-products company
John Smith started Dalotek in 1960.	George and James Hawkins began Green Shoots in the 1920s.

1 ~~John Smith started Dalotek in 1960.~~
2 It has a workforce of 2,500.
3 Dalotek exports to over 12 countries.
4 It manufactures car parts.
5 It introduces one or two new components each year.
6 It employs about 35 people.
7 Green Shoots sells some of its products abroad.
8 It makes garden products.
9 ~~George and James Hawkins began Green Shoots in the 1920s.~~
10 Green Shoots supplies the gardening industry.
11 It launches 12 new products a year.
12 Dalotek provides components for the car industry.

B Underline the verbs or verb phrases which mean the same thing in each pair of sentences in the chart in Exercise A.

John Smith <u>started</u> Dalotek in 1960.

George and James Hawkins <u>began</u> Green Shoots in the 1920s.

C Use the verbs you underlined in Exercise B to complete this company profile.

GNK Services

GNK Services <u>began</u>¹ in 1989 when Dieter Norland left his job as an engineer in the computer industry. The company ....² high-tech security alarms and ....³ its products all over the world. It ....⁴ 150 people at its factory near Rotterdam, although the company's head office is in Amsterdam and ....⁵ a staff of 20. The company ....⁶ a number of new products each year. GNK Services ....⁷ products to the security industry and ....⁸ domestic alarms for the general public.

See the DVD-ROM for the i-Glossary.

D Now write a similar profile for your company or a company you know well.

UNIT 9 ▸▸ COMPANIES

LISTENING
A favourite company

Jeremy Keeley

A 🔊 **CD2.17** Jeremy Keeley, a specialist in change leadership, is talking about his favourite company. Listen to the first part of the interview and complete these notes.

> **LEADERS**
> - decent people who ....[1] their workers
> - care about their ....[2]
> - want to meet customers' ....[3]
> - care about the ....[4]
>
> **WORKERS**
> - believe they're helping people when they most ....[5] it

B 🔊 **CD2.18** Listen to the second part of the interview and answer these questions.

1 What type of company would Jeremy like to work for?
2 What sort of things would that company produce or do?
3 What do the best companies have in common?
4 Which of the following does Jeremy mention?
   a) wanting workers to work at their best
   b) understanding customers' needs
   c) looking after the environment
   d) promoting equality
   e) being ethical and legal

Watch the interview on the DVD-ROM.

C 🔊 **CD2.19** Listen to the final part. What are these companies famous for?

1 Rolls Royce 2 Apple 3 Google 4 Fairtrade 5 Body Shop

D In pairs, what is your favourite company and why?

LANGUAGE FOCUS 1
Present continuous

> - We use the present continuous to talk about temporary situations and actions that are happening now.
>   *We can't find an office in the centre of town, so now we **are** (we**'re**) **looking** in the business park.*
>   *'What **is** Helene **doing**?' 'She **is** (She**'s**) **having** lunch with a customer.'*
>
> - We also use the present continuous to talk about developments and changes.
>   *The cost of energy **is rising** quickly.*
>   *Costs are lower in Vietnam, so we **are** (we**'re**) **moving** production there.*
>
> - The present continuous is formed with *be* and the *-ing* form of the main verb.
>
> ➡ page 153

A Complete these sentences with the present continuous form of the verbs in brackets. Use contractions where possible.

1 Matti isn't in the office today. He*'s meeting* (meet) customers all day.
2 Marta's on the phone. She .... (call) about the sales figure.
3 I can't come to the meeting. I .... (write) a report. I must finish it this morning.
4 We .... (build) a new factory in Spain. The work is nearly finished.
5 The marketing team is very busy right now. They .... (work) on the launch of a new product.
6 Our business in Japan .... (not go) well at the moment.
7 We have a lot of orders, so production .... (hire) 40 extra staff.

UNIT 9 ▸▸ COMPANIES

B Work in pairs. Ask and answer these two questions. Use your own ideas and words from the box in your answers.

| build   change   develop   improve   introduce   prepare   open   organise   write |

A: *What are you working on at the moment?*
B: *I'm preparing a presentation for a seminar.*
A: *What is happening at your company/university?*
B: *They're improving security.*

READING
Gamesa

A Discuss these questions.

1 How popular is wind energy in your country?
2 Which of these points are advantages and disadvantages for wind energy? Add other points you can think of.
   • safe   • clean form of energy   • wind is not constant   • noisy   • ugly

B Before you read the article, match the words and phrases (1–6) to their meanings (a–f).

1 to install   a) to start something new
2 manufacturing plant   b) a company that is owned by another larger company
3 subsidiary   c) to put equipment in position, so it is ready to use
4 to set up   d) a company that you buy from
5 component   e) a factory that makes machines and equipment
6 supplier   f) a part of a machine

C Read this article about a company in the wind-energy business. Is it doing better in its home market or in international markets?

New markets for Gamesa

Four new wind turbines, beside a banana farm in a southern Indian village, turn in the wind, producing electricity for the local community. The turbines are made by Gamesa, a world leader in wind technology.

The Spanish company designs, manufactures and installs wind turbines all over the world. It has sales offices in 20 countries and 30 manufacturing plants in Europe, the US, China and now in India and Brazil, too. It employs nearly 8,000 people worldwide.

Because of weakness in its traditional European and US markets, Gamesa's strategy for growth is to expand its business in India and Latin America, especially Brazil. The strategy is working. In the first half of 2011, revenues rose by 26% to €1,297 million. In the same period, sales were up 29%. For the first time in its history, 100% of its sales were from outside Spain.

D Complete this fact file.

Company	*Gamesa*[1]	Products	............[3]
Nationality:	............[2]	Growth markets	India and ....[4]
Numbers of: • employees • countries with sales offices • manufacturing plants	............[5] ....[6] ....[7]	Results (first half 2011) • Revenues: • Sales:	............[8] ....[9]

85

UNIT 9 ▸▸ COMPANIES

E **Work in pairs.**

Student A: Turn to page 134.
Student B: Turn to page 141.

Share the information in your notes with your partner. How is Gamesa's strategy the same in each country? How is it different?

F **Work in pairs. In each box, match words and phrases from the articles on Gamesa to make word partnerships.**

1	wind	a)	plant(s)	5	enter	e)	quality
2	sales	b)	centre	6	set up	f)	the (Brazilian) market
3	manufacturing	c)	turbines	7	recruit	g)	a subsidiary
4	technology	d)	offices	8	improve	h)	(more) workers

G **Use the notes you made in Exercise E to write a short text for a green-energy website about Gamesa's activities.**

LANGUAGE FOCUS 2
Present simple or present continuous

Complete these rules with *present simple* or *present continuous*.

- We use the .... to describe permanent situations, ones which won't change.
  I **work** in Paris.

- We use the .... to describe temporary situations, ones which happen for a short time.
  I**'m working** in Paris this month.

➡ page 153

A **Which tense are these time expressions normally used with? Put them in the correct column of the chart below.**

always   at the moment   currently   every day   normally   now
this time   today   usually

Present simple	Present continuous
always	*at the moment*

B **Choose either the present simple or the present continuous form of the verb to complete these sentences.**

1 I *stay* / *am staying* at the Ritz every time I'm in New York. I *stay* / *am staying* at the Ritz at the moment.

2 Jan *works* / *is working* from home today. She usually *works* / *is working* at the company's training centre.

3 She often *calls* / *is calling* Russia. Right now, she *calls* / *is calling* a customer in Moscow.

4 I don't usually *deal* / *dealing* with the paperwork. I *deal* / *am dealing* with all the paperwork while Susan is away.

5 Deliveries *take* / *are taking* over two months at present. Usually they *take* / *are taking* just six weeks.

6 Most of the time we *use* / *are using* DHL for deliveries. This time, we *use* / *are using* a different company.

UNIT 9 ▸▸ COMPANIES

C Complete this article with the present simple or the present continuous form of the verbs in brackets.

Profile PRET A MANGER

Pret A Manger .....is.....¹ (be) a UK company and one of the world's leading sandwich chains. It ....² (sell) freshly made sandwiches in busy city centres. At the end of each day, the shops ....³ (give) any unsold products to the homeless. Currently, Pret ....⁴ (do) very well in the south of England.

Pret ....⁵ (operate) a total of 232 UK outlets, and this year it ....⁶ (plan) new outlets for London. In the US, it ....⁷ (have) 23 outlets in New York and another 10 in Hong Kong.

Pret's international activities ....⁸ (grow) in importance. This month, as part of the next stage of expansion, Pret ....⁹ (open) its first two shops in Paris. At the same time, the marketing team ....¹⁰ (work) with Lewis PR, a global PR company, to improve the brand's international image.

D Work in pairs. Role-play this situation. Take it in turns to show each other around your company. Say what happens in each area and what is happening now.

Student A

EBB Bank

Area	What happens	What is happening now
main hall	serve customers	cashier / talk / to a customer
currency section	exchange foreign currency	customer / change / dollars into euros
loans section	Assistant Manager arranges loans for customers	Assistant Manager / talk / to a customer on the phone
Manager's office	Manager works	Manager / meet / an important client
reception desk	staff answer questions from customers	receptionist / listen / to a customer's complaint

This is the main hall. We serve customers here. At the moment, a cashier is talking to a customer.

Student B

Goldcrest Hotel

Area	What happens	What is happening now
kitchen	prepare and cook meals	chefs / prepare / today's lunch
restaurant	serve breakfast, lunch and dinner	waiter / clear / the tables
reception	welcome guests, answer calls	receptionist / talk / to a guest
gift shop	sell souvenirs	sales assistant / help / a customer
a bedroom	guests stay	maid / clean / the room

This is the kitchen. We prepare and cook meals here. At the moment, the chefs are preparing today's lunch.

UNIT 9 ▸▸ COMPANIES

SKILLS
Starting a presentation

A 🔊 CD2.20 **Listen to the start of a presentation. Number these items (a–f) in the order you hear them.**

a) There are three parts to my presentation. Firstly, … ☐
b) By the end of my presentation, you will understand clearly our future plans. ☐
c) Good afternoon, everyone. My name's Robert Ford. ☐ 1
d) If you don't mind, let's leave questions to the end. ☐
e) I'd like to talk about our new marketing strategy. ☐
f) Finally, the details of the costs … ☐

B 🔊 CD2.20 **Listen again. Match the headings (1–5) to the items (a–f) in Exercise A. One heading goes with two items.**

1 Topic of the talk
2 Aim
3 Greeting the audience
4 Plan of the talk
5 Dealing with questions

Watch the presentation on the DVD-ROM.

C **Work in pairs. Prepare an introduction to a presentation. Then introduce the presentation to each other. Choose Role A or Role B below, and use the notes to introduce your presentation. Add any information you wish.**

Role A	Role B
Topic The launch of your company's new product	**Topic** Your company's new teleconferencing system
Plan 1 The background to the launch 2 The features of the new product 3 The advertising and marketing plans	**Plan** 1 The background – why we need to change 2 The new system and its benefits 3 How to use it and to report faults
Aim To give a clear idea of the sales potential of the product	**Aim** To give a clear idea of how the new teleconferencing system improves communication in the company

USEFUL LANGUAGE

GREETING
Good morning/afternoon. I'm …
Hello, everyone. Nice to see you again.
Hi, I'm …. Good to see you all.

TOPIC
My subject today is our new product launch.
I'd like to talk to you about the bonus scheme.
I'm going to talk about our sales strategy.
The subject of my presentation is overseas expansion.

PLAN OF THE TALK
There are three parts to my presentation.
My presentation is in three sections.
Firstly, …
Secondly, …
Finally, …

AIMS
By the end of my presentation, you will have a clear idea of the new system.
By the end of my talk, you will understand how/why this benefits us all.
At the end of the presentation, you will know more about the direction we plan to take.

88

Presenting your company

How to make a good impression

Background

You are beginning a training course on giving presentations. The trainer has provided a structure for an introduction (see below). She asks you to introduce yourself and the company you work for. You are all from different parts of the world and different industries.

> 🔊 **CD2.21** At the beginning of the course, the trainer gives a model presentation. Listen, then answer these questions.
>
> 1 What is the aim of the presentation?
> 2 Where is Fiestatime's most important store?
> 3 What are its turnover and profit?
> 4 What does the company plan to do next year?

Structure for presentation

A Greeting
- Your name
- Your position

B Topic
- Subject/purpose of talk

C Plan of talk
- Sections/parts of talk

D Facts and figures
- Company products or services
- Important figures: number of employees, turnover, profits
- Your main competitors
- Your duties

E Future developments
- Your plans for next year

Task

1 Work in small groups. Read your company profile.

  Student A: Turn to page 133.
  Student B: Turn to page 142.
  Student C: Turn to page 143.

2 Prepare a short presentation about yourself and the company you work for. It should last approximately one minute.

3 Make your presentation to the other members of your group. Try to answer any questions they ask.

4 As a group, decide what you liked about each presentation. Why was it interesting?

Writing

You are a representative of your company. Write a short profile of the company for the company website. Include some of the information from your presentation.

➡ *Writing file* page 129

Case study 9

3 Doing business internationally

A A meeting in France

What do you know about business in France? In pairs, decide whether these statements are true (T) or false (F).

1. It is common for people to work for lots of different companies in their career.
2. Business lunches are usually very short and focus on work.
3. People's educational background is very important.
4. Most major French companies have their headquarters in Paris.
5. Appointments are not usually necessary and are often made just a day in advance.
6. July and August is a common holiday period and not the best time for arranging meetings.

Task 1

1. 🔊 CD2.22 Ryan Miller is a salesman for a medical equipment distributor in the south of France. He is new to French culture and is now talking to the Head of Sales, Sylvie Martin. Listen and answer these questions.

   1. Where was the business meeting?
   2. When was the business meeting?
   3. Where were the headquarters?
   4. Did Ryan go to a university?

2. 🔊 CD2.22 Listen again and discuss what Ryan did not understand about French culture. Use the answers from Exercise A to help you. If necessary, look at the audio script on page 165.

WORKING ACROSS CULTURES ▸▸ DOING BUSINESS INTERNATIONALLY

B Doing business in Russia

Task 2

1 ◆) CD2.23–2.25 **Listen to three people talking about their business trips to Russia on a business radio programme and answer these questions.**

 1 Which cities did the people visit?
 2 Which speaker had the most successful business trip?
 3 Which speaker had the least successful business trip?

2 ◆) CD2.23–2.25 **Listen again and take notes about the key points in each extract.**

3 **Write a list of tips for someone going on a business trip to Russia.**

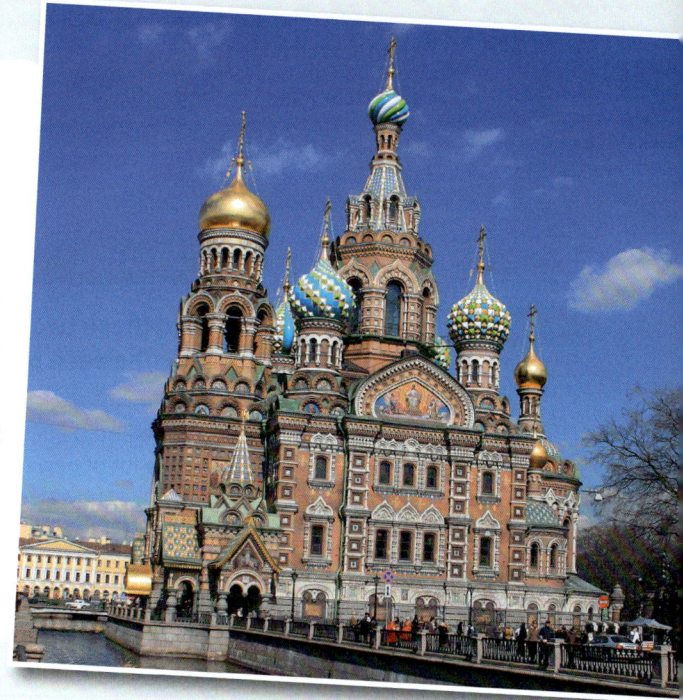

C In a Colombian home

Susan Forbes is a cultural-awareness consultant specialising in Latin America. She is running a workshop on doing business in Colombia. She talks about her first business trip to Bogotá, when she was invited to a Colombian home. Before you listen, read these tips for doing business in Colombia.

1 For social occasions, it is normal to arrive 30 minutes after the invitation time.
2 When invited to a home for a meal, bring flowers, chocolates, nuts or fruit. Wrapped gifts are opened in private. Do not mention the gifts again.
3 Always allow the host to make the first toast.
4 Good topics for conversation are culture, soccer, history, literature and coffee.
5 It is rude not to accept a cup of coffee at someone's home.

Task 3

1 ◆) CD2.26 **Listen to Susan Forbes talking about her first business trip. Take notes on what she did well and what mistakes she made. The tips above will help you.**

2 **In groups, discuss what Susan did well and what mistakes she made.**

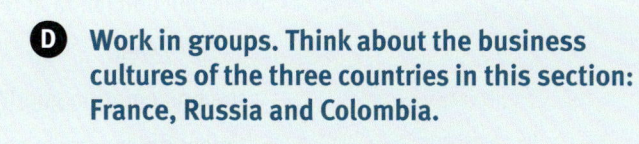

D Work in groups. Think about the business cultures of the three countries in this section: France, Russia and Colombia.

1 Which of these countries would you like to visit? Discuss your answers with other members of your group and give reasons.
2 Choose one of the three countries. How does your own business culture differ from the country you have chosen? In what ways is it similar?

91

UNIT C Revision

7 People

VOCABULARY

Read these two descriptions, then tick (✓) the words below that best describe each person.

> Ahmed Adib spends a lot of time on his work and he does a very good job. He also has a lot of new ideas. He likes to be on time for work and for meetings, but he's also usually very calm. He works very well, and he encourages other people to work well.

> Elizabet Martens always does what she promises to do. This is probably because she wants to reach the top in her career. She's very good at making things work, and she likes to do things for other people. In fact, she really likes to spend time with other people, and other people like to spend time with her.

	Ahmed Adib	Elizabet Martens
ambitious	☐	☐
creative	☐	☐
hard-working	☐	☐
helpful	☐	☐
motivating	☐	☐
practical	☐	☐
punctual	☐	☐
relaxed	☐	☐
reliable	☐	☐
sociable	☐	☐

PAST SIMPLE: NEGATIVES AND QUESTIONS

Complete these sentences with *was*, *wasn't*, *were*, *weren't*, *did* or *didn't*.

1 Benoît .... born in France, he was born in Switzerland.
2 We .... play golf at the weekend because the weather was terrible.
3 .... you see Alfredo yesterday?
4 Elena and Piet .... in the office last week because they were at a conference in Tokyo.
5 How .... your holiday?
6 A: I saw Mikhail and Jenna at the conference yesterday.
  B: .... they well?
7 .... the presentation good?
8 I .... meet Helena because she wasn't in the office.
9 The underground trains .... running yesterday because there was a strike.
10 A: I visited the Hamburg office last week.
   B: Oh, good. .... you see Karl?

UNIT C ▸▸ REVISION

SKILLS

Complete the conversation below using the words from the box.

'll 'm 's do don't have is look need think

A: I ....¹ some training in accounting to ....² my job properly.

B: I ....³ sorry. It's just not possible.

A: It ....⁴ really important for me.

B: The problem ....⁵, we don't ....⁶ the money for this. Why ....⁷ you buy a self-study course?

A: OK, I ....⁸ take a look at one.

B: I think you should ....⁹ for one at an online bookshop.

A: OK, I'll ....¹⁰ about it.

8 Advertising

VOCABULARY

Complete the missing numbers.

1	....	four thousand, five hundred
2	36,589	....
3	....	eight hundred and thirty-nine thousand, two hundred and thirty
4	1,433,900	....
5	....	fourteen point six per cent
6	2,870	....
7	....	fifty-six thousand, eight hundred and one
8	217,418	....
9	....	five million, two hundred and eighty-four thousand, five hundred and sixty-six
10	98.3%	....

COMPARATIVES AND SUPERLATIVES

Look at these sales figures for three electronics retailers. Then complete the article below with the correct words and phrases from the box.

	Sales €m	% change
Teevee Land (38 shops)	27	+7
Planet Electronica (22 shops)	15	+15
EGS (10 shops)	16	+19

a little fewest lower more interesting much the most the most impressive

The three most popular electronics retailers performed well last year. If we look at the sales figures, we can see that Teevee Land's sales were ....¹ higher that its competitors', while Planet Electronica's sales were just ....² lower than EGS's. But the percentage change in sales is ....³ than the sales figures. Teevee Land, the company with ....⁴ shops, shows much ....⁵ growth than its competitors. It is, in fact, EGS, the company with the ....⁶ shops, which has ....⁷ growth in sales.

UNIT C ▸▸ REVISION

WRITING

Use the information in this table to write a short report (about 100 words) comparing the two shampoos.

	Bottle size	Selling price	Target market	Main outlet	Sales	% change (year-on-year sales)
HairGlow	250ml	€14	18–25	hairdressers	1st quarter €141,500 2nd quarter €232,000	+9
Sheen	300ml	€10	26–50	supermarkets	1st quarter €202,500 2nd quarter €195,000	+11

9 Companies

VOCABULARY

Complete the text below using the words from the box.

ITS Electronics ....^{1} electronic components. The company ....^{2} the home electronics industry – companies that ....^{3} TVs, stereos and so on. Isomu Takahashi ....^{4} ITS in 1989. The company ....^{5} about 90 people and ....^{6} to about 10 countries. ITS does its own research and development and ....^{7} six or eight new products each year.

employs   exports   introduces   manufactures   produce   started   supplies

PRESENT SIMPLE OR PRESENT CONTINUOUS

Complete this text with the best form of the verbs in brackets: present simple or present continuous.

My company ....^{1} (*manufacture*) and ....^{2} (*export*) frozen fish products. We ....^{3} (*buy*) our fish directly from local fishermen. Right now, we ....^{4} (*make*) plans to increase our production. So we ....^{5} (*need*) to find different suppliers for fish. Our main customers ....^{6} (*be*) restaurant chains abroad. However, right now, we ....^{7} (*plan*) a new range of frozen meals because we ....^{8} (*want*) to enter the consumer market. So at the moment, our marketing team ....^{9} (*do*) a lot of research. They ....^{10} (*try*) to understand our target market.

SKILLS

Complete this introduction to a presentation with the correct prepositions.

Hi, I'm Elena Martinez. Good to see you all. I'd like to talk ....^{1} you ....^{2} the new computer network. My presentation is ....^{3} three sections. The subject ....^{4} the first part ....^{5} my presentation is the installation schedule. After that, I'm going to talk ....^{6} the benefits of the new software. Finally, I'll explain the training programme. By the end ....^{7} my presentation, you will have a clear idea ....^{8} the new network.

Cultures 3: Doing business internationally

A Choose the best word to complete each sentence about France.

1. It isn't common for people to work for *one company / lots of different companies* in their career.
2. Business lunches are usually long and *focus / don't focus* on work.
3. People's educational background *is / isn't* very important.
4. *Most / Only a few* major French companies have their headquarters in Paris.
5. Appointments *should / don't have to* be made well in advance.
6. July and August is a common holiday period, *so it can be a good / and not the best* time for arranging meetings.

B Complete the sentences below about Russia using the words from the box.

| Allow   Avoid   Confirm   Go   Make   Plan |

1. .... business appointments as far in advance as possible.
2. .... your meetings as soon as you arrive in Russia.
3. .... meetings in the first week of May.
4. .... your socialising in advance.
5. .... straight to a senior manager if you need an answer.
6. .... plenty of thinking time after you ask a question.

C Match the sentence halves about Colombia.

Part 1

1. It's normal to
2. A host should
3. It's rude to

a) always make the first toast.
b) refuse a cup of coffee at someone's home.
c) arrive about 30 minutes after the invitation time for a social occasion.

Part 2

4. In conversation, it's usual to
5. You shouldn't
6. When you visit a home,

d) take flowers, chocolates, nuts or fruit.
e) talk about culture, soccer, history, literature and coffee.
f) mention gifts after you give them.

3.1 Negotiations

Objectives

Speaking
- Can conduct very simple transactions using basic language.
- Can ask someone to repeat a specific point or idea.
- Can ask for and provide things using simple phrases.

Lesson deliverable
To participate in a basic negotiation, practising language to conduct very simple transactions and discuss what to do next.

Performance review
To review your own progress and performance against the lesson objectives at the end of the lesson.

A SPEAKING

Work in pairs. Who do you negotiate with in your daily life? What about?

- with your family (*for example, jobs in the house, where to go on holiday*)
- with your friends
- with your flatmates or neighbours
- with your manager
- with your work colleagues or classmates

B VOCABULARY 1

🔊 **BSA3.1.12 You are going to listen to a British businesswoman, Gayle Bradley negotiating a deal with Zhang, Chief Engineer in Shanghai. Look at the words in the box and tick (✓) the ones you hear.**

delivery rates ☐	delivery date ☐
fish and chips ☐	electronic chips ☐
convenient ☐	warehouse ☐
urgent ☐	moment ☐
13th ☐ 31st ☐	14th ☐ 41st ☐
calendar ☐	helpful ☐
specifications ☐	examinations ☐
ship ☐	shipment ☐
it's a deal ☐	it's real ☐

C LISTENING

1 🔊 **BSA3.1.12 Match the sentences (1–7) to what Zhang says (a–g). Then listen again to the negotiation and check your answers.**

1. We would like to discuss the delivery dates for the electronic chips.
2. Is that convenient for you?
3. Are you saying that you prefer to send the chips a little later?
4. When do you think you can send us the electronic chips?
5. I said 13th, not 30th.
6. What about Tuesday 14th?
7. So, to confirm, I'll send you the specifications in an e-mail …

a) A little later, yes.
b) Oh, I'm sorry.
c) Yes, of course.
d) Friday 10th is … too early for us.
e) I'm not sure. I need to talk to the warehouse manager.
f) And you will have the order on 15th July.
g) Erm, perhaps.

2 **What's the final date of delivery?**

3 **Circle the best word to complete the summary.**

Gayle found it *easy/difficult*[1] to close the deal with Zhang because it wasn't easy for Zhang to say *yes/no*[2]. Finally she asked Zhang to *suggest/cancel*[3] a date.

BUSINESS SKILLS: NEGOTIATIONS

D VOCABULARY 2

1 🔊 **BSA3.1.13 Listen to ten useful expressions from the listening exercise and match them to the correct category (a–e).**

a Checking   c Saying 'no'   e Confirming
b Suggesting d Correcting

2 🔊 **BSA3.1.13 Listen again and practise the pronunciation and word stress.**

Task

Pre-task: Context

A client is negotiating a delivery date with a supplier. The client needs a large quantity of electronic chips as soon as possible for an urgent order.

Part 1: Negotiations 1

Work in pairs and read the information on your card. Role-play the conversation between the buyer and the supplier to negotiate delivery dates.

Student A: You are the buyer. Turn to page x.

Student B: You are the supplier. Turn to page xi.

Look again at the Useful language box for Dealing with problems on page 72, *much / a lot / a little / a bit* on page 79 and Participating in discussions on page 80.

Part 2: Rethinking your position

Discuss with your partner. Were you happy with the result of the negotiation? Is there anything you want to change?

Change roles and negotiate again.
Student A: You are the supplier. Turn to page xi.

Student B: You are the buyer. Turn to page x.

Part 3: Negotiations 2

Now, in your pairs and using the cards, negotiate quantity.

Student A: You are the buyer. Turn to page xii.

Student B: You are the supplier. Turn to page xiii.

Part 4: Writing

After the final negotiation, write a short e-mail to your partner to confirm the delivery date and quantity of chips that you agreed. When you have finished, compare your e-mails to check you understood the same information.

E PEER REVIEW

Work with your partner from the Task and discuss these questions:

- Did you negotiate a 'win-win' situation in your negotiation? Why? / Why not?
- Did you both understand the same date?
- What questions did you ask to check understanding?

F SELF-ASSESSMENT

Look again at the lesson objectives and think about the feedback from your teacher and colleagues. Write a sentence for each of these questions.

- Which learning objectives did you achieve?
- Which expressions did you use from the listenings or the Useful language on page 72? Which ones did you forget to use?
- What will you try to do next time when negotiating dates in English?

G PROFESSIONAL DEVELOPMENT AND PERFORMANCE GOALS

Think of ways to practise negotiation language in your education centre or workplace. Choose a situation for a simple negotiation, write a dialogue and then practise and record it with a colleague.

3.2 Meetings

Business skills

Objectives

Speaking
- Can ask for and provide things using simple phrases.
- Can make simple references to the past using was/were.

Listening
Can recognise when speakers disagree in a conversation conducted slowly and clearly.

Lesson deliverable
To plan, prepare and participate in a meeting.

Performance review
To review your own progress and performance against the lesson objectives at the end of the lesson.

A SPEAKING

Discuss the following questions with a partner. Then compare your ideas with the class.

1. What well-known toy manufacturers do you know?
2. What are the most popular toys and games in your country?
3. Have they changed much since you were a child? Explain.

B LISTENING 1

🔊 BSA3.2.14 Playland is a toy manufacturer. Its managing director, Hans, calls a meeting with the other two senior managers. Listen to the meeting and choose the correct answers.

1. Why has Hans called the meeting?
   a) to talk to his team about toys
   b) to get ideas for a product relaunch
   c) to talk about sales

2. How old is Playland?
   a) 30
   b) 40
   c) 50

3. What was Lucia's favourite thing?
   a) a doll
   b) a game
   c) a bike

4. Who liked games when he or she was a child?
   a) Kate
   b) Lucia
   c) Hans

5. Does Kate agree with Lucia?
   a) yes
   b) no

6. Does Hans agree with with Kate?
   a) yes
   b) no

7. What do they decide to do?
   a) choose a game
   b) choose a toy
   c) look at sales figures

C LISTENING 2

1. 🔊 BSA3.2.14 Listen to the meeting again. Complete these sentences. Then compare your answers with your partner.

   1. Lucia: When I was ten, it was .... time of my life.
   2. Lucia: She was .... doll.
   3. Lucia: The thing I played with .... was my bicycle.
   4. Hans: It was one of .... toys.
   5. Kate: Well, my .... toy wasn't a Barbie either.
   6. Kate: I'm .... Maybe numbers aren't important.
   7. Hans: I .... , Kate.
   8. Kate: On .... something you can play alone, like Lego, would be more successful.

2. Which sentences are about disagreeing?

BUSINESS SKILLS: MEETINGS 2

D LISTENING / SPEAKING

🔊 **BSA3.2.15 Listen to the phrases about disagreeing and practise saying them. Then work with a partner and take it in turns to say something and disagree with it. You can use these sentences, or ideas of your own.**

- How about a special anniversary bike?
- I think we should relaunch an old best-seller!
- We want a toy that will sell well today.

Task

Pre-task: Preparation

You are going to hold your own meeting to think of ideas for your toy company's product relaunch.

On your own, use the card on page ix to prepare your ideas for the meeting.

Part 1: Meeting

Work in small teams and hold your meeting. Ask for and share ideas with your colleagues. Remember, you can disagree if you want to! Decide together on the best toy to be relaunched.

Turn to page pages 49 and 80 for useful meetings and discussions language. Turn to page 58 for useful language for describing products.

◎ **EXTRA PRACTICE: DVD CLIP AND WORKSHEET 3**

E PEER REVIEW

Work in your groups from the Task. Discuss how successful you think your meeting was and complete the Meeting Review notes on page ix.

F SELF-ASSESSMENT

Look at the objectives at the beginning of the lesson. Write sentences about yourself.

I can ....

I can't .... yet.

G PROFESSIONAL DEVELOPMENT AND PERFORMANCE GOALS

List two situations where you can practise your meetings skills in your organisation.

1 ....
2 ....

A12

UNIT 10 Communication

'There is only one rule for being a good talker – learn to listen.'
Christopher Darlington Morley (1890–1957), US writer and journalist

OVERVIEW

VOCABULARY
Internal communication

LISTENING
Networking online

LANGUAGE FOCUS 1
Talking about future plans

READING
Communication technology at work

LANGUAGE FOCUS 2
will

SKILLS
Making arrangements

CASE STUDY
Blakelock Engineering

STARTING UP   How do you communicate? Do this quiz, then compare your answers with a partner.

1 How many mobile phones do you have?
a) none
b) one
c) two or more

2 How long do you spend online each day?
a) less than two hours
b) between two and four hours
c) more than four hours

3 How many e-mails or text (SMS) messages do you send each day? How many do you receive?
a) fewer than 10
b) between 10 and 25
c) more than 25

4 When was the last time you …
a) sent an e-mail?
b) sent an SMS message?
c) sent a fax?
d) wrote a letter (on paper)?

5 How often do you check your work e-mails when you are on holiday?
a) every day
b) every few days
c) never

6 How often do you use Skype or conference calling?
a) every day
b) once a week
c) more than once a week
d) never

7 How many people do you speak to face to face each day when you are working/studying?
a) fewer than five
b) between five and 10
c) more than 10

8 How important are gestures (hand movements, etc.) for you when communicating?
a) not important
b) quite important
c) very important

9 When you communicate, do you prefer to …
a) meet people face to face?
b) speak on the phone?
c) send e-mails
d) send SMS messages?

96

UNIT 10 ▸▸ COMMUNICATION

VOCABULARY
Internal communication

A How do companies communicate with employees? What methods can you think of?

B Complete the text below using the words from the box.

company intranet   electronic   face to face   print   workplace

These days, companies are spending more time and money on improving internal communication. This is the communication which takes place inside an organisation. Communication will be downwards (from managers to junior staff), upwards (from staff to managers) and across (between staff), as well as between individuals and groups of people. There are various channels which can be used. These can be divided into five main areas:

1 ....: paper-based communication, e.g. magazines, newspapers, newsletters, letters, notes and messages

2 ....: direct contact with other people, e.g. one-to-one meetings, team meetings, forums, conferences, briefings

3 ....: physical objects in the working environment or workspace, e.g. notice boards, signs

4 ....: communication using computers, phones, televisions, etc., e.g. DVD, e-mail, voicemail, SMS messages, electronic newsletters, conference calls

5 ....: using social media to create an internal community, e.g. posting profiles, writing blogs and wikis, starting discussion forums, etc. Many leaders write internal blogs. Employees may join chat rooms, forums or message boards to post ideas and comments or upload images and discuss with other employees around the world. They may also be able to download information from the intranet.

Improvements in communication lead to better-informed, happier and more motivated employees, who will become more loyal to their company.

C Match each of the words in red in Exercise B to one of these definitions.

1 move information from a network to a PC
2 web page written by an individual
3 put information from a PC onto a network (*2 words*)
4 methods of communication
5 knowledge-sharing site
6 chances for people to discuss subjects
7 meetings where information or instructions are given

D Work in pairs. How do you prefer to communicate with these people? How do they communicate with you?

At work	At college
your colleagues/co-workers	other students
your boss/manager	lecturers/teachers
your customers/clients	librarians, etc.

See the DVD-ROM for the i-Glossary.

UNIT 10 ▸▸ COMMUNICATION

LISTENING
Networking online

Ros Pomeroy

A In pairs, discuss which of these social networking sites you use, and why you use them.

Facebook   Twitter   LinkedIn   MySpace   Mixi   Orkut   VKontakte   Google+
specialist professional networking sites   dating websites

B 🔊 CD2.27 Listen to the first part of an interview with Ros Pomeroy, a management consultant. Which of the social networking sites in Exercise A does she use?

C 🔊 CD2.28 Listen to the second part of the interview. Which two advantages and one disadvantage of social networking does Ros mention?

D 🔊 CD2.29 Listen to the third part of the interview. Who is the best communicator that Ros knows?

E 🔊 CD2.29 Listen again and complete this text.

He always had a real ....¹ for his subject – whatever he was talking about, he was ....². He made sure that he knew his ....³ very well, and the one thing that made a big ....⁴, I think, is that when he ....⁵ to an audience, he made that audience feel as if they were very ....⁶.

F 🔊 CD2.30 Listen to the final part of the interview. Make a note of whether Ros likes (L), does not like (NL) or does not mention (NM) these forms of communication.

1 letters
2 face to face
3 e-mail
4 handwritten notes
5 corporate newsletter
6 corporate magazine
7 telephone calls

Watch the interview on the DVD-ROM.

G In pairs, think of a good communicator you know. Describe the person and say why they are good at communicating.

LANGUAGE FOCUS 1
Talking about future plans

- We often use the present continuous to talk about arrangements that are fixed.
  *What **are** you **doing** on Friday?*
  *I'm **having** a meeting with my team all morning.* (It's already fixed.)
  *Mario **is meeting** me for lunch.* (It's already fixed.)
  *I'm **not having** any meetings with clients.* (It's already fixed.)

- We also use *going to* to talk about things we intend to do in the future.
  *What **are** you **going to** do when the course finishes?*
  *We're **going to** start our own company.* (It's an intention.)
  *I'm **not going to** look for a job for a few months.* (It's an intention.)

➡ page 154

A Complete these sentences using the present continuous form of the verbs in brackets.

1 .... Max .... to the meeting tomorrow? (*come*)
2 No, he's not in the office. He .... on business all week. (*travel*)
3 He .... not .... back until next Monday. (*come*)

UNIT 10 ▸▸ COMMUNICATION

B **Complete this text using the present continuous form of the verbs in brackets.**

I 'm meeting ¹ (meet) Mr Yamashiro next week. He ....² (arrive) on Tuesday night. On Wednesday, I ....³ (take) him to the factory. I ....⁴ (not see) him on Thursday, but I ....⁵ (drive) him to the airport on Friday.

C **Look at your diary. Talk about three or four things you are doing next week.**

I'm attending a seminar on Friday morning.

I'm visiting friends at the weekend.

D **Complete these sentences using *going to*.**

1 The computers are very slow. What .... we .... do about it?
2 We .... not .... buy new computers. I think it's too expensive.
3 We .... upgrade the software instead.

E 🔊 **CD2.31 Listen to Janine and Patrick talking about their plans for next year. Decide whether these sentences about their plans are true (T) or false (F). Correct the false ones.**

1 Janine is going to change her job. T
2 She is going to do a course.
3 She is going to go abroad for her summer holiday.
4 Patrick is going to change his job.
5 He is going to move to a new house/flat.
6 He is going to buy a new car.

F **Tick (✓) the plans below which are true for you. Add four more plans to each list.**

Fixed arrangement for next week	Intentions for next year
Go away for the weekend.	Change jobs.
Go on a business trip.	Do a course.
Attend a meeting.	Go abroad on holiday.
Write a report / an essay.	Move to a new house/flat.
Entertain business visitors.	Do more exercise.

G **Work in pairs. Tell your partner about your plans for the future.**

READING
Communication technology at work

A **Work in pairs. Ask and answer these questions.**

1 What mobile phone do you have?
2 How often do you use it each day?
3 What do you mainly use it for?
4 Do you use the same mobile for business and private calls?

B **Read the article on page 100 about Vittorio Colao, CEO of the mobile-phone company Vodafone. Do you find anything surprising in his use of communication technology?**

UNIT 10 ▸▸ COMMUNICATION

FT

I'm a fan of Facebook, but not of video calls

by Ingrid Lunden

1 Vittorio Colao, the CEO of Vodafone, has four phones and never switches them off. He loves Facebook, too, but only for friends – not for business networking.

2 Mobile technology is making a big difference to how people work. With smartphones and the right mobile applications, companies will be able to organise meetings and team working anywhere.

3 Mr Colao says that he always carries two or three mobile phones with him. "Right now, I have a BlackBerry, an iPhone and a Samsung 360," he says. "I use the BlackBerry for business e-mail and to swap SMS messages with colleagues. I use the Samsung for social contact and to access Facebook."

4 Mr Colao sees differences in the ways other executives use mobile technology. "It depends on the culture and age. In southern Europe, every executive carries a mobile and uses it all the time. Northern Europeans are more disciplined. They only use mobiles when they need to."

5 He is less enthusiastic about video calling: "I'm not a fan and I don't know many people of my age who are. I don't want to see people when I talk on the phone. Maybe it's because, when I'm on the phone, I like to take notes." He is more positive about conference calling. "Conference calls are useful, especially for keeping up to date on projects."

6 He only uses one social network: Facebook. "I don't have time to use others. I have 98 friends there – but they are real friends." He uses Facebook to send messages and to see what friends are doing.

C Read the article again and answer these questions.

1 How many mobile phones does Mr Colao have?

2 What does he use these phones for?

   a) BlackBerry   b) Samsung 360

3 According to Mr Colao, do executives use their mobiles more in northern or southern Europe?

4 Why doesn't he like video calling?

5 How does he use these communication technologies?

   a) conference calling   b) Facebook

D Find words in the article with these meanings.

1 to exchange (paragraph 3)

2 to get into (paragraph 3)

3 behaving in a controlled way (paragraph 4)

4 someone who likes something very much (paragraph 5)

E Work in pairs. Ask and answer questions about your use of communication technology.

Do you use …?

What do you use it for?

What other equipment would be useful?

How similar is Mr Colao's use of this technology to yours?

LANGUAGE FOCUS 2
will

- We use *will* + infinitive to talk about future events and predictions.
  *Mobile phones **will** replace desk phones in the next few years.*
  *Our company **will not (won't)** survive without investment in new technology.*

- We also use *will* + infinitive for offers and promises.
  *I can see you're busy. **I'll** finish the report for you.*
  ***I'll** have the document ready this afternoon.*

- We often use these time expressions to refer to the future.
  tomorrow, tomorrow evening, the day after tomorrow, next Friday, next month, at the end of May, in the next two years, in three years' time

➡ page 154

A Work in pairs. Find the sentences with mistakes and correct them.

1 Desk phones and desktop computer disappear in the next five years.
   Desk phones and desktop computers will disappear in the next five years.
2 Most companies will be open for business 24/7.
3 As a result, it not be easy for staff to have a good work–life balance.
4 I will think most companies use social networking tools for internal communication.
5 In many big companies, video conferencing will replace face-to-face meetings.
6 As a result, managers no spend as much time travelling for work.
7 I no think companies will use e-mail, except for external communication.

Do you agree with the predictions?

B Work in pairs. Make a list of three or four changes you think will happen in office communication. Share your ideas with another pair.

C Complete the sentences below with future time expressions from the box.

| end of   five years'   in the next   July   ~~next~~   the day after   time   tomorrow |

1 Sales of luxury cars will double by **next** year.
2 I'll send you a copy of the report .... morning.
3 We'll finish the work before the .... June.
4 I'll be back in the office .... tomorrow.
5 We'll finish the work on the new building next ....
6 In two weeks' .... , we'll review the budget.
7 We will need to modernise our factory .... two years.
8 Most people will have a fast broadband connection at home in .... time.

D Match the statements (1–5) to the offers (a–e).

1 I don't have a hard copy of the report.   a) I'll carry one for you.
2 I can't find Sara's address.   b) I'll print it out for you.
3 I think it's time to go home.   c) I'll get a drink from the machine.
4 These boxes are so heavy.   d) I'll give you a lift to the station.
5 I'm very thirsty.   e) I'll e-mail it to you.

UNIT 10 ▶▶ COMMUNICATION

E Work in groups. You have to organise the launch of your new website. Offer to do as many things as possible. Give reasons. Use the list below and your own ideas.

- inform the local media
- design the invitations
- send out the invitations
- order snacks and drinks
- make a welcome speech
- give a presentation about the website

OK. I'll inform the local media. A friend of mine is a journalist. I'm sure she can help us.

SKILLS
Making arrangements

A ◆)) CD2.32–2.35 Listen to four people making arrangements by phone. Match each call (1–4) to the correct situation (a–d).

a) changing an existing appointment ☐
b) apologising for missing an appointment ☐
c) making an appointment ☐
d) suggesting an alternative day ☐

B ◆)) CD2.32–2.35 Listen again and complete these extracts.

Call 1

Jamie: What's a good day for you?
Chris: I can ..*make*..¹ Wednesday. How about 10 o'clock?

Call 2

Lesley: How about ....² in the week? Is Friday OK?
Sam: Yes, I can do Friday morning after 11.
Lesley: Yes, that's ....³ for me. Friday at 11.30. ....⁴ ....⁵ then.

Call 3

Lesley: Sorry, but I need to ....⁶ the time of our meeting. I ....⁷ make it on Monday now.

Call 4

Dan: I'm very sorry I ....⁸ our meeting this afternoon. My flight was delayed. I'll ....⁹ you again later.

Watch the phone calls on the DVD-ROM.

C Work in pairs. Role-play these situations.

1 The Managing Director of Cargo Printing calls a customer to arrange a meeting next week. The MD suggests a time and date. The customer agrees.

2 The MD calls a supplier and suggests a meeting on Friday 20th March. The date and time are not suitable for the supplier. The supplier suggests another date and time. The MD agrees.

3 A customer leaves a message for the MD. The customer was ill and missed a meeting at 9.30 a.m. The customer will call the MD later in the day.

USEFUL LANGUAGE

ASKING

What time is good for you?
What's a good day for you?
What time/day suits you?

AGREEING

I can make five o'clock on Wednesday.
I can do next Monday.
Tuesday the fifth is fine for me.

SUGGESTING A DIFFERENT TIME/DAY

How about 4.15?
Is July 28th OK for you?

DECLINING

I'm afraid I can't make August 2nd.
I'm sorry, I can't do Thursday afternoon.

APOLOGISING

I'm sorry I missed our meeting at 9.30 / on Tuesday.
Sorry I didn't make it on time.

GIVING AN EXCUSE

My flight was late.
The traffic was very bad.
I'm afraid I was delayed/unwell, etc.

Blakelock Engineering

A company has some bad news to communicate

10 Case study

Background

Blakelock Engineering is losing money. To cut costs and improve profits, it is going to reduce its employees by 100. This represents about 10 per cent of the workforce. There are two important decisions to make:

1. who will leave the company;
2. how to communicate with two groups: the staff and the company's shareholders.

🔊 **CD2.36.** Listen to a company director talking to the Head of Human Resources. Note down the three ways they could use to decide who leaves the company. Are there any other ways they could consider?

Arrangements for a meeting

Helen Dawson joined Blakelock six months ago. She works in the design department. Like many staff, she is very worried about losing her job. She calls the Head of Human Resources to arrange a meeting with him. She wants to find out if the company will ask her to leave. The Head of Human Resources does not want to meet her at this time. The management has not yet decided who will have to leave the company. He makes excuses for not meeting her.

Work in pairs. Role-play their conversation.

Task

Work in pairs. You are directors of the company.

1. Discuss the various ways of choosing who will leave the company. What are the advantages and disadvantages of each way? Which way is the best?
2. Decide on the best way to communicate your decision to a) the staff, and b) the shareholders. Say who should communicate your decision.
3. Compare your solutions with another pair.
4. Work as one group. Discuss how the company can help the employees who will be leaving Blakelock Engineering.

Writing

You are the Managing Director of Blakelock Engineering. Write an e-mail to all the staff, announcing a meeting to discuss the present situation of the company. Give the date, time and place of the meeting. Mention that all the directors will attend. Say that you will talk about the company's plans for improving profits.

➔ *Writing file* page 126

UNIT 11 Cultures

'I dislike feeling at home when I am abroad.'
George Bernard Shaw (1856–1950), Irish playwright

OVERVIEW

VOCABULARY
Company cultures

LISTENING
Cultural mistakes

LANGUAGE FOCUS 1
should/shouldn't

READING
Cultural differences

LANGUAGE FOCUS 2
could/would

SKILLS
Identifying problems and agreeing action

CASE STUDY
The wind of change

STARTING UP

cards   clothes   date
customs   food   gifts
hours   language
leaders   money
~~sport~~

A Imagine you are visiting a country for the first time to do business. Complete the tips below using the words from the box on the left.

1 Find out about the most popular *sport* in the country.
2 Always take .... in US dollars.
3 Find out about the normal working ....
4 Be careful how you write the ....
5 Find out about the most important .... and festivals.
6 Learn to speak a little of the local ....
7 Try some of the .... before you go.
8 Wear formal ....
9 Translate your business .... into the local language.
10 Take some .... for your hosts which are typical of your own country.
11 Learn something about the most famous business .... and celebrities.

B Which of the tips in Exercise A do you think are: a) very useful? b) useful? c) not useful?

Why? Compare your ideas with a partner.

C Add some other tips for visitors to your country.

UNIT 11 ▸▸ CULTURES

VOCABULARY
Company cultures

A Different companies have different cultures and ways of working. Complete these sentences with the items in brackets. One of the items in each section cannot be used.

Dress (uniforms / ~~casual Fridays~~ / weekend clothes)

1 We don't have to wear business suits at the end of the week. My company has a system of *casual Fridays*.
2 In many banks, staff can't wear what they like. They have to wear ....

Timekeeping (flexitime / part-time / shift work)

3 For two weeks each month, I work at night. I can't sleep during the day. I hate ....
4 We have a .... system in our office. Some people choose to work from 9 a.m. to 5 p.m.; others work from 10 a.m. to 6 p.m.

Time off (childcare / annual leave / public holiday)

5 I am so busy at the moment that I worked on New Year's Day, which is a(n) ....
6 How many days' .... do you get in your company?

Reporting procedures (written report / face to face / e-mail)

7 We often speak on the phone, but never ....
8 He uploads a(n) .... on the company intranet each month.

Types of meeting (informal / formal / social)

9 Our department starts every day with a(n) .... meeting. It is very relaxed.
10 Companies have an Annual General Meeting (AGM) once a year. It is a very .... meeting, with a lot of people.

Names (job title / first name / family names)

11 In some countries, the company culture is formal. Staff use .... when they speak to each other.
12 What's your .... now? Are you Chief Executive?

B Would you like to work for an organisation which has:

• uniforms?   • a lot of formal meetings?   • casual Fridays?   • flexible hours?

C Match each phrase (1–5) to its explanation (a–e).

A positive company culture …

1 empowers employees.
2 supports innovation.
3 is customer focused.
4 rewards good performance.
5 encourages trust at all levels.

a) New ideas and change are welcome.
b) Relationships between employees and managers are open and honest.
c) Staff have a lot of control over their work.
d) The needs and wants of the customers always come first.
e) There is an incentive scheme for efficient employees.

D Work in pairs. Put the five characteristics in Exercise C in order of importance for you, and explain why.

*See the **DVD-ROM** for the i-Glossary.*

E What are the beliefs and values of your organisation? Discuss in groups.

UNIT 11 ▸▸ CULTURES

LISTENING
Cultural mistakes

Three people talk about cultural mistakes.

A 🔊 **CD2.37 Listen to John's story and answer these questions.**

1 What meal was John invited to? *dinner*
2 What did he look at?
3 What was his mistake?
   a) He talked during an important silence.
   b) He talked about his host's table.
   c) He didn't want a gift.

B 🔊 **CD2.38 Listen to Cameron's story and answer these questions.**

1 Where was Peter's new job?
2 What was his mistake?
   a) He did not use first names.
   b) He did not speak French.
   c) He did not use family names.
3 How did the staff feel when Peter used first names?

C 🔊 **CD2.39 Listen to Susan's story and answer these questions.**

1 Where did Susan make her mistake?
2 Who did she go out for a meal with?
3 What was her mistake?
   a) She poured her own drink.
   b) She did not laugh.
   c) She poured too many drinks.
4 What did she forget to do?

D 🔊 **CD2.40–2.42 Listen to Liz, Jeremy and Ros talking about cultural mistakes.**

Which speaker …	Liz	Jeremy	Ros
1 was working in East Africa?			
2 was working with a Dutch colleague?	✓		
3 got straight down to business?			
4 writes long e-mails?			
5 often adds funny comments in e-mails?			
6 thought a colleague was abrupt and rude?			

Liz Credé

Jeremy Keeley

Ros Pomeroy

Watch the interviews on the DVD-ROM.

E **It is easy to make mistakes in other cultures. What other examples do you know?**

LANGUAGE FOCUS 1

should/shouldn't

- We use *should* and *shouldn't* to give advice and make suggestions.
  We **should** wear formal clothes to the dinner.
  You **shouldn't** be late for meetings.

- We often use *I think* or *I don't think* with *should* to say something is or isn't a good idea.
  I think you **should** go on a training course.
  I don't think you **should** interrupt her.
  '**Do you think** I **should** learn to speak the local language?' 'Yes, **I do**. / No, **I don't**.'

  ➡ page 155

A Complete the sentences below using *should* or *shouldn't* and a phrase from the box.

> speak to our boss   buy an expensive computer system
> be late   ~~develop a better website~~   stay three days

1 Our online business is bad.
  We *should develop a better website*.

2 Our team is working too many hours.
  We ....

3 The meeting is very important.
  We ....

4 She wants to visit a lot of customers in Spain.
  She ....

5 We have to control our costs.
  You ....

B Give the opposite advice by using *should*, *shouldn't* or *I don't think*.

1 I think he should get a salary increase.
  I don't think he should get a salary increase.

2 I think we should launch the new product now.

3 She shouldn't take customers to expensive restaurants.

4 We should take every customer complaint seriously.

5 I think staff should fly economy on every trip.

C Work in pairs. Your colleague is going on a business trip. Take turns to ask for and give advice using the notes below.

A: *I'm going on a business trip. Do you have any advice?*
B: *You shouldn't stay in an expensive hotel.*

- Stay in an expensive hotel. ✗
- Take plenty of business cards. ✓
- Arrange a lot of appointments on the same day. ✗
- Be late for appointments. ✗
- Write a short report after each meeting. ✓
- Keep all your receipts for travel and restaurants. ✓

UNIT 11 ▸▸ CULTURES

READING
Cultural differences

A Do you agree with these statements?

1 All meetings should have fixed start and finishing times.
2 Being on time is equally important in all situations.
3 It's more important to learn about the culture of the country you do business with than to learn the language.
4 There's no point having a detailed plan before you start a project. Things always change, and you need to be very flexible.

B As you read the article below, think about this question.

What are two main causes of cultural misunderstanding between Brazil and China?

FT

Lessons in cultural difference

by Samantha Pearson

1 It is 9.05 a.m. and a group of Chinese businessmen are outside a hotel conference room in São Paulo, waiting for their Brazilian hosts. The seminar was scheduled to start five minutes ago, but, like many meetings in Brazil, it did not start on time. The Brazilians arrive, complaining loudly about the morning's traffic and go immediately to breakfast. Cultural differences between the two countries become clear.

2 In 2009, China replaced the US as Brazil's biggest trading partner. As a result, Brazilian companies are keen to understand the Chinese better and find the best way to do business together.

3 For companies already working with China, getting to know the culture is a priority. At Chinbra, São Paulo's biggest Chinese language school, students, who mainly work in the import business, take evening classes in Mandarin. About half the lesson is about cultural issues. They ask questions such as "Should I give my business card with two hands?" and "What presents should I give – something Brazilian?".

4 Some business deals fail because of small things like a misunderstood e-mail. "In addition to language problems, there is also a lack of cultural understanding between the two countries," says Charles Tang, president of the Brazil–China Chamber of Commerce.

5 One big issue is timing. For successful deals with the Chinese, it is important to be on time for meetings and to meet deadlines. Another issue is planning. In Brazil, because of high inflation during the 1980s and early 1990s and many failed plans, long-term planning was not a priority. Today, many companies still prefer to plan as they go along and fix problems when they happen. The Chinese are completely different. They like to plan everything in advance and in detail.

C Decide whether these statements about the article are true (T) or false (F). Correct the false ones.

1 Brazil's biggest trading partner today is the US.   F (It's now China.)
2 At Chinbra, students spend most of the time learning Mandarin.
3 Charles Tang thinks deals go wrong mainly because of language problems.
4 For the Chinese, being on time is very important.
5 Brazilians don't give a lot of importance to planning.

D Work in pairs. Read the situation at the beginning of the article again (paragraph 1) and discuss these questions.

1 What happened?
2 How do you think both sides felt about the situation?
3 For the next meeting with the Chinese, what could the Brazilians do differently?

UNIT 11 ▸▸ CULTURES

E **Find words in the article with these meanings.**

1 planned (paragraph 1) *scheduled*
2 very important and needing attention (paragraph 3)
3 problems (paragraph 3)
4 to be unsuccessful (paragraph 4)
5 when there is not enough of something (paragraph 4)
6 the last possible date for doing something (paragraph 5)

F **Work in pairs. What practical advice would you give about studying or doing business in your country? Discuss two or three of these points.**

- appointments
- giving gifts
- planning and deadlines
- meetings/seminars
- greetings
- making friends

LANGUAGE FOCUS 2
could/would

- We often use *could* to make a polite request.
  Could I use your mobile phone, please?
  Could you send me a copy of the report, please?

- We often use *would you like* to make an offer.
  Would you like a brochure?

➡ page 155

A **These questions were asked on a plane journey. Decide whether they were asked by the flight attendant (F) or the passenger (P).**

1 Could I have another drink, please?
2 Would you like a newspaper?
3 Could you show me how to turn on the light, please?
4 Would you like another drink?
5 Could I have some mineral water, please?
6 Would you like coffee or tea?
7 Could you fasten your seat belt, please?
8 Could you help me find the movie channel, please?

B **Which of the questions in Exercise A are offers, and which are requests?**

C **You are at a hotel reception desk. Use the verbs in brackets to make polite requests.**

1 You need a map of the city. (*have*) *Could I have a map of the city, please?*
2 You want to go to a good restaurant. (*recommend*)
3 You didn't hear that. (*say*)
4 You want a photocopy of a document. (*copy*)
5 You want your bill. (*have*)
6 You want a taxi. (*call*)

D 🔊 **CD2.43 Listen to the requests in Exercise C to check.**

E 🔊 **CD2.43 Listen again. How does the other person reply?**

109

UNIT 11 ▸▸ CULTURES

F Work in pairs. You are organising a visit to your company's factory. Take turns to make and reply to the requests on page 133.

A: Could I have last month's production figures?
B: Yes, I'll e-mail them to you this afternoon.

SKILLS
Identifying problems and agreeing action

A ◆) CD2.44 Louise, a project manager, is in a meeting with Tom, one of the project team leaders. They are talking about Paul, a foreign consultant hired by head office to work on the project. Listen to the conversation. Decide whether these statements are true (T) or false (F). Correct the false ones.

1. Tom does not have a good relationship with Paul.
2. Tom would like Paul to communicate more face to face.
3. Paul gets on well with the customers because of his knowledge.
4. Paul does not meet his colleagues very often after work.
5. Louise is going to have a meeting with all the team members first.

B ◆) CD2.44 Listen again and complete these extracts.

L: What............¹ is the problem?
T: You see, Paul's not very good at............².
T: Well, how can I put it? They respect him, he's got a lot of............³.
L: Well, I think the............⁴ thing to do is for me to have a talk with him. I'll give him some good............⁵.

Watch the meeting on the DVD-ROM.

C Work in pairs. Look at the audio script on page 166. Imagine you are the project manager. What advice are you going to give Paul? Make a list of three points.

D Complete these sentences (1–4) with suitable endings (a–d).

1. The problem is,
2. I think you should
3. The best thing to do
4. OK. So you're going

a) to have a meeting with him first.
b) he's not good at communicating.
c) talk to him first.
d) is to explain what his role is.

E Role-play this situation. Two managers in the same department have a problem with an employee, Ken Darby. They meet to discuss what to do.

Student A: Turn to page 137.
Student B: Turn to page 142.

USEFUL LANGUAGE

OPENING
There's something I'd like to talk to you about.
I need to talk to you about something.
Could I have a word with you?

STATING THE TOPIC
There's a problem with Paul.
The problem is, we don't have a good relationship.

SUGGESTING ACTION
We could meet the other members of the team.
I think / don't think we should meet Paul every week.
One thing we could do is talk to him.
We should/shouldn't move him to another department.
The best thing to do is explain his role to the team.

RESPONDING TO SUGGESTIONS
I agree. We'll meet him as soon as possible.
Fine. Let's talk to him.
Yes. I think that would be very helpful.
I'm not sure that's a good idea.
Well, I'm not sure about that.
Mmm. I don't think that's a good idea.

The wind of change

11 Case study

A manager wants to bring in new ideas and change the company culture

Background

Kate Maskie is the new General Manager in an overseas branch of Far Eastern Traders, an international clothing company. She wants to bring the best new ideas from head office to the overseas branch.

Kate wants:	Overseas branch culture now
all staff to use first names.	Staff use family names.
all staff to dress casually at work.	Staff dress formally at all times.
to introduce a system of flexible working hours.	Working hours are fixed (9.00 a.m. to 5.00 p.m.).
to keep all meetings to 30 minutes only.	There are many long, formal meetings.
to introduce hot-desking* to the open-plan office.	Most staff have their own space in the open-plan office.
an 'open-door' policy, so staff can see a manager at any time.	Staff need an appointment to see any manager.

* 'Hot-desking' is a system where you do not have your own desk in the office, but use any desk that is free.

🔊 **CD2.45** Listen to Kate Maskie as she talks to Stuart Adams, her manager at head office, about the problems. Discuss these questions.

1 Why does Kate want to change the culture in the branch office?
2 What problem will she face?
3 What will Kate do at the meeting?

Task

Kate and Stuart meet some of the senior staff to discuss the ideas for a new company culture.

1 Work in groups of four and choose a role.

   Kate Maskie: Turn to page 139.
   Director of Human Resources: Turn to page 141.
   Stuart Adams: Turn to page 140.
   Finance Director: Turn to page 144.

2 Look at your role cards and prepare for the meeting.

3 Meet and discuss Kate's ideas. Decide what you will change and what you will keep the same.

Writing

Write the action minutes of the meeting.

FAR EASTERN TRADERS

Subject: New ideas from head office   Date:
Participants:

Agenda item		Decision	Reason	Action	Name
1	Staff to use first names				
2	Staff to dress casually on Fridays only				

➡ *Writing file* page 128

UNIT 12 Jobs

'All jobs are easy to the person who doesn't have to do them.'
Holt's Law

OVERVIEW

VOCABULARY
Skills and abilities

LANGUAGE FOCUS 1
Present perfect

LISTENING
My ideal job

READING
Professional networking sites

LANGUAGE FOCUS 2
Past simple and present perfect

SKILLS
Interview skills

CASE STUDY
Nelson & Harper Inc

STARTING UP

A Look at these jobs. Who do you think should get the highest salary? Put the jobs in order, highest salary first.

- lawyer
- nurse
- professional footballer
- accountant
- fashion model
- postal worker
- firefighter
- teacher
- advertising executive
- air-traffic controller
- doctor
- banker
- architect
- sales assistant
- farmer

B Which jobs have the highest/lowest salaries in your country? Compare your ideas with a partner.

C Which of the following would you like (✓) or not like (✗) in a job?

1. a lot of telephone work
2. writing lots of reports
3. working with the same people
4. working with a lot of different people
5. working on your own
6. working flexible hours (including weekends)
7. using English at work
8. sharing an office
9. casual dress
10. a lot of targets and deadlines
11. travelling to other countries
12. a uniform

D Which is more important to you, a high salary or a job you enjoy? Why?

VOCABULARY
Skills and abilities

A Complete the first part of the advertisement below with the verbs from the box. Use the words in brackets to help you.

> cope with   develop   improve   increase   ~~lead~~   set up   train

KARADA MODE PLC
EUROPEAN MANAGER €95K + CAR

Are you the person we are looking for?

THE ROLE

We are looking for a talented person for this position. In this exciting job, you will need to:

- _lead_ ¹ a team of 25. (*be in charge of*)
- ....² a new branch in Amsterdam. (*start*)
- ....³ new staff. (*teach*)
- ....⁴ sales in all markets. (*make more*)
- ....⁵ new products. (*create*)
- ....⁶ communication between our head office and local branches. (*make better*)
- ....⁷ strict deadlines and work well under pressure. (*manage*)

B Complete the second part of the advertisement with the verbs from the box.

> deal with   manage   motivate   organise   plan

THE PERSON

In your present job, you:

- ....¹ a large department in the clothing industry. (*control*)
- ....² budgets. (*think about the future*)
- ....³ sales conferences and trade exhibitions. (*arrange*)
- ....⁴ customers, suppliers and their problems. (*take action*)
- ....⁵ employees and sales teams to get the best results. (*encourage*)

C Describe your role in your present or a past job. Use the verbs from Exercises A and B.

In my present job, I lead a team of three.

In my last job, I trained staff to use the new IT system.

*See the **DVD-ROM** for the i-Glossary.*

UNIT 12 ›› JOBS

LANGUAGE FOCUS 1
Present perfect

- We use the present perfect to talk about situations that began in the past and continue in the present.
  *I **have worked** for IBM for five years.* (And I'm still working here now.)
  *They **have lived** in Barcelona for two years.* (And they are still living there now.)

- We often use the present perfect to talk about life experiences.
  *I **have had** three jobs since I left university.*
  *She **hasn't had** any experience in marketing.*
  *'**Have** you ever **worked** abroad?' 'Yes, I **have**.' / 'No, I **haven't**.'*

- The present perfect is formed with *have/has* + the past participle of the main verb.

➡ page 156

A Complete these sentences with the present perfect form of the verbs in brackets.

1 I *have given* (*give*) two presentations this month.
2 I .... (*not send*) any e-mails today.
3 He .... (*change*) jobs recently.
4 Magda .... (*be*) away on business all week.
5 They .... (*not have*) any experience in negotiating.

B Match the job interview questions (1–5) to their answers (a–e).

1 How many jobs have you had since leaving university?
2 Why have you changed jobs so often?
3 What have you done that shows leadership?
4 In what ways has your job changed since you joined the company?
5 Have you ever worked with a difficult person?

a) I now have more responsibility and I plan the sales strategy for the team.
b) Well, I lead the sales team. I'm also chairperson of a local business association.
c) I wanted to get experience of sales in different industries.
d) Well, the boss in my last company wasn't very easy to work with.
e) I've worked for six companies.

C 🔊 CD2.46 Now listen and check your answers.

D Complete these interview questions using the present perfect form of the verbs in brackets.

1 How *have you changed* (*you change*) over the last five years?
2 What software programs .... (*you use*) recently?
3 What .... (*you learn*) from your other jobs?
4 What sort of problems .... (*you have*) to deal with?
5 What part of your job .... (*you enjoy*) the most?
6 Which countries .... (*you visit*) for work/study?

E Work in pairs. Ask and answer the questions in Exercise D.

UNIT 12 ▸▸ JOBS

LISTENING
My ideal job

A ◆)) CD2.47 **Listen to the first part of an interview with Liz Credé, an organisation development consultant. In pairs, take notes on what she says about:**

1 her current job
2 a job she had over 20 years ago.

Then compare your notes with your partner's.

Liz Credé

B ◆)) CD2.48 **Listen to the second part of the interview and decide whether these statements are true (T) or false (F). Correct the false ones.**

1 Her strengths come from her work as a CEO over the last 20 years.
2 She understands how organisations work by studying them closely.
3 She can see a situation from many different sides.
4 She finds it easy to make decisions.

C ◆)) CD2.49 **Listen to the final part of the interview. Complete these notes on the advice that Liz gives.**

- Take the ....¹ that you are given and ....² as much as you can from them.
- Really ....³ to those around you and pay ....⁴ to what they are saying.
- Build ....⁵ across the organisation.
- Ask a question that demonstrates you're really ....⁶ in the company.

Watch the interview on the DVD-ROM.

D **In pairs, discuss these questions.**

1 What are your strengths and weaknesses?
2 What kinds of people do you work well with?
3 What is your ideal job?

READING
Professional networking sites

A **Ask and answer these questions in small groups.**

1 Do you have a profile on a professional networking website such as LinkedIn? If so, which one? How do you use it?
2 Does your company/university have a profile on a professional networking website? If so, which one?
3 Discuss how a professional networking site can help individuals and companies / educational institutions.

It can be useful for finding a job / getting new business.

B **Look at Helen Braoudakis's profile on a professional networking site on page 116. Put these headings in the correct place on the profile.**

~~Recruitment professional~~   Education   Specialities
Interests   Work experience   Professional summary

UNIT 12 ▸▸ JOBS

Helen Braoudakis
Recruitment professional [1]

Sydney, Australia

Current: **Graduate Recruitment Manager, Deloitte, Sydney**
Past: Graduate Recruitment Assistant, ADM Consulting, Sydney
Education: Macquarie University, Sydney: Master's in Human Resource Management
Recommendation: 10 people have recommended Helen
Connections: 150
Public profile: http://au.teamplayers.com.helenbraoudakis

.... [2]

I am a graduate recruitment specialist with a Master's in Human Resource Management. I have over four years' experience of recruiting in the management-consultancy industry. Recently, I have also taken responsibility for our summer internships. I enjoy the challenge of finding the best possible candidate for a position. I am able to communicate effectively at all levels. I also have excellent planning and organisational skills.

.... [3]

graduate recruitment, planning, project management, presenting, interviewing, internship management

.... [4]

Graduate Recruitment Manager
Deloitte, Sydney
June 2010–now
- Developed new graduate recruitment strategy.
- Set up and ran summer internship programme for 60 candidates

Graduate Recruitment Assistant
ADM Consulting, Sydney
March 2007–June 2010 (3 years 3 months)
- Planned and attended university recruitment events in Australia and SE Asia
- Arranged interviews (Skype, phone and face to face)

Store Manager
Gemini, Melbourne
February 2003–January 2005 (1 year 10 months)
- Managed the day-to-day work of 30 staff, in two stores
- Responsible for all purchasing and stock control

.... [5]

- Macquarie University, Sydney, Master's in Human Resource Management 2006–2007
- University of Melbourne, Bachelor of Commerce 1999–2002

.... [6]

other cultures, teaching scuba diving, playing the guitar, cooking

C Decide whether these statements are true (T) or false (F). Correct the false ones.

1 Helen did her Master's in HRM in Melbourne.
2 She has worked for three different companies.
3 She has always worked in graduate recruitment.
4 She has good communication skills.
5 When she was at ADM Consulting, she was responsible for organising summer internships.
6 She doesn't have any experience outside Australia.

D Write a summary for a professional networking profile. Use the example summary above. Include information about your experience, qualifications, skills and personal qualities.

UNIT 12 ▸▸ JOBS

LANGUAGE FOCUS 2
Past simple and present perfect

- We use the past simple to talk about completed actions that happened in the past.
  *In 1990, I **worked** in Mexico City for a year.* (I now work in another place.)
  *I **changed** my job last year.*

- We use the present perfect to talk about actions that began in the past and continue into the present.
  *He **has worked** in Berlin since 2006.* (He still works there.)
  *I've **lived** in Mexico City for the last two years.* (I still live there.)

➡ page 156

A Read this profile about Martin Reed's career. Choose the past simple or the present perfect form of the verbs to complete it.

I think I *had / have had* ¹ an interesting career. I *studied / have studied* ² at Oxford University from 1997 to 2000. Then I *applied / have applied* ³ for jobs abroad. I *worked / have worked* ⁴ in Hong Kong for three years, and then I *came / have come* ⁵ to Japan in January 2004. I *have been / was* ⁶ here for more than eight years and I still love it. I'll never go back to the UK.

During my career, I *did / have done* ⁷ a number of different jobs, too. I *sold / have sold* ⁸ computer software in Hong Kong. I *taught / have taught* ⁹ English for my first year in Japan. Since then, I *ran / have run* ¹⁰ my own training company. It is very successful.

B Tick (✓) the expressions below that you can use to complete this sentence.

Mr Kato has been very busy …

this week
last week
since Monday
last month
two weeks ago

for the last two weeks
yesterday
today
recently

C Work in pairs. Take turns to talk about:

- jobs you've had in your career
- projects you've worked on recently
- places you've visited in the last three years.

A: *Tell me about the jobs you've had in your career.*

B: *I've had two jobs. When I was at university, I did a placement in an advertising agency. Then, after my degree, I got a job as a marketing assistant in Paris.*

UNIT 12 ▸▸ JOBS

SKILLS
Interview skills

A Work in pairs. Decide which of these interview tips are more for interviewers, and which are more for candidates. Can you think of any other tips? Compare your ideas.

1. Be completely honest at all times.
2. Try to help the candidate to relax.
3. Always wear your best clothes.
4. Do not ask a lot of questions to which people can answer just *yes* or *no*.
5. Listen carefully and make a lot of notes.
6. Arrive half an hour early for the interview.
7. Ask a difficult question at the beginning of the interview.
8. Get an expensive haircut.

B Decide on the best two tips each for interviewers and for candidates.

C 🔊 CD2.50 Listen to part of an interview. Tiffany Martin is applying for a job as an overseas team leader in Germany. Answer these questions.

1. What is her opinion of the company she wants to work for?
2. What does she say about her language skills?
3. Who does she like to work with?
4. Where does she want to be in 10 years' time?

Watch the phone calls on the DVD-ROM.

D 🔊 CD2.50 Look at the Useful language box below. Listen to the interview again and tick (✓) the expressions you hear.

E Role-play this situation. A director of a well-known group of travel agents, Go Anywhere, is looking for someone to manage the sales office in Tokyo, Japan.

Student A: See below.   Student B: Turn to page 144.

Student A

Director of Go Anywhere

Use these prompts to find out information about the candidate.

1. Did / find / office easily?
2. Why / want job?
3. What strengths / have?
4. Can / work under pressure?
5. What / learn from / last job?
6. What / not like about / last job?
7. What / main interests?
8. Do / have any questions?

USEFUL LANGUAGE

SKILLS

What are you good at?

Do you have any special strengths?

People say that I am good at ...

My main skills are ...

EXPERIENCE

What did you learn from your last job?

What didn't you like about your last job?

I learned (how) to ...

Well, I had a problem with ...

INTERESTS

What do you do in your free time?

What are your main interests?

I really enjoy ...

I spend a lot of time ...

FUTURE PLANS

What do you want to do in the future?

Where do you want to be in 10 years' time?

My main aim is to ...

I plan to be ...
I hope to have ...

Nelson & Harper Inc.

An international business wants to recruit the best staff for its expansion

Background

Nelson & Harper Inc. is a multinational company with a head office in Philadelphia, US. It provides consumer products in the areas of beauty, health and household care. It sells its products globally. In the next five years, it plans to increase its factories and sales offices all over the world. To do this, it needs to hire staff and train them for future management positions.

Job opportunities with Nelson & Harper Inc. at head office and overseas

Nelson & Harper is recruiting candidates internationally in these parts of the company:

- Business administration
- Research and development
- Sales
- Purchasing
- Finance and accounting
- Marketing
- Human resources
- Manufacturing

If you decided to apply for a job at Nelson & Harper, which area(s) would interest you? Discuss your choice(s) with a partner.

🔊 **CD2.51** Listen to a director of Nelson & Harper. He is talking to the company's Vice-President of Human Resources. They are discussing the requirements for people who apply for a job with the company. Make notes under these headings:

- Personal qualities
- Experience
- Skills and abilities
- Interests

Task

1. Work in pairs.

    Student A: Turn to page 133.
    Student B: Turn to page 142.

2. Read your role card and prepare for the interview.

3. Hold the interview.

4. Interviewers: discuss the candidates. What were their strengths and weaknesses? Candidates: discuss the interviews. Which questions were easy or difficult to answer?

Writing

Write a letter to the successful candidate. Give the name of the position, the starting date, the salary and number of days of annual leave. Add any other information that will be useful.

➡ *Writing file* page 128

12

Case study

4 Team working

A In small groups, discuss these questions.

1. Do you prefer to work on your own or with others?
2. Describe a good and bad personal experience of working in a team.

B Work in groups. In which of these countries do you think people prefer to usually work a) in groups? b) on their own?

| China Denmark Finland Greece |
| Indonesia Italy Japan Malaysia |
| Norway Portugal Singapore |
| South Korea Spain Sweden |

C 🔊 CD2.52 An expert in cultural communication is talking about attitudes to team working in different cultures. Listen to the first part of her talk and decide whether these statements are true (T) or false (F). Correct the false ones.

1. The speaker mentions Indonesia, Japan, South Korea, Malaysia, China, Denmark, Sweden and Norway.
2. Asian cultures usually like working towards individual targets.
3. You need to spend a lot of time on team-building activities with Asian teams.
4. The individual is not as important as the group in Asian teams.
5. Strong disagreement should be avoided.

D 🔊 CD2.53 Listen to the second part of the talk and answer these questions.

1. Which two groups does the speaker divide Europe into?
2. Which countries does the speaker mention in each group?
3. What sort of leaders do southern European teams need?
4. In northern Europe, how do team members like to work?
5. How is Finland different to other Scandinavian countries?

E In pairs, do Exercise B again.

F In pairs, write a short summary of the attitudes to team working in Asian, northern European and southern European countries for a colleague who missed the talk.

Task

A Japanese advertising agency wants to increase its number of international clients. Three months ago, it hired two British staff. However, business is bad, and now the company can only keep one person. Read about the two people on page 121. In groups, discuss the strengths and weaknesses of each person. Decide who the company should keep.

WORKING ACROSS CULTURES ▸▸ TEAM WORKING

Name:
Martha Saunders
Age: 32
Education:
Degree in economics and management, Oxford University
Experience:
10 years in advertising with a Japanese company

Comments from other team members:

- Gets on well with everyone and has a good sense of humour.
- Spends a lot of time on building personal relationships with team members.
- Is sometimes not available for evening client entertainment.
- Does not prepare a lot for meetings and does not like writing detailed reports.
- Always patient at meetings and consults with everyone.
- Very popular with all Japanese team members, as she always puts the team first.

Name:
Suzie Rose
Age: 36
Education:
Degree in management studies, Cambridge University
Experience:
seven years in advertising with one British and two Japanese companies

Comments from other team members:

- Very hard-working – works long hours preparing detailed reports.
- Very good at reporting and informing all team members.
- Likes to get agreement before formal meetings.
- Thinks meetings take too long; is impatient.
- Often tells jokes at formal meetings – some team members do not like this.
- Good at interacting with British clients and was able to win a big contract with a British company.

UNIT D Revision

10 Communication

VOCABULARY

Complete the text below using the words from the box.

> blogs and wikis   briefings   channels   download   electronic
> face-to-face   intranet   post   print   upload   workplace

At my company, we use various ....¹ of communication. Sometimes people talk about the 'paperless' office, but at my company, ...² communication – letters, notes and messages – are very important. But I think ....³ communication – direct contact with other people in meetings, team meetings, forums, conferences and ....⁴ – is probably the most important.

One form of communication we rarely use is ....⁵ communication. We don't have any notice boards or signs around the office. Instead, we use ....⁶ communication – mostly computers, for e-mail. And we actively use our company ....⁷, which has really helped to create an internal community. We often post profiles, write ....⁸, and participate in discussion forums. We use electronic message boards to ....⁹ ideas and comments and we sometimes ....¹⁰ images from our computers to discuss with other employees around the world. They may also be able to ....¹¹ information from the intranet to their computers.

TALKING ABOUT FUTURE PLANS; WILL

Correct each sentence by putting *to*, *will* ('*ll*) or a form of *to be* in the correct position.

1 You have a meeting now, so you can't phone Dimitri. But don't worry, I do it.
2 What Lance doing on Monday morning?
3 We meeting the legal team on Tuesday.
4 They're not going attend the conference.
5 Mr Shen and Mr Lee going to give a presentation together.
6 After we upgrade our network, computer security not be a problem.
7 OK, then. I write an e-mail to Jean-Luc.
8 We're going redesign our website next month.

SKILLS

Match the responses (a–f) to the questions/statements (1–6).

1 What time is good for you next Tuesday?
2 How about 10 o'clock on Tuesday?
3 I'm sorry I missed the meeting last Monday. My flight was late.
4 What's a good day for you?
5 Is next Monday morning OK for you?
6 Oh, you're here. Come in!

a) Yes, that's fine for me.
b) Sorry I didn't make it on time. The traffic was very bad.
c) I can make six o'clock. We can have dinner together.
d) I'm sorry, I can't make Monday.
e) Don't worry, I'll tell you about it.
f) Monday.

UNIT D ▸▸ REVISION

11 Cultures

VOCABULARY

Complete the sentences below using the words from the box.

| annual leave   casual Fridays   childcare   flexitime   formal   informal |
| job title   part-time   public holiday   shift work   social   uniform |

1 I don't wear business clothes to work at the end of the week, because we have .... in my office.

2 In our factory, all the workers wear the company ....

3 The factory runs 24 hours a day. So for two weeks each month, some workers work at night. .... keeps the factory going, but some workers hate it.

4 We have .... in my office, so I can choose to work from nine to five or from 10 to six.

5 Pietro's company gives him 14 days' ....

6 Raul has a .... job as an accountant for a small marketing firm. He works 20 hours per week.

7 Next Monday is a .... , so the office will be closed.

8 When children are ill and off school, it can be difficult to arrange .... , so parents often have to miss a day of work.

9 My .... is Marketing Director.

10 My office is .... Everyone uses first names when they speak to each other.

11 When the CEO visits the office, we can't relax. We have .... meetings, and everyone is very serious.

12 I enjoy .... meetings with my colleagues outside of work. Sometimes we go out for a meal in the evening, or play golf at the weekend.

COULD/WOULD, SHOULD/SHOULDN'T

Choose the best words to complete these conversations.

A: *Could / Would*[1] I have a copy of the budget, please?

B: Sorry, Mr Cox said I *should / shouldn't*[2] give it to anyone.

C: *Would / Should*[3] you like some help?

D: Yes, please. *Should / Could*[4] you hold the door for me, please?

E: This report isn't complete. There *would / should*[5] be another section.

F: You *should / would*[6] ask Ping about it. He wrote it.

G: There aren't any taxis. What *should / could*[7] we do?

H: We *could / would*[8] phone Marcus and ask for a lift.

UNIT D ›› REVISION

WRITING

You are a manager at the head office of a company. One of your overseas branches has a lot of problems.

Write an e-mail (about 150 words) to Marcos Flores, the Branch Manager. Say what you think are the *three* biggest problems in the list below and suggest a solution to each of them.

Problems identified

- People don't like wearing formal clothes to the office all the time.
- There are many long, informal meetings that take a lot of time.
- Employees who have children find the 8.30–5.30 working day very difficult.
- Staff don't like the new office manager.
- People spend a lot of time writing reports.
- Staff say it's difficult to talk to the manager (Marcos Flores) – they always have to phone or send e-mails.

12 Jobs

VOCABULARY

Choose the best word to complete these sentences.

1 How can we *motivate / deal with* staff to work harder? What can we offer them?
2 Can you *cope with / organise* strict deadlines and a lot of pressure?
3 I have to *manage / train* new employees to use our software.
4 Jeremy helped to *develop / set up* a new branch office in Lisbon.
5 Mr Allegro is on the phone and he isn't happy. Can you *deal with / motivate* his complaint, please?
6 I'd like to *train / organise* a conference for early next year.
7 Alexi *sets up / manages* a team of about 40 people.
8 We have a basic idea in mind, but we really need to *develop / cope with* it.

PAST SIMPLE AND PRESENT PERFECT

Complete this text with the correct form (past simple or present perfect) of the verb in brackets.

Nouf Al Sudais ....[1] (*study*) at the London School of Economics from 2004 to 2008. Then he ....[2] (*apply*) for jobs in London. He ....[3] (*get*) a job in a bank and has worked there since that time. Since last year, he ....[4] (*take*) several classes in finance at the LSE and he's now considering going back for a Master's degree.

Nouf is fluent in Arabic and English and he ....[5] (*study*) some French, too. He ....[6] (*always enjoy*) language study. He loves working in a job where he can use his languages.

Through his work, Nouf ....[7] (*meet*) people from all over the world. His office works closely with an office in Australia, so he ....[8] (*go*) to Australia about 10 times in the past two years. He ....[9] (*visit*) Japan and China on business, too.

Last year, Nouf's friend Jamal ....[10] (*ask*) Nouf to apply for a job at Jamal's company in Jeddah. But Nouf ....[11] (*not apply*). He likes his job in London, and he isn't ready to leave. He visits his family in Riyadh every year, and last year he ....[12] (*see*) them two or three times.

UNIT D ▸▸ REVISION

SKILLS

Put the words in the correct order to make questions.

1 you / at / What / good / are / ?
2 special / any / Do / skills / you / have / ?
3 job / What / your / did / last / you / from / learn / ?
4 about / like / you / your / didn't / last / What / job / ?
5 time / What / free / do / your / you / in / do / ?
6 your / What / main / are / interests / ?
7 in / want / do / to / What / the / you / future / do / ?
8 years' / be / want / do / to / you / Where / in / 10 / time / ?

WRITING

Answer the questions in the Skills exercise above. Invent the answers if necessary.

Cultures 4: Team working

A Choose the best words to complete the text.

> Most jobs require people to work in teams. If you do business internationally, it's good to understand basic cultural information about team work.
>
> Research shows that East Asian cultures – Indonesia, Japan, South Korea, Malaysia, Singapore and China – tend to *like / dislike*[1] working in groups. It feels *awkward / natural and comfortable*[2] in these societies. They tend to put the group *after / before*[3] the individual.
>
> But other cultures value *team work / the individual*[4], too. Scandinavians – Danes, Norwegians and Swedes – are *not good / good*[5] team players. However, teams do not always work closely together in these cultures. Once team members are given a task, they usually want the freedom to complete it without too much control.
>
> Finland, a neighbour of Norway and Sweden, *isn't / is*[6] the same as its neighbours. Finland's attitude to team work is more like some southern European countries, as Finns *rarely / often*[7] prefer to work on their own. In Portugal, Italy and Greece, teams *can often be / aren't usually*[8] individuals working on their own and reporting to a strong leader. They *work / don't work*[9] in close cooperation. In this case, team leaders *need to / don't need to*[10] give a clear focus and direction for each team member.

B Based on the attitudes to team work described in Exercise A, choose the odd country out in each list.

1	Indonesia	Japan	Portugal
2	Malaysia	Spain	Greece
3	Finland	Italy	Indonesia

4.1 Interviews

Objectives

Listening
Can understand enough to manage simple routine exchanges without undue effort.

Speaking
Can describe skills and abilities using simple language.

Reading
Can understand short, simple e-mails on work-related topics.

Writing
Can write a simple e-mail accepting a work-related invitation.

Lesson deliverable
To arrange, prepare and participate in an interview, and follow up.

Performance review
To review your own progress and performance against the lesson objectives at the end of the lesson.

A SPEAKING 1

1 Work in pairs. Put these actions in the order they happen.

 a get an invitation for an interview
 b go to an interview
 c hear if you got the job
 d see a job advert
 e complete the application form / send your CV

2 What communication methods (e.g. e-mail, telephone, etc.) are used for the different actions in question 1?

B LISTENING 1

🔊 **BSA4.1.16** Adam Johnson applied for a job in the marketing department of World Travel, a holiday company. Listen to the voicemail message and answer the questions.

1 How many people will interview Adam?
2 How long will the interview last?
3 What does Adam need to take to the interview?
4 What does Adam need to do before the interview?

C WRITING

Complete Adam's e-mail accepting the invitation with the words in the box.

would be   regards   ~~dear~~   meeting   interview   for

Subject: Re: Invitation for interview

..........*Dear*..........[1] Mr Smith,

Thank you ....[2] your e-mail. I ....[3] very happy to come to an ....[4] next Tuesday. I look forward to ....[5] you both at your office on Monday at 10 a.m.

..........................[6],

Adam Johnson

D LISTENING 2

1 🔊 **BSA4.1.17** Listen to the first part of Adam's interview. Match the questions to the replies.

1	Did you bring your documents with you?	a	That's an easy question for me.
2	Tell me about yourself.	b	Sure, here you are.
3	Why are you interested in the tourism industry?	c	Well, I have a Master's Degree in Communications Marketing…

2 🔊 **BSA4.1.18** Listen to the second part of the interview. What language does Adam use to talk about his strengths and weakness? Complete the phrases.

Strengths:

1 Hmm, let me ..*see*... . Well, I read a lot to …
2 I find reading .... me with my work.
3 I think it's .... to .... about changes before they happen.
4 I'm also .... dealing with customers.

BUSINESS SKILLS: INTERVIEWS

Weaknesses:

5 Well, to be ...., I've always .... to work alone.

6 The courses have been very ....

7 I know I'll .... this in future.

3 🔊 **BSA4.1.19** Listen to the telephone call Adam gets a week later. Did he get the job?

E SPEAKING 2

Work in pairs. Practise answering some common interview questions. Give feedback.

Student A: Turn to page x.

Student B: Turn to page vii.

Task

Pre-task: Research

1 You have applied for the job below and you received an e-mail response this morning. Read the job description and the e-mail and take notes.

INTERNATIONAL BUSINESS REPORTERS

Home based, $50 per hour, 5 hours per week, Business Online

We are a popular international website and we are recruiting people with business knowledge to write short, weekly reports on business news and activities for our international audience. Candidates must speak English, be organised and must be able to communicate ideas to others clearly.

2 weeks ago

Dear Mr / Mrs .... ,

Thank you for your interest in *Business Online*. We have looked at your application and we would like to talk further. Are you able to attend an online interview next Monday, at 4 o'clock?

We look forward to speaking to you.

Rita Chopra,

Content Editor

---

2 Write a short reply to Rita Chopra, accepting the invitation. Use the e-mail in Exercise C to help you.

Part 1: Preparation

1 Work in pairs or small groups. Read the context.

Context: You are going to attend an online interview with Business Online. You need to prepare for the interview.

2 Allocate roles. Who will be the candidate? Who will be the interviewer? Think about the following points.

Candidate:
- the skills and abilities you need/have and examples that show you have them
- phrases to talk about your strengths and examples that show you have them
- phrases to talk about your weaknesses and what you are doing to change them
- why you want the job

Interviewer:
- how you will start the interview
- what questions you need to ask
- how you will end the interview

Part 2: Interview

Hold your interviews.

1 Did you clearly understand the job description?

2 Did you write a clear e-mail accepting the invitation?

3 Could you ask/answer the questions?

4 Could you ask about/describe skills and abilities?

F PEER REVIEW

Think about the interview. Complete the table and discuss it with your partner from the Task.

	Good points	One thing to change
The candidate's understanding of the job they have applied for.		
The interviewer's ability to ask the candidate questions.		
The candidate's description of their skills and experiences.		
The interviewer's job of managing the conversation.		

H PROFESSIONAL DEVELOPMENT AND PERFORMANCE GOALS

Think about the job you would like to do next. Develop an action plan to apply for that job and choose three points to include.

G SELF-ASSESSMENT

Think about the lesson objectives and the feedback from your colleague. Answer these questions.

4.2 Presentations

Objectives

Speaking
- Can describe skills and abilities using simple language.
- Can give basic advice using simple language.

Listening
Can generally identify the topic of discussion around them when conducted slowly and clearly.

Lesson deliverable
To plan, prepare and give a presentation about key skills for different jobs.

Performance review
To review your own progress and performance against the lesson objectives at the end of the lesson.

A SPEAKING 1

What are common differences between speaking in a conversation and speaking in a presentation? Using the list below (1–6), put the advice in the table.

Conversations	Presentations	Both

1. Speak quickly.
2. Organise ideas before speaking.
3. Ask a lot of questions.
4. Nod and smile.
5. Use a lot of pauses.
6. Look at the other person/people.

B LISTENING 1

🔊 BSA4.2.20 Listen to the introduction to a presentation given by Phil Haines. What two things does he mention?

1. What is his job?
2. What do you learn about the audience?
3. What is his presentation going to be about?

C LISTENING 2

1. 🔊 BSA4.2.21 Listen to the main part of Phil's talk. How many key points does Phil talk about? How does he introduce each point?

2. 🔊 BSA4.2.21 Listen again and complete the phrases Phil uses to give advice.

   1. A qualification in Human Resources Management ………… .
   2. You ………… to have three main skills to be successful in this job.
   3. The first is a business skill. ………… a good ………… to work on your communication skills.
   4. Number two, this is a people skill. My ………… is don't just to listen to people, but really read them.
   5. And finally, this is more of a personal quality, you ………… be confident.
   6. You ………… doing something you think is impossible.

D LISTENING 3

1. Look at slides A and B. Which slide is easier to read? Why?

   A

   You need several skills to be a good doctor. You should be able to remember facts because there are a lot of illnesses. It's a good idea to communicate clearly with different people. And my advice is to be patient. Doctors are always busy, but sometimes people need more time.

   B Key skills for a doctor
   - Remember facts
   - Communicate clearly
   - Be patient

A15

BUSINESS SKILLS: PRESENTATIONS

2 Use the information below to complete the slide about architecture.

> To be a good architect, you should understand science, because that's how you make a building safe. You need to be creative, because people want to buy attractive houses, and they like new designs. Finally, my advice is to learn to sell your ideas effectively. You need to find someone to pay for your building, after all.

Key skills for architecture
• ....
• ....
• ....

3 🔊 **BSA4.2.22** Listen carefully to Phil's ending. Make a slide of the key skills for Human Resources.

E SPEAKING 2

Work in pairs and practise giving advice about another skill. When you finish give feedback to your partner.

Student A: Turn to page xi.

Student B: Turn to page xiii.

Task

Pre-task: Research

1 Think alone about the skills and qualities you need for a job you do or would like to do. Make notes.

2 In pairs or small groups, discuss the notes you made. Share ideas about more skills and qualities each person in the group would need, or go online to do more research.

Part 1: Preparation

1 Work in pairs or small groups. Read the task.

> **Context:** You work for a large company. You need to give a presentation for a team-building session about the skills you need for your job, to help staff understand the different skills each person brings to a team.
>
> **Task:** Prepare a 3–4 minute presentation.

2 Prepare a 3–4 minute presentation. Think about the following things. Complete the gaps using phrases from Exercise C and audioscripts BSA4.2.21– BSA4.2.22.

Structure:
- **Introducing the presentation:** Who are you? Why are you giving the presentation? What are you going to talk about?
- **Main part of the presentation:** Describe the skills a person should have to do your job. Cover: facts /information you need to know for the job, business skills, people skills, personal qualities.
- **Ending:** What main points do you need to repeat?

Techniques and language:
- Prepare a title slide, and a slide of key points.
- Some organising phrases I will use are: ....$_1$, ...$_2$, ...$_3$.
- Some expressions of advice I will use are: ....$_4$, ...$_5$, ...$_6$, ...$_7$.
- I will invite questions with the phrase: ....$_8$.

Part 2: Presentation

Give your presentations.

Presenters: Use the structure in Part 1. Give your presentation.

Audience: Make notes on the different skills while you listen. Did the presenter give good reasons why each skill is useful?

F PEER REVIEW

Complete the sentences about another presentation. Give feedback.

You covered these things in the main part of your presentation:

....

You used these techniques / this language when presenting:

....

One thing you did very well was ....

One suggestion to improve your presentation is ....

G SELF-ASSESSMENT

Look back at the lesson objectives. Complete the sentences.

I can ....

I can't ....

H PROFESSIONAL DEVELOPMENT AND PERFORMANCE GOALS

What advice do you need to give in your job? Do you need to give training? Write three sentences about how you could use the skills in this lesson to help you do this.

1 ....

2 ....

3 ....

Writing file

E-mails

E-mails can have a formal business style or a very informal style, similar to spoken English.

From: e.lee@bilder.com
To: tobias.schmidt@schneemans.de
Subject: Dinner invitation

Dear Mr Schmidt

I would like to invite you to dinner after your visit to our company next week if you have time. Our Managing Director, Alison McDermott, will also come.

I will book a table at an Italian restaurant, Via Venezia, for 8 p.m. on Tuesday evening. The restaurant is next to your hotel in Barchester Road.

I hope you can join us. Please can you let me know this week?

Best wishes
Emily Lee

Emily Lee
Head of PR
Bilder Construction PLC
Box 62
London W1

This formal e-mail is similar to a standard business letter, but usually it is shorter. The e-mail should begin with *Dear* ... and finish with *Best wishes* or *Best regards*.

You use this style if you are writing to somebody outside the company or somebody you do not know well.

From: e.lee@bilder.com
To: s.carpenter@bilder.com
Subject: Seminar contact

Hello Sally

I made an interesting contact at the seminar last week. Pablo Almeira is in charge of Research and Development at Rozlin Electronix in Seville. He is very interested in our new training software and wants you to contact him. Here is his e-mail address:

pablo.almeira@rozelex.com

Hope he's useful for you!
CU
Emily

This informal e-mail is for people you know well inside or outside the company. The e-mail often begins with *Hi* or *Hello* and finishes with *Regards* or *CU*. *CU* means *See you*.

Other short forms are:

TX/TNX	= thanks
RUOK	= Are you OK?
FYI	= for your information
BTW	= by the way
ASAP	= as soon as possible

WRITING FILE

Telephone messages

For a telephone message, write down only the important information. Use note form. Make sure you write the correct telephone number of the caller. Include your name as well.

Telephone message

To: Danny Randall   Name of caller: Brett Sinclair

Date: 7th April   Time: 10.15 a.m.

Message: Meeting place with Adriana changed from Grappa's to Café Continental. Be there at 9 p.m.

Action: Call back if problems on 01699 720 7743

Signed: Frank Churchill

Product launch plans

A plan can be written in list form with bullet points to make it easy to follow.

Use headings to group your ideas together.

Use *will* to say what your plans for the future are.

Product launch – 'Flashy' trainers

Slogan
- The slogan for the product will be '*Your feet will fly*'.

Advertising
- We will have 30-second TV ads in prime-time slots, starting on 25th May.
- There will be large posters on city-centre billboards.
- We will book full-page ads in sports/health magazines.

Endorsement
- We will offer Matt Hawkins, world-class sprinter and holder of the current world record, sponsorship in return for product endorsement.

Special events
- We will hold a champagne launch at the Olympic stadium (with the staff all wearing 'Flashy' trainers).
- There will be a 'Flashy' tour bus to go round schools.
- We will organise a competition linked to the London Marathon, with pairs of 'Flashy' trainers as prizes.

Lists

Make sure your list has a clear title.

Give the points a number and a deadline if possible.

Write your list with short notes, not sentences.

Team-building activities for new project

		By	Done
1	Organise kick-off meeting and dinner in hotel	3/3	✓
2	Weekend skiing trip	15/3	✓
3	Two-day team-building seminar	2–3/4	
4	Move team members to same office away from headquarters	7/4	
5	Every team member should have project team partner	7/4	

WRITING FILE

Action minutes

> The headings should look like this. Make sure you note who was present.

Subject: New office equipment
Date: 19th April 201–
Participants: JS, KG, EdeG, CBM, DG

Agenda item	Decision	Reason	Action
1 Change computer supplier	Agreed	Present supplier too expensive	CBM to check companies by 15/5
2 New chairs	Agreed	Staff have back problems	JS to buy by 15/5
3 Take out walls	Not agreed	Difficult to work; too much noise from colleagues	None
4 Install coffee bar on 6th floor	Agreed	Improve communication and atmosphere	DG to check costs by 15/5

> Note each item, the decision, the reason and who has to take the next step.

> It is a good idea to give a deadline for each action item.

Letters

> **Start**
> When you know the name of the reader:
> *Dear Mr/Mrs/Ms Peng*
> When you don't know the name of the reader:
> *Dear Sir/Madam*

> For a formal letter, it is a good idea to put the topic of the letter as a heading.

> Use the pronoun *we* when writing for your company. This is more formal than *I*.

> **End**
> When you know the name of the reader:
> *Yours sincerely*
> When you don't know the name of the reader:
> *Yours faithfully*

> Sign the letter with your first and second names above your typed name and position.

Tilly's Trinkets Ltd
62 Wardour Street • London WC1

Ms Jing Peng
36 Hersham Road
Alton-on-Thames
Surrey
KT1 3JR

3rd May 201–

Dear Ms Peng

Re: Job application

We are pleased to inform you that you have been successful in your application for the position of Secretary to the Managing Director at Tilly's Trinkets.
   As agreed in the interview, we would like you to start on 1st October in our Wardour Street office. Your starting salary will be £20,000 per annum. You can take 20 days' annual leave.
   Please sign and return a copy of the enclosed contract to confirm acceptance of this offer. We look forward to hearing from you soon.

Yours sincerely

Karen Gilbert

Karen Gilbert
HR Manager

Enc. Contract
Cc: Elaine de Groove
     Managing Director

Common abbreviations

Re: regarding (about)
Enc. documents are enclosed with the letter
Cc: copies (the names of the people who receive a copy of the letter)

Short product descriptions

> Short product descriptions are often found in catalogues.

> Technical product descriptions are normally written in bullet points.

> The text focuses on technical details that are important for the reader.

> Product descriptions for cosmetic products focus more on colour, smell or taste, and how you will feel when you use the product.

GVC home movie system

- Digital miniDV camcorder with nylon carrier and 60-minute cassette
- 6.4 cm LCD colour monitor
- 700x digital zoom and digital colour night scope for colour pictures in the dark
- Long-play function and digital picture stabiliser

Bianca toothpaste

Wake up with **Bianca**! Bianca toothpaste is made of a refreshing mixture of peppermint and eucalyptus, leaving your mouth clean, fresh and ready to start the day.

Short company profiles

> Short company profiles are often found in publicity material.

> They tell the customer what your company does.

> They should be short, easy to read and interesting.

> Make sure the customer can see why your company is the best for him/her.

> Use bullet points to highlight the main points.

Basle Banking Services

Our mission
Basle Banking Services (BBS) is the main provider of solutions in the market for business-to-business financial services. We want to be the number-one partner for your business.

Our services
BBS offers a wide range of services, including sales and investment financing, fund management and insurance.

Benefits for our customers
With our customers, we want to create growth. To do this, we:

- connect industry and technology know-how with the financial markets;
- offer new financial products and solutions, which we develop together with our customers;
- give fast and friendly support.

Activity file

1 Introductions, Starting up, Exercise G, page 7

Student A

Spell the first names, surnames and e-mail addressess of these people for your partner.

1 Our Accounts Manager is Li Hai. That's L-I and then H-A-I. Her e-mail is l.hai2@GHN.cn.
2 Our new Sales Assistant is Ana Torres. That's A-N-A, and then Torres, T-O-double R-E-S. Her e-mail address is a.tor6@BTG.es
3 The Human Resources Manager is Tom Sims. That's T-O-M, and then Sims, S-I-M-S. His e-mail is t.sims@albets.co.uk

Now listen to your partner and write down the first names, surnames and e-mail addresses of three other people.

1 .... 2 .... 3 ....

3 Problems, Vocabulary, Exercise B, page 23

Student A

1 **Match the adjectives (1–8) to their opposites (a–h).**

   1 long   a) difficult
   2 heavy   b) quiet
   3 early   c) boring
   4 slow   d) dangerous
   5 safe   e) light
   6 noisy   f) late
   7 easy   g) fast
   8 interesting   h) short

2 **Your partner has the answers to Exercise 1. Ask him/her questions to check your answers.**

   What's the opposite of 'long'?

3 **Now answer your partner's questions.**

   The opposite of   big   is   small.
                     hot   cold.
                     narrow   wide.
                     high   low.
                     soft   hard.
                     right   wrong.
                     cheap   expensive.
                     relaxing   stressful.

5 Food and entertainment, Vocabulary, Exercise H, page 45

Student A

You are in a restaurant with a visitor from your overseas office.

- Ask about / offer a starter.
- Recommend the Russian salad or soup.
- Ask about the main course.
- Explain *moussaka* (aubergine, tomato and lamb).
- Order the same.
- Agree to order dessert later.

ACTIVITY FILE

4 Travel, Vocabulary, Exercise E, page 37

Student A

1 **Ask your partner for the missing information.**

What is Mr Asafiev's flight number?

Visitor

Name: ....Mr Asafiev............ Flight number: ....

Airport: .... Terminal: ....

Gate number: .... Take-off time: ....

Destination: .... Arrival time: ....

Hotel: ....

2 **Give your partner the information he/she needs.**

Mrs Bendhiba is booked on flight TAY616, from London Heathrow Terminal 4, gate 23. Take-off is at 08:40. She arrives in Berlin at 11:25. She is staying at the Metropole Hotel.

3 **Check the information with your partner.**

6 Buying and selling, Skills, Exercise C, page 58

Student A

You are the Store Manager of a lighting equipment store. You are at a trade fair and you want to buy some table lamps for your store.

Use these prompts to prepare your questions. Ask the manufacturer about:

- the most popular model (*What / your / most popular model?*)
- the target market (*What / your target market?*)
- the features (*What / special features / have?*)
- its weight and measurements (*How much / weigh? How tall / the lamp?*)
- the colours (*What colours / come in?*)
- the cost (*How much / cost?*)
- the delivery (*When / deliver / the lamp?*)

If you like the product, say how many lamps you want to order.

7 People, Skills, Exercise E, page 72

Student A

Office worker

You work for a car-hire company near an airport. You want to come to work at 9.30 a.m. instead of 9.00 a.m. because:

- you have to take your son to school before you begin work. Your partner goes to work early in the morning.
- your new house is further from the airport. You drive to work, but the traffic is bad.
- you are doing an extra part-time job in the evening. You get to bed very late.

8 Advertising, Starting up, Exercise A, page 74

1 c   2 a   3 b   4 c   5 b   6 a   7 b   8 b   9 b

9 Companies, Starting up, Exercise A, page 82

1 b   2 b (It's Italian.)   3 a   4 b   5 a (over 2 million)
6 a (398,000m² in Everett, Washington)   7 b   8 c (It's based in Redmond, Washington.)
9 b (21.5 million units)   10 c (for the 4th year running in 2011)

ACTIVITY FILE

1 Introductions, Vocabulary, Exercise C, page 8

Student A

Ask about: Answer Student B's questions about:

1	McDonald's	2	Samsung – Korean
3	Ikea	4	Zara – Spanish
5	Prada	6	Gazprom – Russian
7	Michelin	8	Mercedes – German
9	Telcel	10	Tata Group – Indian
11	Petrobras	12	Tesco – British

3 Problems, Language focus 1, Exercise C, page 25

Student A

1 You start work at 7.30 a.m.
2 You finish work at 4.30 a.m.
3 You work in Frankfurt.
4 You report to the Financial Director.
5 You never work at the weekend.

4 Travel, Skills, Exercise C, page 42

Student A

You are a business traveller. You phone Big Bird Airways to book tickets for yourself and a colleague.

- Give your name. Ask for two premium economy tickets to New York on 4th June, returning on 9th June.
- Ask the price.
- Ask if there is a pick-up service and car hire.
- Give your credit-card details:
  American Express number: 3871 2239 1026 8892
  Expiry date: 08/15   Security number: 445

5 Food and entertaining, Case study, Task, page 51

Student A

Customer: Tiffany (American)

She prefers:
- hot, spicy food
- quiet restaurants, no music
- restaurants in the centre.

She does not like:
- seafood
- travelling a long distance by car.

If there is no spicy food, she sometimes orders a meat dish.

6 Buying and selling, Case study, Task, page 59

Student A

RC1 SPACESHIP TOY

Manufacturer: Toys Unlimited

Product description: a radio-controlled spaceship, made of plastic and steel; goes backwards and forwards; can turn 360 degrees.

Price: $40

Target market: children aged 3+

Colours: blue and green

Selling points: Press a button and the front rises; hand control easy to use.

Discounts: 5% for new customer, 3% for early payment

ACTIVITY FILE

8   Advertising, Skills, Exercise D, page 80

Student A

You start the meeting with a suggested name for the biscuits.

Name: Classic Taste

Price: €3

Promotion: Advertise in top-class magazines and quality newspapers

9   Companies, Case study, Task, page 89

Student A

Position:	Advertising Manager, Omnia Supermarkets Head office: Paris, France
Duties:	• plan advertising campaign • prepare budgets • lead and motivate staff
Company profile:	A group of supermarkets and convenience stores in France; sells food, household products and furniture
Employees:	Approximately 1,500
Turnover:	€220 million
Profit:	€18.4 million
Competitors:	Carrefour, Auchamp, other supermarket chains
Plans:	• to build more convenience stores • to sell more 'own label' products

11   Cultures, Language focus 2, Exercise F, page 110

Requests	Replies
You want:	
last month's production figures	Yes – e-mail them this p.m.
a meeting with the Quality Manager	No – away on holiday
a copy of the quality report	No – not ready yet
a hotel near the company	Yes – book a room at …
the agenda for your visit	Yes – send it later today

12   Jobs, Case study, Task, page 119

Student A

Vice-President of Human Resources

It is your task to interview the candidate,
then decide if you wish to hire him/her.

1   Ask questions about the candidate:

- What area of the company he/she is interested in
- What position he/she is applying for
- Why he/she wants a job with your company
- What his/her personal qualities are
- What his/her skills and abilities are
- What qualifications he/she has
- What work experience he/she has
- What his/her interests are

2   Ask any other questions you want to.

3   Ask the candidate if he/she has any questions.

Benefits

You can offer:
- a competitive salary for all positions
- three weeks' annual leave
- a company car (for management positions)
- health insurance

ACTIVITY FILE

1 Introductions, Skills, Exercise D, page 12

Student A

Fill in the missing information. Add any other information you wish.
Then develop a conversation with your partner.

Your name: ....

Where you are from: ....

Your position: *Business Manager, JC Electronics.*

Reason for your visit: *to meet important customers of your company*

How your business is doing: *very well – many new customers*

Weather in your country: ....

Where you are staying: *Empire Hotel*

What the hotel is like: *small rooms, but comfortable bed; big television; good service*

Say goodbye.

5 Food and entertaining, Skills, Exercise E, page 49

Manager A

- You suggest a football match and meal in an expensive international restaurant because everyone likes football and international food.
- You think the Grand Theatre and casino is a bad idea because there is not enough chance to talk. The casino is good for later in the evening.
- You think the local restaurant and cabaret/dancing show is a bad idea; the cabaret/dancing show is OK, but the local restaurant is too cheap.

9 Companies, Reading, Exercise E, page 86

Student A

Read about Gamesa's progress in Brazil and complete the notes below.

Gamesa in Brazil

Progress in 2010
Following a decision to enter the Brazilian market, Gamesa set up a subsidiary in São Paulo in early 2010. Just six months later, in July 2010, it opened its first manufacturing plant in Brazil. The plant is in Camaçari in the north-east of Bahía and employs 100 people. It took six months to build, at a cost of $32 million.

Current developments
Gamesa plans to buy 60% of the components for the wind turbines locally. Currently, the company is developing its network of local suppliers. With strong orders for the coming year, Gamesa is already expanding the Camaçari plant and plans to recruit more workers. It is planning to use Brazil as a base for developing business in the neighbouring countries of Argentina, Chile and Uruguay.

Notes

Progress in Brazil

Key events
- *early 2010 – set up a subsidiary*
-

Current projects
- *developing a network of local suppliers*
-
-

2 Work and leisure, Case study, Task, page 21

Student B

Choose one of these roles.

Role card 1
Receptionist

Your job: Receive visitors; answer phone calls; book meeting rooms

Hours: 8 a.m.–5 p.m. Monday to Friday. You sometimes work on Saturdays.

Breaks: One 15-minute break in the morning

Lunch: 1 p.m.–2 p.m. You never go out for lunch because the restaurants in the area are very expensive.

Feelings about job:
You are *not* happy.

- The reception desk is always very busy, so the work is tiring and stressful.
- You have a two-year-old daughter. You take her to a childminder every morning before you go to work. The childminding is very expensive.
- You want more flexible hours, longer breaks, a restaurant and a free day-care centre in the company.

Role card 2
Website developer

Your job: Build software programs; design web pages, graphics and images; advise clients how to improve their software

Hours: 8 a.m.–5 p.m., but often later and at the weekend

Breaks: No regular breaks

Lunch: You usually have a sandwich at your desk.

Feelings about job:
You enjoy the job. You like your colleagues, but you do not like your boss because he:

- does not give you clear goals
- tries to tell you how to do your job
- asks you to give him reports each day about your work.

Role card 3
Writer

Your job: Write creative, original content for company websites; research topics on the Internet

Hours: 9 a.m.–5 p.m., often later

Breaks: No regular breaks

Lunch: Flexible times

Feelings about job:
You are very unhappy because you:

- are always under pressure and stressed. The company needs more content writers.
- want to spend two days a week working at home. The owners won't let you do this.
- want the company to provide free private health care.

Role card 4
Graphic designer

Your job: Meet clients to discuss what they want; produce new ideas for clients and help them to improve their website design

Hours: No fixed times, but always very long hours

Breaks: No fixed times

Lunch: You always have lunch at your desk. Usually fast food / a takeaway meal.

Feelings about job:
You want to leave the company because:

- the owners do not listen to you when the website developers and designers discuss new projects.
- the owners get angry if you have a hospital or dental appointment, or when you are late because you take the children to school.
- some of the younger designers need training, but the owners do not want to send them on training courses.

ACTIVITY FILE

1 Introductions, Starting up, Exercise G, page 7

Student B

Listen to your partner and write down the first names, surnames and e-mail addresses of three people.

1 ………………………………   2 ………………………………   3 ………………………………

Now spell the first names, surnames and e-mail addresses of these people for your partner.

1 The Production Manager is Olga Karpyn. That's O-L-G-A for Olga, and then Karpyn K-A-R-P-Y-N. Her e-mail is karpyn@VLK.pl

2 Our Marketing Manager is Kaori Monchi. That's K-A-O-R-I, and then Monchi M-O-N-C-H-I. Her e-mail is k.mon23@ILG.jp

3 The new Customer Service Manager is Leila Mehrzad. That's Leila L-E-I-L-A, and Mehrzad M-E-H-R-Z-A-D. Her e-mail is l.mehrzad@petco.sa

4 Travel, Skills, Exercise C, page 42

Student B

You are a reservations executive at Big Bird Airways. A customer phones to buy tickets.

- Answer the phone and give the name of the company.
- Check if booking is for business or economy class.
- Ticket prices: economy £550, premium economy £770, business £999
- Pick-up service: no
  Car hire: yes
- Ask for credit-card details.

5 Food and entertaining, Skills, Exercise E, page 49

Manager B

- You suggest a local restaurant and cabaret/dancing show because it is good for visitors to try local food and the cabaret/dancing show is exciting to watch.
- You think the football match is a bad idea because some of the visitors are women. You think the international restaurant is too expensive.
- You think the casino is a bad idea because not everyone likes to gamble. The Grand Theatre is good for early in the evening. The play is interesting.

6 Buying and selling, Skills, Exercise C, page 58

Student B

You are a salesperson for a lighting equipment manufacturer. You are at a trade fair and a Store Manager is asking you about one of your lights. Read the description of the light and answer the Store Manager's questions. Add any other details you wish.

- Your most popular model: AC50
- Target market: students, musicians
- Features: bends in all directions, long-lasting batteries and bulbs
- Weight: 4.5kg
- Measurements: 65cm high x 35cm wide
- Colours: black, blue, brown
- Price: 48 euros
- Delivery: within three days

Working across cultures 2, Exercise A, page 60

1 Germany   2 the US   3 China

3 Problems, Vocabulary, Exercise B, page 23

Student B

1 **Match the adjectives (1–8) to their opposites (a–h).**

1	big	a)	wide
2	hot	b)	wrong
3	narrow	c)	hard
4	high	d)	stressful
5	soft	e)	cold
6	right	f)	low
7	cheap	g)	expensive
8	relaxing	h)	small

2 **Now answer your partner's questions.**

The opposite of	long	is	short.
	heavy		light.
	early		late.
	slow		fast.
	safe		dangerous.
	noisy		quiet.
	easy		difficult.
	interesting		boring.

3 **Your partner has the answers to Exercise 1. Ask him/her questions to check your answers.**

What's the opposite of 'big'?

4 Travel, Language focus 1, Exercise G, page 39

Student B

Part 1

A visitor from head office (Student A) contacts you about a visit. Use the notes to answer his/her questions.

A: *Can I rent a car at the airport?*
B: *No, you can't. It's a very small airport.*

- No, ... It's too far. You need to take a taxi.
- No, ... It's a very small airport.
- Yes, ... We have Wi-Fi.
- Yes, ..., but the exchange rate is not good.

Part 2

You plan to visit one of your company's overseas offices for a week. Student A works there. Ask him/her for this information.

- use a computer?

  Can I use a computer?

- get lunch in the canteen?
- meet you on Monday at 8 a.m.?
- visit some customers on Tuesday?

11 Cultures, Skills, Exercise E, page 110

Student A

Manager 1

- You think Ken is not happy working in your country.
  - He doesn't understand the culture.
  - He isn't interested in learning the country's language or its customs.
  - He's often late for work and for meetings.
  - He doesn't shake hands with other staff at the beginning of the day, but everyone else does.
  - He uses first names with everyone, with senior managers too. No one else does that.
- You think it's best if he moves to a different department or leaves the company.

Try to agree on a solution with Manager 2.

ACTIVITY FILE

1 Introductions, Vocabulary, Exercise C, page 8

Student B

Ask about:

2 Samsung
4 Zara
6 Gazprom
8 Mercedes
10 Tata Group
12 Tesco

Answer Student A's questions about:

1 McDonald's – American
3 Ikea – Swedish
5 Prada – Italian
7 Michelin – French
9 Telcel- Mexican
11 Petrobras – Brazilian

3 Problems, Case study, Task, page 29

Student B

Manager at High-Style Business Rentals

You receive a telephone call from an unhappy guest.

- Listen to the guest.
- Say you are sorry about the problems.
- Offer him/her a bigger apartment (price: $10 more per day).
- Offer him/her a lower internet price ($6 an hour).

Information: You have more furniture for guests in your building.
You will get some new televisions next week.

4 Travel, Vocabulary, Exercise E, page 37

Student B

1 **Give your partner the information he/she needs.**

Mr Asafiev is booked on flight IB231 from New York JFK, Terminal 2, gate 14.
Take-off is at 07:35. He arrives in Madrid at 15:25. He is staying at the Hilton Hotel.

2 **Ask your partner for the missing information.**

What is Mrs Bendhiba's flight number?

Visitor

Name:	Mrs Bendhiba	Flight number:	
Airport:		Terminal:	
Gate number:		Take-off time:	
Destination:		Arrival time:	
Hotel:			

3 **Check the information with your partner.**

6 Buying and selling, Case study, Task, page 59

Student B

ROBOT 'MEMEME' TOY

Manufacturer: WCTV Enterprises

Product description: a small battery-operated robot; made of plastic and rubber; wears big rubber boots; talks in a funny voice, always about itself; based on a character in a TV programme.

Price: $30

Target market: children aged 5+

Colours: red and yellow

Selling points: Can sing five songs; goes fast backwards.

Discount: 6% for new customers

ACTIVITY FILE

4   Travel, Language focus 2, Exercise C, page 41

Student B

Part 1

Student A has a new job abroad. You live in that country. Use these notes to answer his/her questions.

A: *Is there an international school?*
B: *Yes. There's a very good American school.*

- Yes. … some, but … more apartments.
- Yes. … very good American school.
- Yes, … and it's very cheap.
- No, but … lots of small shops and a market every day.

Part 2

You have a new job abroad. Student A lives there. Ask him/her about these points.

- good restaurants
  Are there any good restaurants?
- tennis courts
- swimming pool
- cinemas

5   Food and entertaining, Case study, Task, page 51

Student B

Customer: Hanna (German)

She prefers:
- vegetarian dishes
- lively restaurants with music
- delicious desserts.

She does not like:
- meat or seafood dishes
- expensive restaurants.

7   People, Skills, Exercise E, page 72

Student B

Manager

You work for a car-hire company near the airport. You do not want the office worker to start at 9.30 a.m. because:

- many people come to the company early in the morning to hire a car. It's a very busy time.
- other employees will want to work later if you let this worker start at 9.30 a.m.
- you think the worker is lazy. He/She just doesn't want to get up early in the morning.

8   Advertising, Skills, Exercise D, page 80

Student B

You disagree with Student A's suggestions.

Name: Take-a-break

Price: €1.2

Promotion: Advertise on radio and TV and in cinemas

11   Cultures, Case study, Task, page 111

Kate Maskie

You want to introduce all the new ideas. You think the:

- image of the overseas branch is not good.
- branch will lose customers if it doesn't change.
- staff will enjoy a more relaxed, informal atmosphere.
- staff will be more motivated and will work better as a team.
- branch office will keep more staff if the working hours are flexible.

ACTIVITY FILE

1 Introductions, Skills, Exercise D, page 12

Student B

Fill in the missing information. Add any other information you wish.
Then develop a conversation with your partner.

Your name: ....

Where you are from: ....

Your position: *Marketing Director, Universal Travel*

Reason for your visit: *to visit tourist offices and get information about tourist attractions*

How your business is doing: *not very well at the moment – too many competitors*

Weather in your country: ....

Where you are staying: *Eastern Hotel*

What the hotel is like: *good value for money; big room; large bed, armchair and desk; lots of lights*

Say goodbye.

4 Travel, Case study, page 43

Meeting rooms and seminar rooms

The Conference Centre has three meeting rooms and four seminar rooms.

The meeting rooms

- *Rossini*
  - Seating capacity: 100
  - Video conferencing, large screen (5m x 4m), no direct access to the terrace and garden, technical support at all times
- *Puccini*
  - Seating capacity: 75
  - Video conferencing, projector + screen (4.5m x 4m), direct access to the terrace and garden
- *Verdi*
  - Seating capacity: 50
  - Film projector and screen (4m x 3.5m), six laptops ($20 a day), technical support

5 Food and entertaining, Vocabulary, Exercise H, page 45

Student B

You are in a restaurant with a colleague from your head office.

- Say yes. Ask about a recommendation.
- Choose Russian salad or soup.
- Ask for help. You don't know what *moussaka* is.
- Choose moussaka.
- Suggest ordering dessert and coffee later.

11 Cultures, Case study, Task, page 111

Stuart Adams

You are against all the changes. You think:

- the staff prefer a formal style of management.
- a flexitime system will be difficult to organise.
- hot-desking will not be popular. Staff prefer to have their own desk.
- long meetings are good for team-building and decision-making.
- junior staff will feel uncomfortable with an 'open-door' policy. It is unusual in their culture.

ACTIVITY FILE

5 Food and entertaining, Case study, Task, page 51

Student C

Customer: Takashi (Japanese)

He prefers:
- high-quality seafood and delicious desserts
- quiet restaurants with relaxed atmosphere
- beautiful restaurants with soft music.

He does not like:
- hot, spicy food
- long trips by car.

9 Companies, Reading, Exercise E, page 86

Student B

Read about Gamesa's progress in India and complete the notes below.

Gamesa in India

Progress in 2010

In early 2010, Gamesa decided to enter the Indian market by setting up a subsidiary. Soon after, in February 2010, the company started production at its first manufacturing plant, near the city of Chennai in south-east India. The plant has a workforce of 100. The following month, as part of its strategy for developing the Indian market, it opened a technology centre, also near Chennai.

Current developments

The technology centre employs 45 engineers. Currently they are working with local suppliers to improve quality. The centre is also setting up research projects with universities. Business is growing fast, and Gamesa has large orders in India and also in the neighbouring country of Sri Lanka. As a result, the company is expanding its production capacity and is building new plants in the northern state of Gujarat and in Tamil Nadu in the south of India.

Notes

Progress in India

Key events
- early 2010 – set up a subsidiary
-
-

Current projects
- technology centre working with local suppliers to improve quality
-
-
-

11 Cultures, Case study, Task, page 111

Director of Human Resources

You like some of Kate's proposals but not all of them. You think:
- shorter meetings are a good idea.
- a more relaxed, informal style will help the company's image.
- hot-desking will be good because it reduces office costs.

You do not want to introduce any other changes during the next year.

ACTIVITY FILE

9 Companies, Case study, Task, page 89

Student B

Position:	Production Manager, Miriam Palmer Health Care Head office: Munich, Germany
Duties:	• to manage and control production • to check product quality • to supervise and motivate the factory workers
Company profile:	makes beauty and skin-care products; sells its products in 25 countries
Employees:	2,500
Turnover:	US$85 million
Profit:	US$10.2 million
Competitors:	L'Oréal, Henkel
Plans:	• to set up factories in Africa • to launch a new hair shampoo in the US

11 Cultures, Skills, Exercise E, page 110

Student B

Manager 2

- You think Ken has a problem but you're not sure what it is.
- You like him.
- He is good at his job and helpful to colleagues.
- He often does overtime in the evenings, but he doesn't socialise with colleagues or attend social events organised by the company.
- You want to keep Ken in the company and you are happy for him to stay in your department.

Try to agree on a solution with Manager 1.

12 Jobs, Case study, Task, page 119

Student B

Candidate

It is your task to answer the questions of the Vice-President of Human Resources and to persuade him/her to hire you. There are positions available in all the areas listed, both at head office and overseas. You can join the company as a trainee, junior executive or manager. You may use information from your own life or invent your profile.

Preparing for the interview

Think about:

- the area of the company you wish to work in
- the position you would like to have
- why you want a job with Nelson & Harper
- your personal qualities
- your skills and abilities
- your qualifications
- your work experience
- your interests.

Think also of questions you wish to ask the interviewer, for example, what the salary is, how many weeks' annual leave, etc.

5 Food and entertaining, Case study, Task, page 51

Student D

Customer: Nigel (English)

He prefers:

- vegetarian dishes
- lively restaurants with a lot of customers
- friendly waiters and fast service.

He does not like:

- spicy food or meat dishes
- expensive restaurants that are not value for money.

5 Food and entertaining, Skills, Exercise E, page 49

Manager C

- You suggest the Grand Theatre and a casino because the play at the theatre is very good and the casino is very fashionable.
- You think the local restaurant and cabaret/dancing show is a bad idea because the cabaret/dancing show is too noisy. The local restaurant is fun, but the food is not good quality.
- You think the football match and international restaurant is a bad idea because the international restaurant is not interesting for the visitors. The football match is good for the afternoon, but the weather may be cold and wet.

6 Buying and selling, Case study, Task, page 59

Student C

SKATEBOARD 'INSIDE TRACK'

Manufacturer: Elite Sports Goods

Product description: a two-wheel skateboard; very fast, doesn't make much noise; best-selling skateboard in China and Brazil

Price: $60

Target market: skateboarders aged 15+

Colours: eight bright colours

Selling points: Skateboards have colourful designs by a famous artist; Jeff Rollins, skateboard champion, advertises the product

Discount: 15% for orders over 3,000 items

8 Advertising, Skills, Exercise D, page 80

Student C

You like Student's A's name and you agree with Student B's price, but you disagree with their promotion ideas.

Name: Classic Taste

Price: €1.2

Promotion: Advertise on posters and websites popular with the target market (young professional people)

9 Companies, Case study, Task, page 89

Student C

Position:	Conservation Officer, The Forest Life Trust Headquarters: Vancouver, Canada
Duties:	• to raise money for wildlife projects • to persuade government officials to protect wildlife in their country
Company profile:	A non-profit organisation to protect all wildlife; it has thousands of members and supporters worldwide.
Employees:	10 full-time employees at Head Office; many unpaid workers
Turnover:	US$12.6 million
Profit:	Non-profit organisation
Competitors:	other wildlife organisations
Plans:	• to organise a worldwide campaign to protect large animals • to contact famous people to appear in an advertising campaign for the Trust

ACTIVITY FILE

11 Cultures, Case study, Task, page 111

Finance Director

You like some of Kate's proposals, but not all of them. You think:

- a flexitime system will be popular with staff.
- staff should dress casually at work.
- an 'open-door' policy is an excellent idea.

You do not want to introduce any other changes during the next year.

12 Jobs, Skills, Exercise E, page 118

Student B

Candidate for the job of Sales Manager, Tokyo office

Use these prompts to answer the Director's questions.

1. Yes / came by taxi
2. like working with people / interested in Japanese culture
3. good with numbers / speak Japanese fluently
4. stay calm at all times / Lot of pressure / previous job / no problem
5. how to deal with customers / work well in a team
6. long hours / lot of unpaid overtime / long journey to work
7. cycling, watching baseball
8. company benefits? / free parking?

3 Problems, Language focus 1, Exercise C, page 25

Student B

1. You start work at 9.30 a.m.
2. You finish work at 7.00 p.m.
3. You work in London.
4. You report to the Customer Care Manager.
5. You work on Saturday mornings.

Working across cultures 1, Exercise B, page 30

1 c   2 a   3 d   4 b   5 c   6 b   7 d   8 b   9 d

144

Grammar reference

1 *to be*; *a/an*; *wh-* questions

to be
Form

+	I'm (= am)	a student.
	He's/She's/It's (= is)	from Poland.
	You're/We're/They're (= are)	at work.
–	I'm not (= am not)	American.
	He/She/It isn't (= is not) *or*	here.
	He's/She's/It's not	Chinese.
	You/We/They aren't (= are not) *or*	lawyers.
	You're/We're/They're not	
?	Am I	late?
	Is he/she/it	at the office?
	Are you/we/they	tired?

Questions with *to be*

- We put the form of the verb *to be* at the beginning.

  Am I early?   **Is** it here?
  Is he a manager?   **Are** you Spanish?

- We do not use the short form of the verb in answers.

  Are you a consultant?   Yes, I **am**. (NOT ~~Yes, I'm~~.)
  Is she married?   Yes, she **is**. (NOT ~~Yes, she's~~.)
  Are they OK?   Yes, they **are**. (NOT ~~Yes, they're~~.)

a/an

1. *a/an* with singular nouns
   - We use *a* before words beginning with a consonant sound (for example *c, p, y, j*).
     a city   **a** European   **a** picture   **a** problem   **a** university
   - We use *an* before words beginning with a vowel sound (for example *a, e*).
     an address   **an** answer   **an** hour   **an** interest   **an** office

2. *a/an* with jobs

   We use *a/an* with jobs.
   He's **a** designer.   (NOT ~~He's designer~~.)
   She's **an** architect. (NOT ~~She's architect~~.)

3. We don't use *a/an* with plural nouns.

wh- questions

What	's	your job?
	are	their names?
Who	's	your boss?
	are	they?
Where	's	my case?
	are	the files?

145

2 Present simple; adverbs and expressions of frequency

Present simple
Form

+	I/You/We/They **work**.
	He/She/It **works**.
−	I/You/We/They **don't work**.
	He/She/It **doesn't work**.
?	**Do** I/you/we/they **work**?
	Does he/she/it **work**?

Uses

We use the present simple:

- to talk about habits and work routines.

    I *get up* early in the morning.
    She *works* from home.
    They *go* to work by train.

- to talk about facts and things that are generally true.

    They *have* offices in Seoul.
    It *rains* a lot in Manchester.
    She *earns* a high salary.

- with verbs that describe permanent states.

    I *like* meeting people.
    She *has* three children.
    I think he *lives* in a flat.
    I *know* his boss very well.

- with adverbs and expressions of frequency.

    She **always wears** blue.
    He **usually/generally takes** work home at the weekend.
    They **often go** home early on Fridays.
    I **sometimes play** tennis with a colleague.
    Do you **ever go** to the theatre?
    I **never go** to the theatre.

Adverbs and expressions of frequency

1 Adverbs of frequency usually go before the main verb, but after the verb *to be*.

   I **sometimes** make phone calls to the USA.
   My boss is **usually** friendly.
   We don't **generally** stay up late.

2 For emphasis, *usually*, *generally*, *often* and *sometimes* can go at the beginning of a sentence.

   Sometimes, I don't like my job.
   Generally, we take clients out to a good restaurant.

3 Expressions of frequency can go at the beginning or the end of a sentence, but not in the middle.

   Once a year, we have a sales conference.
   We have a sales conference **once a year**.
   (NOT ~~We have once a year a sales conference.~~)
   Does he play golf **every Saturday**?
   (NOT ~~Does he every Saturday play golf?~~)

3 Present simple: negatives and questions; *have*; *some* and *any*

Present simple: negatives and questions

Points to remember

1. In questions, the *-s* is on the auxiliary verb, not the main verb.
   ***Does** he **drink** coffee?* (NOT *Does he drinks coffee?*)
2. We do not use the full verb in a short answer.
   '***Do** you **like** meeting customers?*' '*Yes, I **do**.*' (NOT *Yes, I like.*)
3. Spelling rules
   - For *he*, *she* and *it*, we add *-s* with most verbs.
     *She **comes** from Brazil.*
     *The job **pays** a good salary.*
   - When the verb ends with a consonant + *y*, the ending becomes *-ies*.
     *He often **flies** to Amsterdam.*
   - When the verb ends in *-ch*, *-sh*, *-s*, *-ss*, *-x* or *-z*, the ending becomes *-es*.
     *He **finishes** every day at six.*
     *She **faxes** the invoice to us.*

have

Form

+	I/You/We/They **have**	a German car.
	He/She/It **has**	a CD player.
−	I/You/We/They **haven't** (= have not) / **don't** (= do not) **have**	the time.
	He/She/It **hasn't** (= has not) / **doesn't** (= does not) **have**	a good printer.
?	**Do** I/you/we/they **have**	a ticket?
	Does he/she/it **have**	a reference number?

Uses

- We use *have/has* to indicate possession.
  *She **has** a fast car.*
- We also use *have/has* to talk about plans.
  *I **have** a meeting this Tuesday, but I'm free on Wednesday.*
- In British English, we use *have got* in the same way.
  *He**'s got** a job interview next week.*

Some and *any*

- *Some* and *any* are used with plural nouns when the quantity is not specified.
- If the sentence is positive, we use *some*.
  *There are **some** deliveries due in today.*
- If the sentence is negative, we use *any*.
  *There aren't **any** deliveries due in today.*
- If the sentence is a question, we use *any*.
  *Are there **any** deliveries due in today?*

4 can/can't; there is / there are

can/can't
Form

+	I/You/He/She/It/We/They **can**	go.
−	I/You/He/She/It/We/They **can't** (= **cannot**)	go.
?	**Can** I/you/he/she/it/we/they	go?

Remember: *can* stays the same with *he*, *she* and *it*. (NOT ~~He cans go~~.)

Short answers

Yes, you **can**.

No, I **can't**.

Uses

- We use *can* to talk about ability.

  He **can** write computer programs.
  She **can** fly a helicopter.

- We use *can* to ask for permission.

  Can I make a phone call, please?   Yes, go ahead.
  Can we park in this space?   Sorry, you can't park here. It's reserved.

- We use *can* to talk about what is possible.

  Can you come next Thursday?   Sorry, I'm afraid I have another appointment.
  Can we put another desk in here?   No, the room's too small.

- We do not use *to* after *can*.

  (NOT ~~She can to ride a motorbike.~~)

there is / there are
Uses

- We use *there is (not) a* + singular noun to say that something exists or doesn't exist.

  There's a coffee machine on the second floor.
  There isn't a swimming pool in this hotel.

- With plural nouns, we use *there are* with *some* in positive statements, and *there are not* with *any* in negative sentences.

  There are some people in the room.
  There aren't any flights on Sundays.

- We use *is there / are there* + *a/any* to ask a question.

  Is there a message for me?
  Is there any baggage?
  Are there any good nightclubs in the city?

5 *some/any*; countable and uncountable nouns

some/any
Form

	Plural countable nouns	Uncountable nouns
+	We need **some** machines.	We need **some** equipment.
–	There aren't **any** restaurants.	There isn't **any** food.
?	Would you like **some** carrots?	Would you like **some** spaghetti?
	Do you have **any** coins?	Do you have **any** money?

Uses

- We use *some* to make an offer when we think the answer will be 'yes'.

  Would you like **some** tea?   Yes, I would.
  Can I offer you **some** coffee?   Yes, please.

- We use *any* to make an offer when we don't know the answer.

  Do you want **any** coffee?   No, thank you.

Countable and uncountable nouns

1. Countable nouns include individual things, people and places and have a plural.

   a computer   *some computers*
   a secretary   *two secretaries*
   a restaurant   *good restaurants*

2. We do not use *a/an* with uncountable nouns. They do not have a plural.

   *It's difficult to find **good staff**.*   (NOT ~~a good staff~~)
   *I don't often use **public transport**.*   (NOT ~~public transports~~)

many, much and *a lot of*

1. We can use *many* or *a lot of* in positive statements.

   *I have **many** English customers.*
   *I've got **a lot of** English customers.*
   Many is more formal than *a lot of*.

2. We do not normally use *much* in positive statements.

   *They've got **a lot of** money.*   (NOT ~~much money~~)

3. We use *many* with plural countable nouns in questions and negative sentences.

   *Do you have **many** visitors?*
   *There aren't **many** vegetarian restaurants.*

4. We use *much* with uncountable nouns in questions and negative sentences.

   *Do you do **much** advertising?*
   *I don't have **much** time.*

5. We use *a lot of* in positive and negative sentences and questions with both plural countable and uncountable nouns.

   *I have **a lot of** baggage.*   *I have **a lot of** bags.*
   *We don't have **a lot of** time.*   *We don't have **a lot of** books.*
   *Do you have **a lot of** money?*   *Do you have **a lot of** American clients?*

6 Past simple; past time references

Past simple
Form

1 Regular verbs

Verb	Ending	Example
Ends in a consonant (e.g. *work*)	+ *-ed*	I **worked** at home yesterday.
Ends in *-e* (e.g. *decide*)	+ *-d*	He **decided** to take a taxi.
Ends in a consonant + *y* (e.g. *study*)	change *-y* to *-ied*	She **studied** law at university.
Ends with a consonant + vowel + consonant (e.g. *stop*)	double the final consonant + *-ed*	They **stopped** smoking two years ago.

But if the final consonant is in an unstressed syllable, we do not double it (e.g. *develop* → *developed*; *market* → *marketed*).

2 Irregular verbs

Many frequently used verbs are irregular.

buy – bought   cost – cost   know – knew   make – made
meet – met   put – put   send – sent   write – wrote

(See the list of irregular verbs, page 157.)

Uses

We use the past simple to talk about a:
- completed single action in the past.
  He **met** her at the sales conference.
  We **gave** them a lot of money.
- past state that is now finished.
  I **lived** in Italy in 1999.
  We **had** an agent in Asia at that time.
- repeated action in the past.
  We **went** to the beach every day.
  I always **wrote** to him in English.

Past time references

1 We use the past simple with expressions that refer to a definite moment or period in the past.

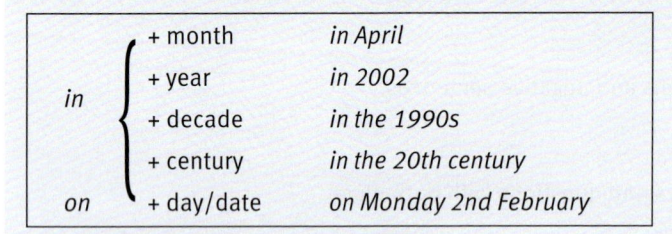

in	+ month	*in April*
	+ year	*in 2002*
	+ decade	*in the 1990s*
	+ century	*in the 20th century*
on	+ day/date	*on Monday 2nd February*

He first **set up** in business **in 1999**.
The 1960s were relatively prosperous.
We **signed** the contract **on 3rd April 2003**.

2 Other expressions

We **had** a meeting **last** Friday.
I **visited** the factory **yesterday**.
He **left** the firm five years **ago**. (= five years between now and the moment he left)

7 Past simple: negatives and questions; question forms

Past simple: negative statements

We use *did not / didn't* + infinitive without *to* to make negative statements about the past.

Form

+	−
I went by train.	I **didn't go** by train.
She saw you.	She **didn't see** you.
They had a very good time.	They **didn't have** a very good time.

Past simple: questions

We make questions about the past with *did/didn't* + subject + infinitive without *to*.

Did you check the figures?   **Did** they have a good time?   **Didn't** Paul tell you?

Question forms

Questions with *to be*

To make questions with the verb *to be*, we put the subject after the verb.

Was he at the meeting?
Were there any messages for me?
Were they pleased?

Questions with a modal verb

To make questions with a modal verb, we put the subject after the verb.

Can I see you now?
Would you like a coffee?

Question words: *what, where, when, why* and *how*

We put question words at the beginning of the sentence before a form of *do, be,* a modal or an auxiliary.

	Question word	Form of *do, be,* modal or auxiliary	Subject	
I prepared some invoices.	**What**	did	you	**do** yesterday?
She went to Beijing.	**Where**	did	she	**go**?
They learned about it on Friday.	**When**	did	they	**learn** about it?
She needs a holiday.	**Why**	does	she	**need** a holiday?
She gets on very well with her colleagues.	**How**	does	she	**get** on with her colleagues?
It cost a lot of money.	**How much**	did	the machine	**cost**?
I see my suppliers once a month.	**How often**	do	you	**see** your suppliers?
I can do it next week.	**When**	can	you	**do** it?
He was happy.	**Why**	was	he	happy?

Be careful not to use two past forms in the same sentence.
Where did you stay? (NOT ~~Where did you stayed?~~)
Be careful with the word order. (NOT ~~Where did stay you?~~)

8 Comparatives and superlatives; *much / a lot, a little / a bit*

Comparatives and superlatives
Form
Comparative adjectives are forms like *older, more expensive*.
Superlative adjectives are forms like *the oldest, the most expensive*.

- For the majority of one-syllable adjectives, add *-er, -est*.
  cheap → cheaper → the cheapest
- For one-syllable adjectives ending in *-e*, add *-r, -st*.
  late → later → the latest
- For short adjectives ending in one vowel + one consonant, double the consonant.
  big → bigger → the biggest
  hot → hotter → the hottest
  BUT don't double *w*.
  new → newer → the newest
- For adjectives ending in consonant + *-y*, change *y* to *i*.
  easy → easier → the easiest
  healthy → healthier → the healthiest
- Some adjectives are irregular.
  good → better → the best
  bad → worse → the worst
  far → further → the furthest (or *far → farther → the farthest*)

Uses

1. When we compare two things, we use the comparative + *than*.
   *France is **bigger than** Belgium.*
   *I think a Porsche is **less expensive than** a Rolls Royce.* (NOT ~~that~~)

2. When we compare three or more things, we use the superlative.
   *December is **the busiest** month in all our stores.*
   *Our products are not just good – they're **the best** in the world.*

much / a lot, a little / a bit

We can use *a lot / a bit* (especially in conversation) or *much / a little* (more formal) before comparatives.

- For large differences, we use *much / a lot*.
  *We have a **much lower** margin on computers than on software.*
  *Our new range is **a lot more successful** than the previous one.*
- For small differences, we use *a little / a bit*.
  *This time he seemed **a little more interested** than last time.*
  *Our prices are **a bit higher** than theirs.*

9 Present continuous; present simple or present continuous

Present continuous
Form

+	I'm He's/She's/It's You're/We're/They're	waiting.
–	I'm not He/She/It **isn't** You/We/They **aren't**	working.
?	**Am** I **Is** he/she/it **Are** you/we/they	coming?

Short answers

Yes, I **am**. No, I'**m not**.
Yes, he/she/it **is**. No, he/she/it **isn't**.
Yes, you/we/they **are**. No, you/we/they **aren't**.

Spelling rules

- Most verbs add *-ing*.
  She'**s talking** to a client.
- For verbs ending in *-e*, take away *e* and add *-ing*.
  He'**s making** some coffee.
- For verbs ending in consonant + vowel + consonant, double the final consonant and add *-ing*.
  Is anyone **sitting** here?
  But we do not double the final consonant if it is in an unstressed syllable (e.g. *developing, marketing*).

Uses

We use the present continuous:

- to talk about actions in progress at the time of speaking.
  I'**m using** the photocopier at the moment.
  Not now, I'**m talking** to a customer.
- for actions that are not necessarily in progress at the time of speaking, but have not finished.
  I'**m** still **writing** that report.
  We'**re trying** to enter new markets.
- for temporary situations.
  We'**re staying** at the Hilton for the next few days.

Present simple or present continuous

- We use the present simple to describe permanent situations which will not change.
  I **work** in Paris.
- We also use the present simple to talk about habits.
  I normally **drive** to work.
- We use the present continuous to describe temporary situations – situations which happen for a short time.
  I'**m walking** to work this week.

GRAMMAR REFERENCE

10 Talking about future plans; will

Forms

- We can use the present continuous, *going to* and *will* to talk about the future.

+	I'm He's/She's/It's You're/We're/They're	flying	to New York on Friday.
–	I'm not He/She/It **isn't** You/We/They **aren't**	planning	any budget cuts this year.
?	**Am** I **Is** he/she/it **Are** you/we/they	organising	the office party?

+	I'm He's/She's/It's You're/We're/They're	going to	be	there tomorrow.
–	I'm not He/She/It **isn't** You/We/They **aren't**	going to	do	that tomorrow.
?	**Am** I **Is** he/she/it **Are** you/we/they	going to	leave	tomorrow?

+	I/You/He/She/It/We/They	will	try.
–	I/You/He/She/It/We/They	won't (= will not)	work.
?	Will	I/you/he/she/it/we/they	go?

Uses

1 We use the present continuous to talk about things we have already arranged for the future.

   I'm meeting Mr Righetti next Thursday.
   We're having a staff party on Friday evening.

2 Sometimes we can use either the present continuous or *going to*.

   We're having a staff party on Friday evening.
   We're going to have a staff party on Friday evening.

3 *going to* is more suitable for strong intentions and predictions.

   I'm going to go to that meeting even if she doesn't want me to.
   We're certain the situation is going to get better.
   It's going to rain.

   Compare: *It's raining.* (now)

4 We use *will* to make:
   - predictions about things we think are inevitable and will happen without any arrangement or individual intention.

     I think there will be an economic crisis soon.
     In the next few years, everyone will be able to access the Internet with their mobile phone.
   - offers.

     I'll get Mr Schmidt a cup of coffee.
   - promises.

     I'll give her your regards if I see her.
     I'll have the report on your desk before Friday.

5 The opposite of *will* is *will not* or *won't*.

   Don't worry, I won't forget.

11 should/shouldn't; could/would

should/shouldn't
Form

+	I/You/He/She/It/We/They **should**	go.
–	I/You/He/She/It/We/They **shouldn't** (= **should not**)	go.
?	**Should** I/you/he/she/it/we/they	go?

Short answers

Yes, I/you/he/she/it/we/they **should**.
No, I/you/he/she/it/we/they **shouldn't**.

Uses

1 We use *should* to say that we think something is the right thing to do.
   We **should** do more to protect the environment.
   You **should** always prepare a presentation in advance.

2 We use *shouldn't* to say something is not the right thing to do or to criticise.
   She **shouldn't** drive if she's broken her glasses.
   He **shouldn't** interrupt people all the time; it's rude.

3 We use *should* to ask for or give advice.
   '**Should** I apologise to him?'
   'Yes, I think you **should**.'

could/would

1 We use *could* and *would* to make requests.
   Could/Would you open the door for me, please?

2 We use *would you like* to make offers.
   Would you like some coffee?

GRAMMAR REFERENCE

12 Present perfect; past simple and present perfect

Form

We form the present perfect with *have/has* + the past participle of the verb.
We form the past participle of regular verbs by adding *-ed* (e.g. *finished, tried, lived*).
Many frequently used verbs have irregular past participles (e.g. *been, gone, made, seen*).
(See list of irregular verbs, page 157.)

+	I've/You've/We've/They've He's/She's/It's	**been** there before. **moved**.
–	I/You/We/They **haven't** He/She/It **hasn't**	**made** an effort. **gone** away.
?	**Have** I/you/we/they **Has** he/she/it	**had** enough time? **made** a mistake?

Short answers

Yes, I/you/we/they **have**.   No, I/you/we/they **haven't**.
Yes, he/she/it **has**.   No, he/she/it **hasn't**.

Uses

We use the present perfect when we think about the past and present together.
In particular, we use this tense to talk about:

- actions that began in the past and continue in the present.

    She**'s worked** here for years. (She still works here.)

- life experiences.

    He**'s had** a number of jobs. He**'s been** a project manager, a financial analyst, and he**'s started** his own internet business.

- the present result of a past action.

Past action		Present result
completed the report yesterday	I**'ve put** it on her desk.	She's reading it now.
advertising campaign last month	Sales **have gone up**.	We're making more money.

Past simple *or* present perfect?

1. When we first give news, we often use the present perfect. When we give or ask for more details, we often change to the past simple.

    '*I***'ve found** your file.' 'Oh great. Where **did** you **find** it?'
    John **has gone** to Tokyo. He **left** last night.

2. We use the past simple with expressions of finished time.

    I **met** her last November.
    I **came** here in 2001.

3. We use the present perfect with expressions of time that take us up to the present.

    He**'s been** CEO since the beginning of last year. (He is still CEO.)
    So far, we **haven't had** any news.

4. We do not use the present perfect with expressions of finished time.

    (NOT ~~I have received a reply yesterday.~~)

Irregular verbs

Verb	Present participle	Past tense	Past participle
be	being	was	been
become	becoming	became	become
begin	beginning	began	begun
break	breaking	broke	broken
bring	bringing	brought	brought
build	building	built	built
buy	buying	bought	bought
catch	catching	caught	caught
choose	choosing	chose	chosen
come	coming	came	come
cost	costing	cost	cost
cut	cutting	cut	cut
deal	dealing	dealt	dealt
do	doing	did	done
draw	drawing	drew	drawn
drink	drinking	drank	drunk
drive	driving	drove	driven
eat	eating	ate	eaten
fall	falling	fell	fallen
find	finding	found	found
fly	flying	flew	flown
forget	forgetting	forgot	forgotten
get	getting	got	got
give	giving	gave	given
go	going	went	gone
grow	growing	grew	grown
have	having	had	had
hear	hearing	heard	heard
hold	holding	held	held
know	knowing	knew	known
learn	learning	learned *or* learnt	learned *or* learnt
leave	leaving	left	left
lose	losing	lost	lost
make	making	made	made
mean	meaning	meant	meant
meet	meeting	met	met
pay	paying	paid	paid
put	putting	put	put
quit	quitting	quit	quit
read	reading	read	read
run	running	ran	run
say	saying	said	said
see	seeing	saw	seen
sell	selling	sold	sold
send	sending	sent	sent
set	setting	set	set
shake	shaking	shook	shaken
show	showing	showed	shown
shut	shutting	shut	shut
sleep	sleeping	slept	slept
speak	speaking	spoke	spoken
spell	spelling	spelled *or* spelt	spelled *or* spelt
spend	spending	spent	spent
steal	stealing	stole	stolen
swim	swimming	swam	swum
take	taking	took	taken
teach	teaching	taught	taught
tell	telling	told	told
think	thinking	thought	thought
understand	understanding	understood	understood
wake	waking	waked *or* woke	woken
wear	wearing	wore	worn
win	winning	won	won
write	writing	wrote	written

Audio scripts

UNIT 1 INTRODUCTIONS

CD1 TRACK 1 (ES = EMMA SCHNEIDER, CP = CHARLES PORTER)
ES: Hi! You must be Charles.
CP: That's right, yes. Sorry I'm late. There was a delay with the flight.
ES: Welcome to Germany. I'm Emma. Emma Schneider, from Habermos in Hamburg.
CP: Oh! Emma … Nice to meet you at last! I've heard so much about you …
ES: Let me help you with your bag.

CD1 TRACK 2 (R = RECEPTIONIST, SJ = SHI JIABAO)
R: Payton Electronics. Good morning. How can I help you?
SJ: Good morning. My name is Shi Jiabao. I'd like to speak to the Marketing Manager, please.
R: I'm sorry, I didn't catch your name. Could you say it again?
SJ: Mr Shi Jiabao.
R: Just one moment, please, Mr Shi. I'll connect you.

CD1 TRACK 3 (AA = AKIM ANYUKOV, HB = HARRY BARKER)
AA: Excuse me, I am looking for Room 205.
HB: That's for the talk about investing in China, isn't it? I'm going there myself, so let's go together.
AA: Great. My name's Akim, by the way. Akim Anyukov. From Astena Consulting.
HB: Nice to meet you. I'm Harry.

CD1 TRACK 4 (NS = NURIA SOSA, AD = ANNA DAVIESON)
NS: Good afternoon. Are you Mrs Davieson?
AD: Yes, that's right.
NS: How do you do. I'm Nuria Sosa, from RTA Seguros.
AD: Pleased to meet you, Nuria. Did you have a nice trip? I think you need to check in at reception. Let me show you.
NS: Thank you.

CD1 TRACK 5
A H J K
B C D E G P T V
F L M N S X Z
I Y
O
Q U W
R

CD1 TRACK 6
1 Ms Schneider's first name is Emma. That's E-double M-A.
2 Shi Jiabao is visiting Payton Electronics. Payton is spelt P-A-Y-T-O-N.
3 He's Akim, and his surname's Anyukov. I'll spell it for you: A-N-Y-U-K-O-V.
4 Nuria Sosa is talking to Mrs Davieson. That's D-A-V-I-E-S-O-N. Nuria's e-mail address is S-O-S-A-at- R-T-A-S-dot-com-dot-A-R

CD1 TRACK 7
Brazil; Brazilian
Germany; German
India; Indian
Mexico; Mexican
Italy; Italian
Russia; Russian
Korea; Korean
Japan; Japanese
China; Chinese
Kuwait; Kuwaiti
Oman; Omani
Poland; Polish
Spain; Spanish
Sweden; Swedish
Turkey; Turkish
France; French
Greece; Greek
the UK; British
the USA; American

CD1 TRACK 8 (I = INTERVIEWER, JK = JEREMY KEELEY)
I: Can you introduce yourself?
JK: My name is Jeremy Keeley. I live in a small city in England near London called St Albans. I have three teenage children, and I run my own small business, which works for organisations across the UK and in Europe, where I help leaders to make decisions together and to improve the quality of their leadership.
I: Do you always shake hands when you meet someone?
JK: I like to shake hands. I like people to feel welcome, to feel important, to feel valued, so yes.

CD1 TRACK 9 (I = INTERVIEWER, JK = JEREMY KEELEY)
I: What do you say when you meet a new business contact?
JK: I usually say, 'Hello', 'How are you?', 'Where do you come from?', 'What do you do?' I usually find out what's important to them, why they're there. I usually wait until they've asked me a question before I talk too much about myself.
I: When do you exchange business cards?
JK: I usually wait until the person I'm meeting offers me a business card before I offer them mine, so we'll exchange them at that point.

CD1 TRACK 10 (M = MARISTELLA)
M: My name's Maristella. I'm Brazilian and I'm from São Paulo. I'm a research analyst for an investment bank in New York. I'm married with two children, a boy and a girl. They're at high school in Scarsdale. My husband's American and he's a doctor. My sister's in New York, too. She's a student at Columbia University. We're all interested in sports and movies. My son's a good tennis player.

CD1 TRACK 11 (P = PIERRE)
EXTRACT 1
P: Hi. I'm Pierre. I'm from Switzerland. I work for Foster Wheeler, an international engineering company. I'm an engineer. The company's head office is in Geneva, but I work in the Singapore office. My wife's from Singapore and she's an IT consultant.

CD1 TRACK 12 (G = GUSTAVO)
EXTRACT 2
G: My name's Gustavo. I'm from Argentina. I work for the United Nations. I'm a lawyer and I work in New York. It's a great place. My girlfriend's from New York. She's a journalist for the *New York Times*.

CD1 TRACK 13 (S = SILVIA)
EXTRACT 3
S: I'm Silvia and I'm an architect. I have my own company. It's small, just six people. The office is in Rome, but I'm not from Rome. I'm from Sicily. My family lives in Palermo. Franco – that's my husband – he's a househusband at the moment. He looks after our three children.

CD1 TRACK 14 (B = BOB, J = JIM, P = PAULA)
CONVERSATION 1
B: Hello, Jim. This is our new intern, Paula Atkins.
J: Nice to meet you, Paula. I'm Jim Davis, I work in sales.
P: Pleased to meet you, Jim.
J: How long will you be with us?
P: About three months, maybe longer.
B: OK, Jim, see you later …
J: Bye, Paula, enjoy your visit.
B: Now, Paula, how about a drink? Tea or coffee?

CD1 TRACK 15 (LC = LUCY COLLINS, JB = JENNY BRADSHAW, JR = JONATHAN ROSS)
CONVERSATION 2
LC: Good morning. My name's Lucy Collins, I'm a finance director. I work for a supermarket group.
JB: Hello, I'm Jenny Bradshaw, I'm a director of public relations. I work for a big media company.
LC: How do you do?
JB: Nice to meet you.
LC: Let me introduce you to my colleague, Jonathan Ross. He's my assistant.
JR: Pleased to meet you, Jenny.
LC: Where are you from, Jenny?
JB: I'm from New York. I'm here to attend a conference. How about you two?
LC: We're from Manchester. We're here to visit Head Office.

AUDIO SCRIPTS

CD1 TRACK 16 (J = JEFF, S = SUSAN)
CONVERSATION 3
J: Hi, I'm Jeff. I'm in Sales.
S: Hi, Jeff. I'm Susan. I work in Human Resources.
J: How are things going in your department?
S: Pretty good. I enjoy my work. My colleagues are really nice, and I like my boss. Her name's Judy Barlow. Do you know her?
J: Yes, she's nice. My boss is Richard Mason. He's not very friendly, but he's a good manager.
S: Well, that's the most important thing. OK, what are you having for lunch?
J: I think I'll have a salad. That's what I usually have for lunch here.

UNIT 2 WORK AND LEISURE

CD1 TRACK 17
PERSON 1
Well, I'm a product manager, and what's important for me is a high salary, long holidays and helpful colleagues. I only have two of these in my present job!

CD1 TRACK 18
PERSON 2
I want to be a salesman, so what's important for me is a company car, parking facilities and a mobile phone.

CD1 TRACK 19
PERSON 3
I'm an accountant. What's important for me is a friendly boss, travel opportunities … oh, and job security.

CD1 TRACK 20
PERSON 4
Fast promotion, flexible hours and some sports facilities are what's important for me. I work in customer service.

CD1 TRACK 21
1 at night
2 in the autumn
3 on the 15th of February
4 on Thursday
5 in the afternoon
6 on Tuesday evening
7 in June
8 at New Year (BrE) / on New Year (AmE)
9 at the weekend (BrE) / on the weekend (AmE)

CD1 TRACK 22 (I = INTERVIEWER, RP = ROS POMEROY)
I: Can you describe a typical working day?
RP: Well, what I enjoy the most about the work that I do is that there is no such thing as a typical day. I work for different clients on different projects, and when the client needs me for something, I have to be ready to respond. So I can be in meetings, I can be running a workshop or a discussion, or quite often I can be in my own office in front of a computer screen, or on the phone.

CD1 TRACK 23 (I = INTERVIEWER, RP = ROS POMEROY)
I: Do you have enough time for leisure?
RP: Well, some weeks I do work very long hours, and I also have teenage children. The combination of those two things does sometimes make it difficult to find enough time for leisure, for myself. But, to answer your question, even so … yes, I think I do have enough time for leisure.

CD1 TRACK 24 (I = INTERVIEWER, RP = ROS POMEROY)
I: What do you like doing to relax?
RP: At the weekends, I spend a lot of my time reading the newspaper. I catch up on the news from the previous week. And also I try to go out running. Now, running may not sound like something that is very relaxing, but I think that it's very important to get outside into the fresh air and see the countryside. So that's why I run.

CD1 TRACK 25 (I = INTERVIEWER, M = MARK)
INTERVIEW 1
I: So, Mark, you work for a fashion company in Milan. Tell me about your working life. What do you do when you get to work?
M: First, I say hello to all my colleagues and then I check my e-mail.
I: Where do you have lunch?
M: We have a long lunch break. I sometimes go home for lunch, because it's close to work. The other days I have lunch with colleagues in a restaurant.
I: How much do you travel for your job?
M: Not a lot, but I always go to the fashion shows in Paris and New York.
I: And what do you do on the weekend?
M: On Saturday nights, I meet friends for a meal or we go clubbing.

CD1 TRACK 26 (IN = INTERVIEWER, IS = ISABELLE)
INTERVIEW 2
IN: So what do you do, Isabelle?
IS: I work for a pharmaceutical company. I'm a research assistant.
IN: Can you tell me about your working day? What do you do when you get to work?
IS: I'm always at my desk at seven o'clock. First, I check my e-mail and my diary. Then I have a coffee with my colleagues.
IN: Where do you have lunch?
IS: I don't stop for lunch. I usually have a sandwich at my desk.
IN: How often do you travel for work?
IS: I never travel for work. I'm always in the office.
IN: What about the weekend? What do you do?
IS: I've got two small children, so I like to spend time with them. On Saturday evenings, we sometimes invite friends round for dinner or we go to the cinema. It depends if we can get a babysitter.

CD1 TRACK 27 (I = INTERVIEWER, D = DAN)
INTERVIEW 3
I: What do you do, Dan?
D: I'm a sales manager for Africa and Europe.
I: Tell me about your working day. What do you do when you get to the office?
D: First, I have a meeting with my team. Then I check my BlackBerry and reply to important e-mails.
I: Where do you have lunch?
S: I usually have lunch in the company restaurant. About twice a week, I go out for lunch with visitors.
I: How often do you travel on business?
S: I'm away a lot. I visit the sales office in South Africa three times a year. And I'm in Europe once a month for a week.
I: And what you do on the weekend?
D: I like quiet weekends. I read a lot and listen to music. On Sunday mornings, I play golf.

CD1 TRACK 28 (P = PAT, T = TIM)
P: Hi, I'm Pat. It's Tim, isn't it?
T: Yes, hi, Pat. Nice to meet you.
P: What do you do in your job?
T: I manage a web team at an IT company.
P: Ah, yes. And how many hours a week do you work?
T: Usually between 30 and 35 hours, but sometimes it's a lot more.
P: Yes, it's the same in my job, but I have to travel around quite a lot.
T: Uh-huh, and what do you like best about your job?
P: Well, I work flexible hours, which is great. And I like the people I work with. Do you meet your colleagues after work?
T: Yes, from time to time. We sometimes go for a meal at a nice restaurant near the office.
P: Oh, that's nice. And what do you do in your free time?
T: I love sports. I really like karate and I love playing golf. But I'm not really interested in watching sports on TV. I don't enjoy watching professional golf, for example. What about you?
P: I like golf too, but I'm also into French cinema and jazz music. I like watching DVDs and I really enjoy going to concerts. I also like playing the guitar. I'm interested in computer games, but I'm not very good at them.

CD1 TRACK 29 (HR = HUMAN RESOURCES, MP = MEDIA PLANNER)
HR: I'd like to ask you a few questions about your work. What exactly is your job?
MP: I'm a media planner.
HR: OK, so what do you do at work?
MP: Well, to put it simply, I decide the media we use for our advertising campaigns. I spend a lot of time each day talking to people in radio, television and the press, as well as with internet companies. We use all kinds of modern media for our advertising campaigns.
HR: OK, thank you. What hours do you work?
MP: Hmm. It depends. If we're working on a big advertising campaign, I start at eight and often don't leave the office much before nine or 10 in the evening. There's a lot of pressure in my job.
HR: I can see that. What about breaks? How long do you have for lunch?
MP: Usually, I don't have a break at lunch. I get a sandwich at the local deli and eat it at my desk. I have a proper lunch maybe once or twice a month.
HR: Mmm, you are busy. So tell me, how do you feel about your job? What do you like about it?
MP: There's a lot of variety in my work. I meet lots of interesting people outside the office, and many of my colleagues are also friends. I really enjoy working with them.
HR: Right, so what don't you like about the job?

AUDIO SCRIPTS

MP: Huh, how long have you got? OK, I don't like working such long hours without a break. I have a young daughter and I don't see much of her because I get home so late. I often work on the weekend if we have to plan a really big advertising campaign. So my work–life balance isn't good. Too much work, not enough time for leisure, for fun activities. Not enough time for the family – that's my problem.

UNIT 3 PROBLEMS

CD1 TRACK 30
PERSON 1
Well, I think the biggest problem is when we have late deliveries. Then there isn't enough stock to sell to customers. We also sometimes get difficult customers who want you to spend a lot of time with them, or who want their money back for no reason!

CD1 TRACK 31
PERSON 2
I have big problems with the computer system. It seems to crash once or twice a week. When this happens, it means I can't work. The other big problem is we have a lot of documents, which are sometimes difficult to find. It's a big office, and a lot of documents go missing when people don't return them.

CD1 TRACK 32
PERSON 3
Well, we're always very busy. It's never quiet. I guess the worst problem, apart from that, is people who are rude to you on the phone. People think they can say anything because they can't see you. Sometimes it's difficult to be polite to all the customers.

CD1 TRACK 33
PERSON 4
Well, it can be very noisy at times, but for me, that's not a problem. I think it's normal. The worst problem is when the machinery breaks down and we can't work. We have to stop production and call the engineers. The other big problem is when customers want to change their orders.

CD1 TRACK 34 (I = INTERVIEWER, JK = JEREMY KEELEY)
I: What are typical work problems for you?
JK: As a consultant, I run my own business and I'm often on my own, but my clients have quite complicated problems that they need to resolve. My biggest problem is having enough time to do a good job with the amount of work I've got to do. And then I also face urgent requests for help when I'm already very busy.

CD1 TRACK 35 (I = INTERVIEWER, JK = JEREMY KEELEY)
I: What are the biggest problems in companies you know?
JK: Most of the companies I work with are big, international companies facing complicated situations. Probably the biggest problem they face is the amount of change they have to go through all the time, and they have to go through that change fast, at speed.
Secondly, they find it very difficult to plan their needs and therefore also to plan their resources; in other words, their staff, the equipment, the property, the money they need to satisfy their customers. And their customers expect them to reduce their prices at the same time as these companies have increasing costs. So they have to be much more productive, much more efficient, all the time.

CD1 TRACK 36 (I = INTERVIEWER, JK = JEREMY KEELEY)
I: Can you give an example of a problem you've solved?
JK: My customers usually ask me to help them solve complicated problems, where lots of people need to be involved in designing the solution. Recently, there was a computer system that had to be introduced that affected millions of customers and their bills.
At the last moment, a problem arose that affected the whole system. I brought the technical team, the business team, the project team and the suppliers together in one room, and by understanding the whole problem, and by understanding each others' individual problems, we came up with the solution that solved the problem altogether.

CD1 TRACK 37 (R = RECEPTIONIST, M = MARCIA, H = HARRY)
R: Hello, United Food Corporation.
M: Good morning, my name's Marcia Jones, Hove Stores.
R: Good morning. How can I help?
M: I'd like to speak to Harry Palmer, please.
R: Hold on a minute, I'll put you through …
H: Harry Palmer.
M: Hi, Harry, Marcia here.
H: Hi, Marcia.
M: I need some information. Can you give me the name of your new marketing assistant, please? I need to contact him.
H: Certainly. His name's Jeff Haydon.
M: Could you spell his name for me, please?
H: OK. J-E-F-F H-A-Y-D-O-N.
M: Sorry, could you repeat that, please?
H: J-E-F-F H-A-Y-D-O-N.
M: Right. G-E-F-F H-A-I-D-O-N?
H: No, not G, J. J-E-F-F. And Haydon has a Y, not an I. H-A-Y-D-O-N.
M: Right. OK, I've got that. Thanks very much.
H: No problem.
M: I'll speak to you soon, Harry. Bye.

CD1 TRACK 38 (BS = BEVERLEY SIMPSON, JS = JACKIE SINGER)
CALL 1
BS: Hello?
JS: Hello, Jackie Singer here. Can I speak to Beverley Simpson, please?
BS: Speaking. How can I help you?
JS: I've got a problem. I can't meet your boss, Vanessa Gordon, next Wednesday. Something's come up.
BS: OK, I'll pass on your message. I'm sure we can arrange another time.
JS: Thanks very much. Bye.

CD1 TRACK 39 (MB = MICHAEL BENSON, SC = SHEILA CLARK)
CALL 2
MB: Good morning, this is Michael Benson, PKJ Electronics.
SC: Oh, hello, Michael, this is Sheila Clark. What's the problem?
MB: It's about the delivery of mobile phones. I want 50, not 15.
SC: Sorry about that. I'll deal with it immediately.
MB: Good. I need them by the end of the week.
SC: OK. It's no problem. Bye for now.
MB: Thanks for your help. Bye.

CD1 TRACK 40 (DR = DENISE ROBBINS, MJ = MIKE JACKSON)
CALL 3
DR: Good morning, Harding Kitchenware, Denise Robbins speaking.
MJ: Hello, my name is Mike Jackson. I'm phoning about my dishwasher. There are no instructions in the package.
DR: Oh dear! Sorry to hear that. Which model is it?
MJ: Hold on, I'll check … It's the PT1095 model.
DR: I'm sorry, I didn't catch that. Could you repeat it, please?
MJ: PT1095 model.
DR: Got it. I'll send you some new instructions right away.

CD1 TRACK 41 (DP = DAVID PATTERSON, JR = JIM ROBERTS)
CALL 4
DP: Hello?
JR: Hello.
DP: David Patterson here, Hudson and Company. Can I speak to Jim Roberts, please?
JR: Speaking.
DP: There's a problem with the invoice you sent me.
JR: Oh, really?
DP: Yes, I can't read it very well. The words are not clear.
JR: Ah, sorry about that.
DP: Also, I think the figures are wrong.
JR: I'll look into the matter and send you another invoice. Is that OK?
DP: Fine. Thanks very much.

CD1 TRACK 42
GUEST 1
I don't like my bedroom at all. It's really small and dark. There's no light in the ceiling, and one of the table lights is broken. There's a lot of noise outside the window, and I don't have a view of the city. All the walls are grey, and there are no pictures. The gym has no equipment, and the sauna is never open.

CD1 TRACK 43
GUEST 2
My bedroom's too small. It isn't bright, and the walls are grey. The bathroom isn't well equipped. There's no bath, and the shower doesn't work well.
It has Internet, but it's so expensive to use – $10 an hour! I have an old television in the sitting room. There are no satellite programmes, just three or four local ones, so I can't watch TV in the evening.

CD1 TRACK 44
GUEST 3
I'm not happy with the apartment. The bedroom's too small, and the air conditioning doesn't work. The sitting room doesn't have enough furniture. There is just one old sofa and no desk. I like to swim every day, but the pool's too small, and the water isn't clean. The terrace and garden are nice, but there is no furniture there, no tables or chairs. At night, it's very noisy outside the building.

CD1 TRACK 45
GUEST 4
The apartments look good in the advertisement, but when you get here, everything's different. The beach is about 20 kilometres away, not just a few minutes by car. And there are so many people on it. There's no sand, either. I hate that kind of beach, don't you?

WORKING ACROSS CULTURES 1

CD1 TRACK 46

Understanding dining habits in different cultures is important if you want to build strong business relationships. The key is preparation. So, before you go to another culture, find out about their dining habits.

In this workshop, we are going to look at seven areas that you should research before you travel abroad.

I'll start with arrival. Is it important to be punctual, to arrive on time? For example, in Denmark, it's not good to arrive late. But in Italy, you can arrive at dinner up to 30 minutes late.

Secondly, seating. Who sits where? Should you wait before sitting down? For example, in Germany, it is good manners to wait until you are shown where to sit.

Thirdly, how much to eat? In Norway, Malaysia and Singapore, it is rude to leave food on your plate. But in Egypt and China, leave a little food on your plate to show you are full.

Fourthly, what you use to eat. Do you use a knife and fork, chopsticks or hands? In Arab cultures, you should not eat with your left hand.

I'll move on to drinking. In some cultures, alcohol is not allowed. And in other countries such as Korea, Japan and Russia, it is rude or unlucky to pour your own drink.

Body language is another important area. Is it bad behaviour to rest your elbows on the table, as it is in Germany?

Finally, leaving. In China, it is common to leave soon after your meal. However, in Colombia, it is polite to stay for a while after the meal.

We will now look at each of the seven areas in detail, but remember: if you are not sure what to do at the dining table, then do the same as your host or other guests who know the culture.

UNIT 4 TRAVEL

CD1 TRACK 47 (C = CUSTOMS OFFICER)
EXTRACT 1
C: Do you have any duty-free goods? Please open your suitcase.

CD1 TRACK 48 (P = PILOT)
EXTRACT 2
P: This is your pilot speaking. We are now flying at 30,000 feet.

CD1 TRACK 49 (A = AIRPORT ANNOUNCER)
EXTRACT 3
A: Passengers for flight GA642 to Rome, please go to gate 26.

CD1 TRACK 50 (T = TRAVELLER)
EXTRACT 4
T: The Hotel Excelsior, please.

CD1 TRACK 51 (T = TRAVELLER)
EXTRACT 5
T: A single ticket to the city centre, please.

CD1 TRACK 52 (F = FLIGHT ATTENDANT)
EXTRACT 6
F: Please fasten your seatbelts and switch off any electronic devices.

CD1 TRACK 53 (A = STATION ANNOUNCER)
EXTRACT 7
A: The next train leaves from platform 8.

CD1 TRACK 54 (G = GUEST)
EXTRACT 8
G: Can I have an alarm call at 6 a.m. tomorrow, please?

CD1 TRACK 55
PART 1
Attention all passengers on platform 1. The next train to arrive is the 14:32 to London. Passengers on platform 2, the next train to Manchester is at 14:40.

CD1 TRACK 56
PART 2
Flight BA125 is now boarding at gate 17. Please go to the gate now. Flight JA327 is now boarding at gate 23. Please go to the gate now. Last call for all passengers for flight SA238 at gate 12. The gate closes in five minutes.

CD1 TRACK 57
PART 3
A: Can I check the time of this afternoon's train to Edinburgh?
B: Yes, it leaves at 14:25 from platform 7. No, sorry that's wrong. I'm looking at Saturday. It's 14:16 from platform 5.

CD1 TRACK 58
PART 4
A: Hello, Neptune Travel.
B: Hello. I'd like to book a flight from London to Hamburg on Sunday.
A: Certainly, let's see. Er, there are flights at 9.30 a.m. and 3.30 p.m.
B: The 9.30 is best. What time does it arrive?
A: 11.45.
B: That's fine.
A: So that's BA341 from Heathrow, Terminal 5.

CD1 TRACK 59 (I = INTERVIEWER, LC = LIZ CREDÉ)
I: Why do you go on business trips?
LC: There are two reasons that I go on business trips. The first is to work with my clients, who are based all over the world. At the moment, I travel to Amsterdam about every month. The second reason is to visit my colleagues. They are based in Singapore and Chicago, and I travel to see them about twice a year. And in between times, I contact them by phone and video conferencing.
I: Which is your favourite business location, and why?
LC: My favourite location is our Singaporean office. And the reason I like that a lot is because it's based in the old town of Singapore, and not in the business district. It has a lot of character, and it's great to be able to experience Singapore life, rather than just the hotels for the business side.

CD1 TRACK 60 (I = INTERVIEWER, LC = LIZ CREDÉ)
I: What's your favourite way of travelling?
LC: My favourite way of travelling is to fly business class. That allows me to go into a business lounge and have a meal before I fly. And then once I'm on the plane, I have a seat that turns into a bed, and that's great for getting sleep before I arrive at the other end.
I: Do you like to stay in the same hotels?
LC: Yes, I do. I travel a lot and it's great when I go back to a hotel and they recognise me, they know my name, and they know what I like to do in the hotel. And there's one particular favourite in Amsterdam that I go to, where they remember what my favourite drink is.

CD1 TRACK 61 (PR = PAUL ROBINSON, JP = JUDITH PREISS)
PR: Paul Robinson speaking.
JP: Oh, hello, Paul. This is Judith Preiss here.
PR: Hi, Judith.
JP: Paul, I'm calling about that meeting. Can you make next Wednesday?
PR: I'm sorry, Judith. I can't. But I can make Thursday or Friday.
JP: Well, I can't do Thursday, but Friday is OK.
PR: OK. Friday it is. Can we meet in the morning – say 10 o'clock?
JP: Ten o'clock's fine. Oh, and can I bring my colleague, Sabrina? You met her at the conference.
PR: Of course. I can pick you up from the station if you like.
JP: Great. See you on Friday. Bye.

CD1 TRACK 62 (R = RECEPTIONIST, S = SIMON)
R: Hello, Capri Hotel. How can I help you?
S: Hello. I'd like to book a room from Monday the 10th to Wednesday the 12th of this month.
R: Right. Let me check. Yes, we have some rooms then. Do you want a single room or a double room?
S: Single, please.
R: With a bath or a shower?
S: A bath, please.
R: Fine.
S: How much is it per night?
R: 120 euros.
S: OK.
R: So that's a single room with a bath for two nights. And you're arriving on the 10th and leaving on the 12th?
S: Yes, that's right.
R: What time do you think you'll arrive?
S: About 6 p.m.
R: That's fine. Can I take your credit-card details, please?

CD1 TRACK 63 (CO = CONFERENCE ORGANISER, GCC = GUSTAV CONFERENCE CENTRE)
GCC: Gustav Conference Centre.
CO: Hello, it's Jill Diamond here from JooC Designs.
GCC: Hi, Jill, how can I help?
CO: Well, we want to have more members of staff at our conference. We'd like to have another 30 employees. Is that OK?
GCC: Mmm, I'm not sure, really. So you want 65 people at the conference, not 35?
CO: That's right.
GCC: Mm. Can I call you back? I'll talk to my colleagues and let you know.
CO: OK, please do your best for us. Thanks. Goodbye.

AUDIO SCRIPTS

UNIT 5 FOOD AND ENTERTAINING

CD1 TRACK 64 (M = MAN, W = WOMAN)
- **M:** Would you like a starter?
- **W:** Yes, please. What do you recommend?
- **M:** Well, the escargots – the snails in garlic butter – are very tasty. And the tomato soup is very good here.
- **W:** I'd like the tomato soup.
- **M:** Great. And I think I'll have the snails. What would you like for your main course?
- **W:** Can you help me with the menu? What's paella?
- **M:** It's Spanish. It's a kind of rice dish. It's made with seafood.
- **W:** That sounds nice. I'll have that.
- **M:** Right. I think I'll have the spaghetti. Shall we order dessert later?

***

- **M:** Well, how about some dessert?
- **W:** Actually, I've eaten too much. I'm full. I think I'll just have a coffee.
- **M:** OK. And I'll have the apple pie.

CD1 TRACK 65
- **A:** Would you like a starter?
- **B:** I'd like the soup, please.
- **A:** What do you recommend for the main course?
- **A:** You should try the roast duck. It's delicious.
- **A:** Would you like a dessert?
- **B:** No, thanks. I'm full.
- **A:** Right. I'll get the bill.
- **B:** Thanks very much. That was a lovely meal. I really enjoyed it.

CD1 TRACK 66 (I = INTERVIEWER, JK = JEREMY KEELEY)
- **I:** How do you entertain business contacts?
- **JK:** I like to get to know my contacts. I give them a chance to tell me about themselves and what's important to them, what they need. So I take them places that we can talk – perhaps a coffee, lunch. If I know them well,
  I take them for dinner – places that we can spend time with each other.
- **I:** What's your favourite entertainment?
- **JK:** Recently I met a client at their office, and we walked across a park together … and while we walked, we talked. We had a cup of tea at the other side of the park and then walked back together, spent the time talking about what was really important. I really enjoyed it, and I think they did, too.

CD1 TRACK 67 (I = INTERVIEWER, JK = JEREMY KEELEY)
- **I:** Is a meal in a restaurant the best way to entertain business contacts?
- **JK:** A meal is a good way to entertain contacts. It gives you the chance to talk to them, and to find out about them. I am careful about the noise level and about how private it is, but I enjoy it.
- **I:** Can you give an example of a mistake made when entertaining clients?
- **JK:** I'd say, don't take out a client you don't like, don't waste the time. Don't take a client to a restaurant where they can't eat the food. So if they're vegetarian, don't take them to a steak restaurant. Don't spend too much money, don't make it too expensive, that might embarrass them.

CD1 TRACK 68 (I = INTERVIEWER, JK = JEREMY KEELEY)
- **I:** You have to plan a meal for a mixed group of nationalities. What would you do?
- **JK:** I get to know what they can eat and what they can't eat, and what they like, from them personally. I ask them, I don't assume. I then plan it carefully, but I also relax, so that they can relax and enjoy it.

CD1 TRACK 69 (A = ALEX, M = MEL)
- **A:** How can we entertain our visitors next week? What do you think?
- **M:** We could show them the castle.
- **A:** Hmm, I don't know about that. I think we need something more interesting for them to do.
- **M:** Yes, I agree. I also think it's too far away. Why don't we invite them for dinner?
- **A:** Good idea. Which restaurant do you recommend?
- **M:** The food is always good at Pierre's.
- **A:** That's right, but it's usually very busy.
- **M:** We could try the new restaurant at the Grand Hotel. It's very popular.
- **A:** Yes, that's right, but it's very expensive!
- **M:** How about a restaurant by the river?
- **A:** Yes, that's a great idea. There's a good Italian restaurant there.
- **M:** I think I have a menu in my office. Some of the dishes are fantastic, and everyone loves the atmosphere. Shall I book a table there for eight people for Wednesday night?
- **A:** Yes, please. Can you call the restaurant as soon as possible? Make it for 7.30?
- **M:** Right. We need to check with Jane Stirling, the Head of Marketing. It's important she comes as well.
- **A:** Yes, OK.

UNIT 6 BUYING AND SELLING

CD1 TRACK 70
SPEAKER 1
I buy a lot of books on the Internet. I often look at them in the bookshop, but then buy online. It's much cheaper, and they arrive very quickly. It's great. I guess I buy a book every two weeks, perhaps more.

CD1 TRACK 71
SPEAKER 2
I love the January sales. I buy things like electrical goods because the discounts and special offers are so good. You can get some real bargains, especially in the big department stores. I go every year.

CD1 TRACK 72
SPEAKER 3
I buy my music and movies online. I just download them. It's so easy and convenient. I usually buy something every week. I probably spend too much because it's so easy!

CD1 TRACK 73 (KS = KARL SIMPSON, AD = ALEX DODD)
- **KS:** Hello. Can I speak to Alex Dodd, please?
- **AD:** Speaking.
- **KS:** This is Karl Simpson.
- **AD:** Ah, yes, Mr Simpson. You asked us for a price for some TX7s.
- **KS:** Yes, that's right. Before I place an order, I have some questions.
- **AD:** Sure. Go ahead.
- **KS:** Well, firstly, do you give a guarantee?
- **AD:** Yes. It's two years on all our models.
- **KS:** OK. And what about a deposit?
- **AD:** Well, we ask for a 15% deposit on large orders – that's more than 50 units.
- **KS:** Yes, that's no problem. And do you have the goods in stock?
- **AD:** Yes, we always have goods in stock, and we always deliver on time.
- **KS:** OK, I think that's everything. I'd like to compare prices with Emmerson's, but I'll contact you again this afternoon.

CD1 TRACK 74
1 saved, delivered
2 launched, worked
3 decided, visited

CD1 TRACK 75
started finished advised lived wanted opened missed booked invited

CD1 TRACK 76 (I = INTERVIEWER, RP = ROS POMEROY)
- **I:** What advice would you give to new sales staff?
- **RP:** My advice would be: be patient. Take time to build relationships with the people that you want to sell to, and the sales will come. It is also, of course, important to make sure that you fully understand and are knowledgeable about the product or service that you're selling.
- **I:** What mistakes do salespeople often make?
- **RP:** I think one of the biggest mistakes that salespeople make is to try to sell something to a customer that the customer does not actually need or want. It is much better to take time to understand what the customer wants – with that knowledge a salesperson can find the reasons that the customer may have to buy the product or service. And anyway, customers like to be listened to, not to be talked at.

CD1 TRACK 77 (I = INTERVIEWER, RP = ROS POMEROY)
- **I:** What qualities do you need to be a successful buyer?
- **RP:** To be a successful buyer, I think, requires a lot of preparation. It's about working out the maximum price that you are prepared to pay, it's about contacting several different suppliers, asking for a, a written quotation of the cost and services and products that are being offered; and it's also about being prepared to look at ways of getting additional extras perhaps, or some discount for ordering a higher volume of the product, for example. And finally, it's important to be prepared to walk away from the purchase if you're not happy with what is being offered.

CD1 TRACK 78 (I = INTERVIEWER, RP = ROS POMEROY)
- **I:** What's the best thing you have bought?
- **RP:** I think the best thing that I ever bought was a house. This was about eight years ago, the house had some extra land around it, and the seller was asking for a very high price. I put in a much, much lower offer, which was not accepted. But over a period of 18 months, with lots of different negotiations and some patience on my part, I was prepared to wait all that time, eventually I bought the house at a much lower price than had originally been asked for.

CD1 TRACK 79 (I = INTERVIEWER, W = WOMAN)
- **I:** So tell me a little about Mikael Ohlsson's early life.
- **W:** Well, he was born on December the 27th in 1957, in a town in the south of Sweden. He studied industrial design and marketing at Linköping University. That was in the late '70s.

I: What about his career in IKEA?
W: Well, Mr Ohlsson got his first job in 1979. He worked as a carpet salesman in the IKEA store in Linköping. Two years later, in 1981, he became the manager of a store in Sundsvall. Ohlsson moved up the career ladder quickly, with management jobs in training and marketing.
I: When did he get his first international experience?
W: He got a job in Belgium in 1988. He was the Country Manager there. In 1991, the company moved him to Canada for another four years. In 1995, he returned to Sweden as Managing Director – a job he did for five years. Mr Ohlsson's next big job was Regional Manager for Southern Europe and North America. And then, on September the 1st, 2009, IKEA named him as Chief Executive – a position he still has today.

CD1 TRACK 80
Hi everyone! I'm Carol, and this is the new Kachet bag from Teena Fashions. It's stylish and fashionable. It's for smart, professional women. It's made of soft material. It's very easy to clean and take care of. It's got a special feature on the inside of the bag. I'm sure you all love the extra pocket at the front. It's really useful!
It's got a padded handle and a wide shoulder strap for easy carrying. As you can see, you can close it easily. Just zip it up.
Take a look inside. There's plenty of space, isn't there? It's got lots of pockets and a special compartment to keep things safely. It's got a big compartment in the centre and one at the back, so it's very roomy. But it's lightweight. It's much lighter than most bags. It weighs about half a kilo when empty. And it's just 35 centimetres long.
It comes in three colours: black, blue and brown. It's a great bag for all seasons. You can carry it all day long. It's just 75 euros. Order now, and we'll deliver within a week. Postage and packaging, five euros extra.

CD1 TRACK 81 (GM = GENERAL MANAGER, J = JIM)
GM: Let's talk about new products, Jim. Do you remember last year we bought that electronic tennis game from Sportsline? It was a great product, it brought a lot of people into our stores.
J: Yeah, it was one of our best buys. I seem to remember our sales increased a lot after it went on sale in November.
GM: Mmm, I want to do the same thing this November. Buy a really exciting product, advertise it on television and get plenty of customers into our stores.
J: Good idea. Are you thinking of a new sports game?
GM: Well, maybe, but any toy that's exciting and will get people into our stores. Something we can sell at a high price and make a good profit on. Any ideas?
J: Mmm, OK, if it's a new sports product – how about skateboards? Skateboarding's very popular with young people, and the market's growing fast. They'll pay a lot for a skateboard that's a bit different.
GM: Yeah, good idea. OK, what about other new toys? Something big and expensive. Maybe something children can try out when they visit our stores.
J: Mmm, there are a lot of toys to choose from. There's a new robot coming on the market soon. I saw it at a toy fair and liked it. Another company had a space toy on show. There was a lot of interest in it, too. Both products might be good ones for us. They're radio-controlled. Children love radio-controlled toys, you can charge a high price for them.
GM: OK Jim, let's find out more about the products, then we can discuss which one to order. We don't have enough cash to buy all of them, so we'll have to make a choice.

WORKING ACROSS CULTURES 2

CD1 TRACK 82
When you meet an American for the first time in a business situation, it's usual to shake hands. You should use a fairly firm handshake. Keep good eye contact when you talk to Americans. It shows that you are interested in what they're saying, and it's a sign of respect.
Personal space is important to them. They like to keep a distance of about two to three feet between them and the person they're talking to.
Americans tend to speak in a direct, informal manner. They like to get to the point quickly. This can be surprising for people who have a more indirect style of communication.
If you go to a meeting, arrive on time or even a few minutes earlier. Americans value punctuality. There probably won't be much small talk at the start of the meeting. Agendas for meetings are common and usually followed carefully.
Most Americans want to use first names as quickly as possible after meeting businesspeople from other cultures.
There are no special rules about giving and receiving business cards. Many Americans fold or write on a card, but this doesn't mean they don't respect you.

CD1 TRACK 83 (DS = DON SANDERS, GB = GAYLE BRADLEY)
DS: So, Gayle, what did you learn while you were in Shanghai?
GB: Well, quite a few things. For example, each day, when you meet Chinese colleagues at work, you shake hands. You also shake hands at the end of the day. They often nod their head as well.
DS: What about their way of communicating?
GB: They don't like saying no to you. If a Chinese person says no, it can make the other person feel uncomfortable. The other person 'loses face', and that's not good. So, instead of saying no, they'll say *maybe* or *we'll see* or *perhaps*. But that's really their way of saying no.
DS: So they express themselves more indirectly?
GB: Yes. The Chinese often express themselves more by body language rather than by words. You have to watch their body language, their facial expressions, their gestures, to work out what they really mean.
DS: OK. Interesting. What about other differences?
GB: There are plenty. When you talk to Chinese businesspeople, it's best to use their title, such as Mr, Mrs or Miss, followed by their surname. I always use their last name and their title: for example, I'd say, Good morning, Chief Engineer Zhang.
DS: And what about business cards?
GB: You present your business card with both hands. One side must be in Chinese, and that's the side you show to your Chinese contact.
DS: What about meetings?
GB: OK, the important things are to be on time and to know who the most senior person is. It's usually the oldest person in the room. You mustn't interrupt people in meetings or talk over them. It's important to show respect at all times, so your Chinese colleagues never 'lose face'.

UNIT 7 PEOPLE

CD2 TRACK 1 (I = INTERVIEWER, RP = ROS POMEROY)
I: What kind of people do you like to work with?
RP: I like working with all kinds of people. In particular, I like working with people who are hard-working and, most of all, people who are reliable; that is, those that do what they say they are going to do and on time. But I also like working with creative people, people who are willing to find new ways to solve problems. And I don't like people who give up too easily.

CD2 TRACK 2 (I = INTERVIEWER, RP = ROS POMEROY)
I: Can you tell us about a bad manager you worked with?
RP: Yes, I have worked with some bad managers. I can think of one manager who often criticised members of her team in front of others. And this meant that her team members hid information from her. It also meant that they were not prepared to take any risks, because they knew that if something went wrong, then she would not support them.

CD2 TRACK 3 (I = INTERVIEWER, RP = ROS POMEROY)
I: Can you give an example of a really good manager?
RP: Well, luckily, I have met and worked with several good managers, and these are people who are willing to delegate; that is, they will give a task to a team member to get on and complete. They are less involved in how a task is done, but they are clear about setting the objective and being clear about what results they expect. And a good manager will also give praise and feedback to a team member when they do a good job.

CD2 TRACK 4 (I = INTERVIEWER, J = JACK)
I: So how did you like the job?
J: The work was interesting, but there was too much to do. The deadlines for the projects weren't realistic. Everybody had to work very long hours. Most people didn't leave the office until 8 p.m. And we worked a lot of weekends.
I: Who was your manager?
J: Sophie Turner. She was a really nice person and she knew a lot about the business, but nothing went smoothly. She wasn't a good manager.
I: What was the problem?
J: Meetings didn't start on time and they went on for hours. But the real problem was motivation. She didn't know how to motivate the staff. Everyone was very unhappy. Luckily, she left.

CD2 TRACK 5
1. Where was Steve Jobs born?
2. Who did Jobs start Apple with?
3. When did Apple introduce the famous Macintosh computer?
4. Why did Jobs leave Apple?
5. What did Pixar specialise in?
6. Who did Jobs marry?
7. How much did Apple pay for NeXT?
8. When did Steve Jobs resign as CEO of Apple?
9. How old was Steve Jobs when he died?
10. Who is Apple's new CEO?
11. How many people does Apple employ worldwide?

AUDIO SCRIPTS

CD2 TRACK 6
1. Where was Steve Jobs born?
   In California.
2. Who did Jobs start Apple with?
   He started it with his friend Steve Wozniak.
3. When did Apple introduce the famous Macintosh computer?
   In 1984.
4. Why did Jobs leave Apple?
   Because of disagreements with the CEO, John Sculley.
5. What did Pixar specialise in?
   It specialised in computer animation.
6. Who did Jobs marry?
   He married Laurene.
7. How much did Apple pay for NeXT?
   400 million dollars.
8. When did Steve Jobs resign as CEO of Apple?
   He resigned in August 2011.
9. How old was Steve Jobs when he died?
   He was 56.
10. Who is Apple's new CEO?
    Tim Cook.
11. How many people does Apple employ worldwide?
    More than 46,500.

CD2 TRACK 7 (J = JULIAN, H = HANNA)
J: I'd really like to attend this evening course in Spanish, Hanna. It's important for me. I get calls every day from our suppliers in Colombia and Argentina. Sometimes it's difficult to understand what they're saying. I need to know more Spanish for my job, but I don't have enough money to pay for the classes.
H: Look, I'm really sorry, Julian. The problem is, we don't have enough money to pay for language courses. It's a difficult time for us at the moment. We have to cut costs. And if we pay for your course, everyone will want to go on a course.
J: OK, I understand the problem. Perhaps you could give me a little money towards the cost of the course? It would help me a lot.
H: I'm sorry, Julian – it's just not possible. Why don't you buy one of those self-study courses in Spanish? They're cheap, and you can improve your Spanish a lot if you study hard. I think you should visit the shopping centre. There's a special promotion at the moment for self-study language courses.
J: Really? OK, I'll do that. Will the company pay for a self-study course if I buy one?
H: I can't promise anything, Julian. But bring the receipt to me, and I'll see what I can do for you.
J: OK, thanks a lot.

CD2 TRACK 8 (M = MATTHEW)
M: Good morning, my name's Matthew. I'd like to tell you about a problem I have at work. It's about our project manager. I work in customer relations for a medical insurance company. We're a small team, we help customers if they have problems. But our project manager is no good at all. He makes mistakes all the time, and then customers get angry with us. Some of them even shout at us on the phone.
There's a part of our website which is for employees at a big multinational company. If one of the employees wants to contact us, they can phone us and we deal with the problem. Well, our project manager didn't put the right phone number on the website. He put the number of someone living in our town. Of course, this person was really angry when she received so many calls. She phoned us every day to complain, and I had to deal with her phone calls. I don't know what to do about this problem.

UNIT 8 ADVERTISING

CD2 TRACK 9
six thousand, three hundred
seventy-five thousand, eight hundred and seven
eight hundred and twenty-three thousand, one hundred and twenty
one million, two hundred and fifty-five thousand, five hundred
ten point five per cent

CD2 TRACK 10
Last year, we had a market share of 10.3 per cent. We increased our advertising budget by 13 per cent for the launch of Sparkle Lite. We sold over 850,000 units of Sparkle, our most popular product. The new advertising campaign cost 900,000 euros. Next year, we want to increase our market share to 11.5 per cent and sell over 2,100,000 units of Sparkle.

CD2 TRACK 11
1. smaller
2. faster
3. slower
4. higher
5. worse
6. better
7. more competitive
8. more efficient
9. more interesting

CD2 TRACK 12 (LC = LIZ CREDÉ)
LC: An advert I really don't like is one for a snack product of potato crisps. It's about a man choosing whether he loves the potato crisps more than his partner or not. I think this is completely unrealistic, and it also goes on for a long time.

CD2 TRACK 13 (I = INTERVIEWER, LC = LIZ CREDÉ)
I: What makes an advert really effective?
LC: I think what makes it effective is for it to be very memorable, that you remember a key message or the main product in it. One that I particularly like at the moment is the Honda cars advert, which uses pictures of flowers in the countryside to give a very modern message about the engine and the cars.

CD2 TRACK 14 (I = INTERVIEWER, LC = LIZ CREDÉ)
I: Are there some things that you should not use in adverts?
LC: Yes, I think that adverts shouldn't use claims or promises that don't seem to be delivered at home. I'm thinking particularly about cleaning products, which claim to remove stains, but they don't do it when I try them at home.

CD2 TRACK 15 (C = CHRIS, N = NICKY, S = STEPHEN)
C: Sorry, Stephen, I don't agree with you. It's not the right time to spend money on a big advertising campaign. I think we need to target rich people, famous people, pop stars and also people who plan expensive weddings. What do you think, Nicky?
N: Yeah, you're right. They're the people to aim at and they have plenty of money. Actually, we could do it pretty cheaply, you know.
C: Oh, you think so?
N: Yes. In my opinion, we can use a different way of advertising. I think we should use sites like Facebook and Twitter to advertise our flowers. We could get a lot of business that way. How do you feel about that, Stephen?
S: Well, yes, why not use those sites? I really like the idea. We could reach a lot of consumers on Facebook.
C: OK, Nicky's come up with a great idea. How about starting with a Facebook page, and we'll see if we get any interest?
S: OK.
N: Fine.

CD2 TRACK 16 (L = LAURENCE, T = TRACY)
L: Did you watch TV last night, Tracy? There was a commercial for Palmer and Mason's new chocolate bar.
T: Yeah, I saw it. I thought it was really good.
L: I liked it a lot, too. It was a great idea to use the film star Veronica Pond. And they chose some interesting places for her to advertise the product. I think we saw her in five different countries, so it was a really international advertising campaign.
T: Mmm, and probably very expensive. I think they're also using a lot of billboard advertising. I saw two huge ads on my way to work this morning.
L: Well, one thing's for sure, they'll have a big campaign. They're a much bigger company than us. They have more money to spend, so they'll probably use all the media.
T: Yes, money's certainly not a problem for them. But we can do a good launch if we plan it well. Choosing the right agency will be really important. We need one that's good value for money.
L: I agree – good value for money and also creative. Well, we're looking at three at the moment, so we'll have to choose one of them pretty soon.

UNIT 9 COMPANIES

CD2 TRACK 17 (I = INTERVIEWER, JK = JEREMY KEELEY)
I: Tell us about your favourite company.
JK: My favourite company is a private healthcare insurance company. I really like the leaders, they're decent people, who really look after the people that work for the company, and they care about their customers and want to meet the customers' needs, and they also care about the environment.
What I particularly like is that all the people that work for the company work for the company because they believe they're helping people when they most need it.

AUDIO SCRIPTS

CD2 TRACK 18 (I = INTERVIEWER, JK = JEREMY KEELEY)
I: Which company would you like to work for, and why?
JK: I don't know the name of the company I want to work for, but the company I want to work for has a big purpose, it wants to change things for people in the world for the better. So a company, perhaps, that will produce green energy, or affordable housing for the poorest people in the world, or ways of feeding people who can't currently be fed.
I: What do the best companies have in common?
JK: I think the one thing they have in common is strong leadership. These are leaders who really want to look after the people that work for the company. They want those people to work at their best. They care about their customers and they understand the customers' needs, and they focus the company's resources on meeting those needs. They also look after the environment and the sustainability of the world around them. And they're ethical and legal.

CD2 TRACK 19 (I = INTERVIEWER, JK = JEREMY KEELEY)
I: Which company will do well in the future?
JK: I don't know which company's going to do well in the future, but Rolls Royce is famous for the quality of its leadership, Apple is famous for its innovation and creativity, and Google invests a lot of time in inventing new products for its customers. Fairtrade is renowned for looking after people in the world, and the UK company Body Shop is renowned for being environmentally friendly. And I think the company that does well in the future will bring those elements together.

CD2 TRACK 20
Good afternoon, everyone. My name's Robert Ford. I'd like to talk about our new marketing strategy. There are three parts to my presentation. Firstly, the background to the strategy. Secondly, how we want to change our current operations. Finally, the details of the costs and the effect of the change on staff. By the end of my presentation, you will understand clearly our future plans. If you don't mind, let's leave questions to the end.

CD2 TRACK 21
Good morning, everyone. My name's Nicky Hunter. I'm a director of a medium-sized coffee chain, Fiestatime.
I'm going to talk about our company and its plans for the future. My presentation is in three sections. Firstly, I'll say a few words about our company. Secondly, I'll describe my duties. And finally, I'll talk about our plans for the future.
Fiestatime's head office is in Chicago, and our flagship store is in New York. We own more than 200 stores across the country. Our outlets sell coffee, coffee drinks and pastries. Most of our coffee beans come from Brazil. We have 3,000 employees, and our turnover is approximately 50 million US dollars. Our profit is about 12.2 million. Our main competitors are Starbucks, Dunkin' Donuts and, of course, McDonald's!
I'm responsible for new business. My job is to help the company grow and to hire and supervise managers for our new outlets. We're expanding fast. Next year, we plan to open at least 10 new stores on the West Coast. We'll start by opening a store in San Francisco and after that, we'll expand …

WORKING ACROSS CULTURES 3
CD2 TRACK 22 (S = SYLVIE, R = RYAN)
S: I heard there were some problems with the sales trip. What happened?
R: I tried to arrange a business meeting with our clients in Toulouse in the first week of August, but most people were on holiday. Also the headquarters are in Paris, so I didn't see a senior manager.
S: When did you make the appointment?
R: Two days in advance. That wasn't a good idea.
S: So how did the meeting go?
R: Well, we had lunch first – quite a long lunch, actually. And the person I met, Pierre Dubois, was very friendly. In fact, he didn't seem to want to talk about business. You know me … I like to get down to business straight away, so as not to waste time.
S: Mmm.
R: Anyway, at the end of the meeting, he asked me a bit about myself. I told him I didn't go to university, but I was proud of being a successful businessman. After that, he was very quiet.

CD2 TRACK 23
speaker 1
My business trip to St Petersburg was a complete disaster. I only arranged two meetings in advance, and one of those was cancelled at short notice. Unfortunately, I went in the first week of May, when there were some public holidays. Anyway, my advice to anyone going to Russia is: make appointments as far in advance as possible; confirm your meetings as soon as you arrive in Russia; and avoid meetings in the first week of May.

CD2 TRACK 24
speaker 2
I had a very successful trip to Kazan. Before the trip, I did a lot of preparation and research. I planned a lot of time for socialising and getting to know people before any business was discussed. I printed out all my documentation in both English and Russian. I gave a detailed presentation on our products and was able to answer all the technical questions they asked me.

CD2 TRACK 25
speaker 3
I think my business trip to Moscow was OK. I spent a lot of time trying to build up relationships; because in Russia, relationships are very important. However, I wasted a lot of time trying to get decisions from junior managers. Next time, I'll go straight to senior managers. One other thing is that Russians sometimes like to think in silence before they answer a question. Next time, I'll allow them enough time to answer.

CD2 TRACK 26
I'm going to begin by telling you about my first business trip to Bogotá, 15 years ago. The client I met was very generous and he invited me to his home for a meal. I didn't want to be rude, so I arrived on time. I brought some gifts for his wife and daughter and wrapped them carefully. They didn't open their presents, so I asked them to. I also asked if they liked the presents. They said they did. When dinner was served, I toasted my new friend and his family. The conversation was about culture, soccer, history and literature and seemed to go well. At the end of the evening, he offered me some coffee. Unfortunately I don't like coffee, so I said no.

UNIT 10 COMMUNICATION
CD2 TRACK 27 (I = INTERVIEWER, RP = ROS POMEROY)
I: Do you use social networking sites?
RP: I use LinkedIn, which is a professional networking site, and I'm connected to just over a hundred people that way. I know some people who are connected to more than five hundred people in that way. I also use a couple of specialist professional networking sites, for knowledge-sharing and for sharing expertise about some very specialist topics.

CD2 TRACK 28 (I = INTERVIEWER, RP = ROS POMEROY)
I: What are the business advantages and disadvantages of social networking?
RP: The main advantage for me, I think, has been being able to keep in touch with many more people in my professional field than I otherwise would be able to. I think also there have been times when I have made contact with people who are interested in the work that I do.
The disadvantage can be that other people make contact with me, who are trying to sell me something that perhaps I'm not interested in.

CD2 TRACK 29 (I = INTERVIEWER, RP = ROS POMEROY)
I: Who is the best communicator you know?
RP: The best communicator I think is my ex-boss from about 15 years ago.
I: And why was he good at communicating?
RP: He always had a real passion for his subject – whatever he was talking about, he was enthusiastic. He made sure that he knew his subject very well, and the one thing that made a big difference, I think, is that when he spoke to an audience, he made that audience feel as if they were very important.

CD2 TRACK 30 (I = INTERVIEWER, RP = ROS POMEROY)
I: Which ways of business communication do you like or not like?
RP: Face-to-face communication is, I think, the best for getting information across and for getting things done in business. I also like e-mail and other forms of electronic communication. They are good for making many more people aware of what is going on.
The thing I dislike the most is the corporate newsletter or company magazine. The corporate magazine is always one way, it's about the message the company wants to get across, and is often not that interesting for an employee.

CD2 TRACK 31 (P = PATRICK, J = JANINE)
P: What are you going to do next year, Janine?
J: I'm going to change my job. That's the big decision. I'm going to look for a part-time job, so I have more time for my family. And I'm going to do a course, too. I'm not sure what to study, but maybe something in computer graphics.
P: Computer graphics? I think that's a good area to get into. And what about a summer holiday – any ideas?

AUDIO SCRIPTS

J: I think we're going to stay at home. I need to save money for my course. We may go camping for a week or two … What about you, Patrick? What are your plans?
P: Well, I'm not going to change my job, but I am going to move to a new flat.
J: Move to a new flat?
P: Yes, I'm fed up with all the commuting. Most days it takes me nearly two hours to get to work, so I'm going to move somewhere nearer to work.
J: Sounds like a good idea. Any other plans?
P: Mm. I need to get fitter, so I'm going to do more sport. And I'm going to sell my car and buy a motorbike. I've always wanted a motorbike …

CD2 TRACK 32 (J = JAMIE, C = CHRIS)
CALL 1
C: Hello?
J: Hello. It's Jamie here. We need to meet next week. What's a good day for you?
C: I can make Wednesday. How about 10 o'clock?
J: That's OK for me.
C: Great. See you on Wednesday at 10 o'clock, then.

CD2 TRACK 33 (L = LESLEY, S = SAM)
CALL 2
L: OK, let's meet one day next week. What day is good for you?
S: I can do Monday or Tuesday afternoon.
L: Sorry, I can't make Monday or Tuesday. How about later in the week? Is Friday OK?
S: Yes, I can do Friday morning after 11.
L: Yes, that's fine for me. Friday at 11.30. See you then.
S: OK. Bye.
L: Bye.

CD2 TRACK 34 (L = LESLEY, K = KELLY)
CALL 3
L: Hello, it's Lesley here. Sorry, but I need to change the time of our meeting. I can't make it on Monday now.
K: Oh … How about Tuesday at the same time?
L: Yes, that's fine for me. See you on Tuesday at 10 o'clock.

CD2 TRACK 35 (D = DAN)
CALL 4
D: Hello, this is a message for Jean. I'm very sorry I missed our meeting this afternoon. My flight was delayed. I'll call you again later. By the way, it's Dan here, from Chicago.

CD2 TRACK 36 (D = DIRECTOR, HR = HEAD OF HUMAN RESOURCES)
D: I think there are several ways to do this. We've got eight departments in the company. We could simply reduce each department by 10 workers. And then we can hope the other 20 employees will want to leave for various reasons.
HR: Well, that's certainly one way. Another way, of course, would be the 'last in, first out' system. We ask employees who joined the company recently to leave – for example, everyone who joined us during the last year.
D: Yeah, a lot of companies do that. They think it's fair, but I'm not so sure.
HR: Well, there's a third way. We choose workers who are not essential to the company. We could ask department heads to decide which workers they don't really need any more. It's quite a good way, really. You cut costs, but you don't reduce your profits.
D: So which way do you think we should use? Whatever way we choose, it will be important to help those who are leaving as much as possible.
HR: Hm, I agree. We need to give them a lot of advice and help, so they can move on in their lives. And we need to communicate very clearly to all our staff why we're taking this action.
D: Absolutely.

UNIT 11 CULTURES

CD2 TRACK 37 (J = JOHN)
J: I was in Yemen, in the Middle East, and I was invited to a colleague's house for dinner. There was a long silence during the meal. I felt uncomfortable. I saw a beautiful table and said, 'What a lovely table.' My host laughed and said, 'Oh, then please take it.' I said, 'Oh no, I can't take it.' My host offered it to me three times. It was very embarrassing for us both.

CD2 TRACK 38 (C = CAMERON)
C: My friend Peter joined a French company recently. He made a mistake and used first names rather than family names. The staff were not happy about this. It is always best to be formal at first in France, especially when you start a new job. Peter's last company was an American company. People were more relaxed there, and they always used first names.

CD2 TRACK 39 (S = SUSAN)
S: I was in Osaka in Japan, and we went out for a meal with our Japanese sales staff. There were lots of bottles on the table and, after a while, I poured my own drink. I didn't wait for somebody to pour my drink, and I forgot to pour drinks for the others. The Japanese staff looked a bit embarrassed and started laughing.

CD2 TRACK 40 (I = INTERVIEWER, LC = LIZ CREDÉ)
I: Can you give an example of a cultural mistake in business?
LC: Yes, I think mistakes can come from differences in styles of communication, er, which might be true for some different cultures. I have an example of working with a Dutch colleague, who sent me an e-mail saying, 'I don't like the design – change it', which came across to me as very abrupt and a bit rude, whereas actually he was just meaning to be very clear in what he wanted to happen. And once we had a conversation about that, I was able to change it in the way that he wanted.

CD2 TRACK 41 (JK = JEREMY KEELEY)
JK: I have made a mistake. I was working with people in East Africa, and they had urgent problems to solve. When I was working with them, I rushed the work, I got straight on to the business. And what I learned was that it's rude to start work on the business in East Africa before you have asked each other how you are and what's been going on in your lives. And so when I did the work, I found it hard to get on with it, until I'd given them their space to do it.

CD2 TRACK 42 (RP = ROS POMEROY)
RP: It's easy to make cultural mistakes working internationally. I usually write quite long e-mails. I leave the important part of the message until the end, and that normally comes after perhaps some funny comment. It took me some time to learn that people in other countries find that confusing, they don't understand that I am not being direct. They are confused by the humour, and what I am trying to say then often gets ignored.

CD2 TRACK 43
1 **A:** Could I have a map of the city, please?
   B: Yes, here you are.
2 **A:** Could you recommend a good restaurant, please?
   B: Yes, there's a very good Italian restaurant near here. It's in Seymour Street.
3 **A:** Could you say that again, please?
   B: Yes, Seymour Street. I'll show you where it is on the map.
4 **C:** Could you copy this document for me, please?
   D: I'm sorry, I can't. The office is closed in the evening, but I can do it for you tomorrow morning.
5 **C:** Could I have my bill, please?
   D: Yes, I'll just print it for you.
6 **C:** Could you call me a taxi, please?
   D: No problem. Where do you want to go?

CD2 TRACK 44 (L = LOUISE, T = TOM)
L: So, Tom, things aren't going very well with you and Paul. What exactly is the problem?
T: Well, we don't have a very good relationship – that's it, really. I don't think I can work with him.
L: Why not?
T: Well, it's not just me – I think the whole team feels the same. You see, Paul's not very good at communicating. Or maybe I should say, he communicates in the wrong way. He doesn't like face-to-face meetings, but that's the way we solve most of our problems here. He spends most of his time sending e-mails to all of us. He's very formal, too formal for this country. I suppose it's because of the culture he comes from.
L: What about our customers? Does he get on well with them?
T: Well, how can I put it? They respect him, he's got a lot of knowledge … but they don't really like him. Our customers like to meet us in the evening and get to know us socially. Paul doesn't join in. He's always too 'busy' when a customer invites us for a meal. Maybe that's why the rest of the team doesn't get on well with him. They all enjoy meeting after work and having a good time together. Paul's just not interested in that sort of thing.
L: Mmm, it's a pity. Socialising is important over here. You know, we sent Paul out here to help you, but it isn't working, is it? Your relationship, I mean?
T: No, it isn't. What's the solution, then? What should we do?
L: Well, I think the best thing to do is for me to have a talk with him. I'll give him some good advice.
T: That's a good idea. After that, I think you should talk to the team. Explain what Paul's role is. People don't seem to understand what he's doing here.

AUDIO SCRIPTS

CD2 TRACK 45 (KM = KATE MASKIE, SA = STUART ADAMS)
KM: I really want to change things in the branch office, Stuart. I'd like our style to be more relaxed and friendly, just like it is at head office. That's the kind of image to show to our customers. It would get us a lot more business.
SA: Mmm … sorry, Kate, I can't agree with you.
KM: Why not? What's the problem?
SA: You see, the staff at the branch office don't want to change things. They've been with us for years, and they're quite happy with the way things are.
KM: Maybe, but we do need to change our style. We need a more modern image – I feel strongly about that. I want to meet some of the senior staff as soon as possible to explain why we need to change.
SA: Well, good luck!
KM: I can see you're against changing things, Stuart. But perhaps some of the staff will have a different opinion.
SA: Maybe … OK, let's set up a senior staff meeting for next week. You can present your proposals for change. We'll see how people feel about them.
KM: Right, I'll make the arrangements and let you know when the meeting will be.

UNIT 12 JOBS

CD2 TRACK 46 (I = INTERVIEWER, C = CANDIDATE)
I: How many jobs have you had since leaving university?
C: I've worked for six companies.
I: Why have you changed jobs so often?
C: I wanted to get experience of sales in different industries.
I: What have you done that shows leadership?
C: Well, I lead the sales team. I'm also chairperson of a local business association.
I: In what ways has your job changed since you joined the company?
C: I now have more responsibility and I plan the sales strategy for the team.
I: Have you ever worked with a difficult person?
C: Well, the boss in my last company wasn't very easy to work with.

CD2 TRACK 47 (I = INTERVIEWER, LC = LIZ CREDÉ)
I: What would be your ideal job?
LC: I'm very fortunate, because I think my current job is my ideal job, and I know a lot of people wouldn't be able to say that. I lead the management consultancy of 35 consultants, and I enjoy working with all my colleagues. We do very interesting work with a variety of clients, and although we work very long hours, it's very rewarding, and we have a good laugh as well.
I: Tell us about a job you didn't like.
LC: Thankfully, that was one that I had over 20 years ago. And the reason I didn't like it was because I didn't think the company treated people very well. It didn't involve them or get the best out of them, and I also didn't get on well with my manager. Fortunately, I only stayed there a couple of years.

CD2 TRACK 48 (I = INTERVIEWER, LC = LIZ CREDÉ)
I: What are your strengths and weaknesses?
LC: I think my strengths come from my work as a consultant over the last 20 years. I understand how organisations work through looking at their leadership, their culture and their business strategy, and I'm able to bring that understanding to my new, new projects with new clients. I think my main weakness is that I can see a situation from many different sides, and sometimes that makes it hard to make decisions.

CD2 TRACK 49 (I = INTERVIEWER, LC = LIZ CREDÉ)
I: What advice would you give to young people starting work?
LC: I think there are three main things I'd say to them: one would be take the opportunities that you're given and really learn as much as you can from them; the second would be to really listen to those around you and pay attention to what they're saying; and the third would be to build relationships across the organisation, because that's really going to be helpful to getting the work done.
I: What's the best question to ask in a job interview?
LC: When you go for a job interview, I think it's a good idea to ask a question that demonstrates you're really interested in the company, and that perhaps you've done some research into the organisation. I'm particularly interested in culture, so perhaps you could ask a question about the company culture – 'What's it like to work around here?' Or 'What are the pluses and minuses in the job that you're expecting to do?'

CD2 TRACK 50 (I = INTERVIEWER, TM = TIFFANY MARTIN)
I: Why do you want this job?
TM: First of all, I like meeting people and getting people to work together as a team. And then I like travelling and using my languages. I really want to work for this organisation. It has an excellent reputation.
I: Do you have any special skills?
TM: I'm fluent in German and French. I get on well with people. I'm also good at managing people and getting them to achieve results together. I love organising events for clients, and I think I'm very good at that.
I: What did you learn from your last job?
TM: I improved my marketing skills and I learned to work well in a team.
I: And what mistakes have you made?
TM: Well, I'm not really patient with people who don't meet deadlines.
I: What kind of people do you work well with?
TM: As a team leader, I have to work with all kinds of people. But the people I like best are those who work hard and are reliable.
I: What are your interests?
TM: I have lots of different interests. As I said before, I like travelling and discovering new cultures. I also like aerobics and skiing.
I: What about the future? Where do you want to be in 10 years' time?
TM: I want to be working in an international company as its Marketing Manager.
I: Do you have any questions for us?
TM: If I get the job, when would you like me to start?

CD2 TRACK 51 (D = DIRECTOR, VP = VICE-PRESIDENT, HUMAN RESOURCES)
D: Let's talk about the new people we want to employ, Martia. What kind of candidates are we looking for?
VP: Starting with personal qualities, we want people who'll share our values, people who are honest, open and reliable. I also think they should be sociable and friendly. You know, the sort of people you like to work with. It'll be very useful, too, if they have qualities as future leaders. If they can show that, it'll be a big advantage for them.
D: So what about skills and abilities?
VP: Well, I think we should hire people who are good organisers and also good at teamwork. They're very important skills.
D: That's true. It'll be an advantage, too, if candidates can analyse and solve problems. And they'll need to know how to use our main IT systems. What about language skills?
VP: Well, they should know at least one other language.
D: At least one. A lot of them could be working overseas, so they'll certainly need to be able to learn a foreign language. OK, previous experience: I think we agreed earlier that they should have at least three years' commercial or industrial experience. Right?
VP: Yes, that was the minimum. We also agreed there'll be no age limit, but we think most candidates will be in the 25 to 35 age group.
D: Yes, I don't expect them to be older than that. OK, I think that's about it.
VP: Yes, but there is one other thing. We should ask them about their interests. We don't want to hire someone who has no interests outside work.
D: Fine. It should be interesting.
VP: Let's hope so. You never know what a candidate will tell you at an interview!

WORKING ACROSS CULTURES 4

CD2 TRACK 52
In the case of team working, researchers have found that there are some cultural attitudes that are similar for the majority of people from Indonesia, Japan, South Korea, Malaysia, Singapore and China.
These are societies that usually like working in groups. People in these societies are often happier working towards team goals rather than individual targets. They are naturally good team players, and it's not always necessary to spend a lot of time on team-building training sessions. The individual is not as important as the group, and arguments should be avoided.
Team leaders must avoid situations where team members might lose face or lose respect.

CD2 TRACK 53
It's difficult to find common attitudes towards team working in all European countries. It's easier to find similarities in some southern European countries (say Portugal, Italy, Greece and Spain) and then in some northern European countries. Here, I will discuss Denmark, Norway and Sweden first, and then mention Finland at the end.
Southern European teams can often be individuals working on their own and reporting to a strong leader. Team leaders need to give a clear focus and direction for each team member.
Many Scandinavians like working in teams, and this means that Danes, Norwegians and Swedes are good team players. However, a team leader who gives orders all the time to junior members is not likely to succeed. Once team members are given a task, they want the freedom to complete it without too much control. It's also important that information is shared widely across the group. Finland, however, is different, as Finns often prefer to work on their own.

Market Leader Extra: Business skills
Audio script Elementary

1.1 SMALL TALK

BSA1.1.1 (JW = Jane Wilson, Sc = Silvio Contini)

JW: Good morning, I'm Jane Wilson, the organiser of this event.
SC: Pleased to meet you, Miss Wilson, My name's Silvio Contini from Teso International.
JW: Nice to meet you, too and welcome to our event. Where are you staying?
SC: At the Marriot Hotel. It's near this conference centre so I can walk here.
JW: Do you like walking?
SC: Yes, I really enjoy walking in my free time - but the weather's not very good today.
JW: I know. It's cold for this time of year. What's the weather like in Italy at the moment?
SC: Oh it's very warm, twenty-five degrees or more.
JW: Lovely. Where do you live in Italy?
SC: I live in Florence with my wife and three children.
JW: A wonderful city! Would you like a tea or coffee? There's some on the table over there. Introduce yourself to some of the other participants before the presentation starts.
SC: Thank you. See you later.
JW: Nice talking to you, Silvio.

BSA1.1.2 (WM = Wesley Moore, JW = Jane Wilson, EF = Emi Fujimori)

WM: Hi there, I'm Wesley Moore. You must be Jane.
JW: Yes, I'm Jane Wilson. Pleased to meet you and welcome to our event.
WM: Good to meet you, too.
JW: And this is Emi Fujimori from Japan.
WM: Hi there, Emi. How are things going?
EF: (taken aback by the informality of the greeting) How do you do, Mr Moore.
WM: Oh, er, how do you do Ms Fujimori. What company do you work for?
EF: I work for PKX Energy. I'm their International Manager.
WM: Is that a Japanese company?
EF: No, it's Canadian.
WM: Oh, I didn't know that. Now tell me why your government makes it so difficult for American companies to …
EF: Er…
JW: Oh, Mr Moore, let's not talk about politics now. I'd like you to meet someone else…

BSA1.1.3 (VG = Veronica Gomez, JW = Jane Wilson, HB = Hans Bachmeier)

VG: Excuse me, Jane. Is that Hans Bachmeier over there?
JW: Yes Veronica, it is. Come and meet him. Hans, this is Veronica Gomez.
HB: Good morning, Ms Gomez.
VG: Pleased to meet you, Mr Bachmeier. I've heard a lot about you from Jane.
HB: Oh. Have you? And what do you do, Ms Gomez?
VG: I'm Marketing Manager for WXB Electrics. And you're CEO of Bachmeier Components, aren't you?
HB: That's right.
VG: Is this your first visit to the UK?
HB: Yes, it is. Our business is mainly in South America. Is WXB a global company?
VG: Yes, our head office is in Leeds here in the UK but we've got offices all over the world.
HB: Hm. Do you travel much for your work?
VG: Yes, quite a lot.
HB: What do you like doing in your free time, Ms Gomez?
VG: I really love visiting museums and art galleries and going to classical concerts. What about you?
HB: I love classical music, too. In fact, would you like to come to a concert this evening? I've got an extra ticket and I'm going with some of my colleagues.
VG: I'd love to, thank you. See you later.

1.2 TELEPHONING

BSA1.2.4 (RW = Rob Walker, SM = Sofia Marquez)

RW: Dunedin Language School, good afternoon.
SM: Good afternoon, can I speak to Rob Walker, please?
RW: Speaking. How can I help you?
SM: Hello, this is Sofia Marquez from ELC in Malaga, Spain. It's about our booking with you in September.
RW: Yes, I remember; for your Sales Manager. Let me check on the computer. OK, I've found it. Mr Dupont has a booking for a three-week course in Business English. Are you calling about his accommodation?
SM: Yes. He doesn't want a hotel. He wants to stay with a family.
RW: OK, no problem. Can you give me some information about Mr Dupont?
SM: Of course. What do you want to know?
RW: First, does he have a problem with pets or children in the family?
SM: Sorry, I don't understand. What do you mean by pets?
RW: Animals in the house – like dogs or cats.
SM: Oh, I see. No, he doesn't like pets, but children are OK.
RW: OK, fine. Can he eat all kinds of food?
SM: No, Mr Dupont is vegetarian. He doesn't eat meat or fish. Is that a problem?
RW: No, not at all. Lots of British people are vegetarian. OK. I think maybe the Ross family. They are very nice and they have a beautiful house.
SM: Yes. Can you tell me something about them?
RW: Yes. John Ross is a lawyer. His wife Diane is an architect. They are both good cooks. I think they have one son, but he's at university now. And they don't have animals.
SM: That sounds perfect.
RW: Good. I will check if they are free in September and then I will e-mail you.
SM: Thank you. Oh and one more thing: Mr Dupont loves playing tennis. Are there any tennis courts or clubs near your school?
RW: Sorry, I didn't catch that. Can you repeat it, please?
SM: Are there any clubs where he can play tennis near your school?
RW: I see. Well, I don't know, but I will find out and send you details in the e-mail.
SM: Excellent. Thank you for your help.
RW: You're welcome, goodbye.
SM: Goodbye.

BSA1.2.5 (RW = Rob Walker, SM = Sofia Marquez)

RW: Dunedin Language School, good afternoon.
SM: Good afternoon, can I speak to Rob Walker, please?
RW: Speaking. How can I help you?

SM: Hello, this is Sofia Marquez from ELC in Malaga, Spain. It's about our booking with you in Sept …
RW: Well, I don't know, but I will find out and send you details in the e-mail.
SM: Excellent. Thank you for your help.
RW: You're welcome, goodbye.
SM: Goodbye.

BSA1.2.6 [Track repeated] (RW = Rob Walker, SM = Sofia Marquez)

RW: Yes, I remember; for your Sales Manager. Let me check on the computer. OK, I've found it. Mr Dupont has a booking for a three-week course in Business English. Are you calling about his accommodation?
SM: Yes. He doesn't want a hotel. He wants to stay with a family.
RW: OK, no problem. Can you give me some information about Mr Dupont?
SM: Of course. What do you want to know?
RW: First, does he have a problem with pets or children in the family?
SM: Sorry, I don't understand. What do you mean by pets?
RW: Animals in the house – like dogs or cats.
SM: Oh, I see. No, he doesn't like pets, but children are OK.
RW: OK, fine. Can he eat all kinds of food?
SM: No, Mr Dupont is vegetarian. He doesn't eat meat or fish. Is that a problem?
RW: No, not at all. Lots of British people are vegetarian. OK. I think maybe the Ross family. They are very nice and they have a beautiful house.
SM: Yes. Can you tell me something about them?
RW: Yes. John Ross is a lawyer. His wife Diane is an architect. They are both good cooks. I think they have one son, but he's at university now. And they don't have animals.
SM: That sounds perfect.
RW: Good. I will check if they are free in September and then I will e-mail you.
SM: Thank you. Oh and one more thing: Mr Dupont loves playing tennis. Are there any tennis courts or clubs near your school?
RW: Sorry, I didn't catch that. Can you repeat it, please?
SM: Are there any clubs where he can play tennis near your school?
RW: I see. Well, I don't know, but will…

2.1 MEETINGS

BSA2.1.7 (L = Louise, J = Jurgen, E = Emily)

L: OK, everyone, we need to decide which trade fair to visit this year. It's July already so we don't have much time to decide. I think it would be a good idea to run through a few options. We need a few statistics so that we can compare them. Please do take notes to help you.
: The first fair on the list is the Autumn Fair at the NEC in Birmingham, in the UK. I know we visited this one last year but it is the UK's number one event for gifts. It has over 29,000 visitors…
J: Sorry, Louise, how many visitors did you say?
L: That's 29, two nine, thousand.
J: OK, thank you. That's a lot of visitors.
L: Exactly. From 84 different countries.
J: Hm. And how many exhibitors does it have?
: We want as much choice as possible when we are buying, don't we?
L: Right. Yes. It has over 1,400 exhibitors. We went last year and there were a lot.
E: Sorry, Louise, was that 400 exhibitors?
L: No, one thousand four hundred! Fourteen hundred!
E: Wow! OK.
J: How long does it last?
L: Umm … four days.
E: How much time can we spend there?
L: Two days I think.
E: Can we go to more than one fair this year?
L: Well, … I don't know. Normally we only go to one. We have a small travel budget, so no, I don't think so.

2.2 PRESENTATIONS

BSA2.2.8 (T = Teresa, J = James)

T: Good morning, thank you all for coming today. My name's Teresa Kent, and for anyone who doesn't know me, I'm the Event Coordinator for Darby Tech.
: I'm here today to talk to you about the venue for our annual sales conference. Then I can talk about costs. There'll be time at the end for any questions. So, let's get started. James, over to you.
J: Thank you Teresa. So, our choice for next year's annual sales conference is The Orange County Convention Center in Orlando, Florida, right here in the USA. Let's look at why …

BSA2.2.9 (T = Teresa, J = James)

J: So, our choice for next year's annual sales conference is The Orange County Convention Center in Orlando, Florida, right here in the USA. Let's look at why we chose this place.
To start, it's just fifteen minutes from the busy Orlando airport, which has many cheap flights. This helps to keep the overall costs low for our international sales team.
Now, let's look at facilities. As you can see from these numbers, it's a very big building. There's a large lecture theatre, and there are 74 rooms of different sizes. We can book the smaller rooms for our breakout sessions, such as the regional sales meetings. We'll be in the North Building for all of our sessions, so walking between rooms will be easy.
So, turning to food. I know we had some negative comments about the food last year. I think that's not going to be a problem with this centre. There are three restaurants. They offer a sit-down service for up to 200 guests, so we can make our welcome meal something really special this year.
Finally, of course, the best thing is the entertainment nearby. The centre is located on International Drive, the heart of fun in Florida and near all the best theme parks, like Sea World. It's going to be great. So, note the dates – the 18th to the 25th June next year. Keep those dates clear.
So, Teresa's going to talk now about costs.
T: Thanks Jim that sounds …

BSA2.2.10 (J = James)

1
J: And so … this conference centre is very good – Umm it has lots of rooms and restaurants, and the costs are very low. I think it's the right choice. OK, does anyone have any questions?

2
J: So, to summarise what we saw. I think this conference centre has everything: a great location; easy transport to and from the airport; modern facilities; fantastic restaurants; and overall a low cost. I think you'll agree this will be a very special experience, and make everyone feel like part of the Darby Tech family. Thank you very much for listening. I'll be happy to answer any questions.

BSA2.2.11 (T = Teresa, J = James, S1 = Speaker 1, S2 = Speaker 2, S3 = Speaker 3)

S1: A lot of our sales team are here in the States and like to drive to the conference. What about parking?
T: James, can you answer this?

J: Sure. Parking's no problem. The centre has space for over six thousand cars, and we can reserve parking.

S2: What about restaurants?

J: Do you mean in Orlando?

S2: No, I mean at the centre. Are there any self-service restaurants, too?

J: Yes, there are three restaurants so meals won't be a problem.

S3: You said that the centre is near lots of theme parks. Will the cost of entertainment be included?

T: I can answer that one. We have one free day during the conference and a trip to a theme park is an option for that day, at no extra cost.

3.1 NEGOTIATIONS

BSA3.1.12 (GB = Gayle Bradley, Z = Zhang)

GB: Good morning, Chief Engineer Zhang. It's very good to see you again. How are you?

Z: Good morning, Mrs Bradley. I'm very well, thanks. And you?

GB: We're very happy to do business with you again. As I wrote in my e-mail, in our meeting today we would like to discuss the delivery dates for the electronic chips.

Z: Yes, of course.

GB: So, as I explained, we need the electronic chips on Friday the 10th July. Is that convenient for you?

Z: Erm … perhaps.

GB: I mean, it's really important that the delivery date is no later than Friday the 10th July. Is that possible for you?

Z: Erm … OK, we'll think about it. I need to talk to our director.

GB: Are you saying that you prefer to send the chips a little later?

Z: A little later, yes. That's right.

GB: Right. When do you think you can send us the electronic chips?

Z: Friday the 10th is erm … too early for us. I'm afraid it's a very large order. It's not enough time.

GB: I understand. It was an urgent order. We need the chips for some bank cards.
How about Monday the 13th?

Z: Monday the 30th? Yes, that's good.

GB: I'm sorry but I think you didn't understand me. I said 13th, not 30th.

Z: Oh, I'm sorry. My English is not so good.

GB: Don't worry, your English is better than my Chinese!

GB: We can do a bit later than the 13th. But only one or two days later, is that all right? What about Tuesday the 14th?

Z: Tuesday the 14th? I'm not sure. I need to talk to the warehouse manager.

GB: Chief Engineer Zhang, we need the chips as soon as possible. It will be very helpful if you can tell me the delivery date. Why don't you suggest a date?

Z: Ah, yes. If you send us the specifications today, you can get the shipment on the 15th.

GB: The 15th July. But no later.

Z: I understand.

GB: Fine. We can work with that. So, to confirm, I'll send you the specifications in an e-mail.

Z: And you will have the order on the 15th July.

GB: It's a deal! Thank you.

Z: You're welcome.

BSA3.1.13 (GB = Gayle Bradley, Z = Zhang)

1 **GB:** Is that convenient for you?
2 **GB:** Are you saying that you prefer to send the chips a little later?
3 **GB:** How about Monday the 13th?
4 **GB:** I said 13th, not 30th.
5 **GB:** What about Tuesday the 14th?
6 **GB:** Why don't you suggest a date?
7 **Z:** Friday the 10th is … too early for us.
8 **Z:** I'm not sure. I need to talk to the warehouse manager.
9 **GB:** So, to confirm, I'll send you the specifications in an e-mail.
10 **Z:** If you send us the specifications today, you can get the shipment on the 15th.

3.2 MEETINGS

BSA3.2.14 (H = Hans, L = Lucia, K = Kate)

H: OK, team. Thank you for being on time. As you all know, this year is our fortieth birthday. We'd like to celebrate it with a marketing campaign - to sell a very special edition of a toy or game from the past. I think this is going to be our most exciting year ever!
Er … First of all, I'd like you to think back to when you were around ten years old and decide which of your toys or games you would choose.

L: Ah, how nice it would be to be ten years old again! When I was ten it was the easiest time of my life. There was lots of time for fun and play. Now what was my favourite toy?

K: Wasn't it your Barbie doll? Every girl in Scotland had one when I was a kid.

L: Well, actually, no. I didn't have a Barbie doll. My only doll was handmade by my grandmother. She was the most beautiful doll, but I didn't play with her much. The thing I played with the most was my bicycle! I was always outdoors, cycling with my friends. How about a special anniversary bike? That would be good publicity.

H: In a way, but no good for us since we don't sell bikes!

L: That's true. How about you Hans? Which toy did you like the most?

H: Well, it wasn't a Barbie, that's for sure! When I was a kid, I loved Lego. You could do anything with it. It was one of the most creative toys. I played with it for hours. I know we don't make Lego, but we could choose one of our creative toys, one that kids play with on their own … Er … What about you Kate?

K: Well, my best toy wasn't a Barbie either. It was a game, not a toy. I loved playing board games! I would play with my friends, till very late at night sometimes! I think we should promote a game you can play with your friends.

H: Um. Interesting, a toy and a game. So … which product should we relaunch this year?

L: I think we should look at the sales figures for all the toys we've produced and relaunch an old best-seller.

K: Erm … I'm not sure. Maybe numbers aren't important.

H: Umm, I don't agree, Kate. For the campaign to be a success we want a toy that will sell well today. We don't want a fortieth birthday flop!

L: Well, I think it should be something you can play with your friends.

K: On the other hand, something you can play with alone, like Lego, would be more successful.

H: OK. Let's look at the sales figures first …

K: Yes, OK.

L: Yes, I think that's important.

BSA3.2.15 (K = Kate, H = Hans)

K: I'm not sure.
H: I don't agree, Kate.
K: On the other hand…

4.1 INTERVIEWS

BSA4.1.16 (D = Daniel)

D: Hi, this is a message for Adam Johnson. My name's Daniel Smith and I'm the head of Human Resources at World Travel. Thank you for the application you recently sent. We'd like to invite you to attend an interview on the twenty first of March, at 10 a.m., in our Mill Street office. Your interview will be with the manager of the marketing team, Judith May, and myself, and it should last about forty-five minutes. Please could you bring a copy of your identity documents, as well as a copy of your certificates with you to the interview? Could you please just send an e-mail to confirm if you can come? I look forward to meeting you.

BSA4.1.17 (J = Judith, A = Adam, D = Daniel)

J: Adam? How are you? I'm Judith May, and I think you spoke to my colleague Daniel on the phone?
A: Hi, nice to meet you both.
J: Please take a seat.
A: Uh … Thanks.
D: Actually, before we get started, Adam, did you bring your documents with you?
A: Sure, here you are.
D: That's great. I'll just get those copied.
J: Now, we just have a couple of questions for you. So, tell me about yourself.
A: Well, I have a Master's Degree in Marketing Communications from Bournemouth University. I've worked in the marketing department of an insurance company, Insure Now, for two years, and I enjoyed that, but now I'm keen to move into the tourism industry.
J: And why are you interested in tourism industry?
A: Hm … That's an easy question for me. Tourism is growing at the moment. It employs more people than any other industry, so it's also very important in the world. I think there are going to be a lot of opportunities in tourism.
D: Hmm … that's very true.

BSA4.1.18 (D = Daniel, A = Adam, J = Judith)

D: So, what are your main strengths?
A: Hmm, let me see. Well, I read a lot to stay up-to-date. I find reading helps me with my work. And I've joined a few online professional groups. Sites like Facebook are necessary for marketing, but they change so quickly and I think it's important to know about changes before they happen. That's why the professional groups help. I'm also good at dealing with customers. I made some changes to Insure Now's website two years ago, and they had twenty per cent better customer reviews afterwards.
D: Hmm, that's interesting. And what do you think are your weaknesses?
A: Well, to be honest, I've always preferred to work alone, on my own, but I know that working in teams is very important. I've had training on teamwork. The courses have been very helpful. I decided that, when I get more experience, I want to manage teams, so I know I'll need this in the future.
J: We offer a lot of training here. Just one last question: why do you want to work for us?
A: Well, I like your work. I saw your online marketing when I was researching the industry. It's the kind of thing that I'd like to do.
D: OK, Adam, that's great. We'll take a look at the situation here and call you back next week. It was nice to meet you.
A: Pleased to meet you, too.

BSA4.1.19 (D = Daniel, A = Adam)

D: Hi, Adam?
A: Yes, speaking.
D: Adam, it's Daniel Smith from World Travel. We met last week.
A: Hi, how are you?
D: I'm good, thanks. I'm phoning because I just wanted you to know that we really liked you and we thought that you have the skills we need here in the World Travel marketing team. We'd like to offer you the job.
A: Oh! That's great! Fantastic! Thank you!
D: We just need to go over a few things with you and then discuss when you can start. Does that sound good to you?
A: OK! Well, first …

4.2 PRESENTATIONS

BSA4.2.20 (PH = Phil Haines)

PH: I'm Phil Haines and I'm here to talk to you about the job I do. I'm a Human Resources manager. I've worked in Human Resources for fifteen years. It's my job to find the best employees and help them to do their best work for the business or organisation. I know that a lot of you here today are thinking about working in this field in the future, so I'm going to talk to you about the skills I think you should develop to be great in this field.

BSA4.2.21 (PH = Phil Haines)

PH: Of course, a qualification in Human Resources Management helps, and you need to know a lot of information about employment law, wages and benefits. But what about the skills you need? Well, you need to have three main skills to be successful in this job. We're going to look at each of those now and then I'll answer any questions.

The first skill is a business skill. It's a good idea to work on your communication skills. I mean a really good idea. Even if you're really good at talking with people generally, the communication skills you need for this job are different. Why? Because you need to give presentations and organise training regularly. In interviews, you're going to need to make people feel comfortable. And then there are those conversations no-one wants, when you need to talk about work that's just not good enough, or when two people in the company disagree and your job is to bring them back together. So – Number one – have great communication skills.

Number two – this is a people skill. My advice is don't just listen to people, but really read them. When I say read people, what I mean is, you're going to need to decide if the person in front of you is friendly, hard-working or honest, just by looking and listening carefully. Most people will tell you the things you want to hear. Often, they say things that aren't true because they just want the job, or an easy life. Your job is to find the truth. So - Number two - get good at reading people.

And finally – this is more of a personal quality – you should be confident. The best people in Human Resources are strong people. You could try doing something you think is impossible. You'll soon see that feeling confident comes after doing something difficult, not before. And you can't do this job if you're weak or scared.

BSA4.2.22 (PH = Phil Haines)

PH: So, those are the three most useful skills in my opinion – communicate well, learn to read people, and be confident with people at all levels of management in the company. So, now I'm going to take questions. Yes …?

Market Leader Extra: Business skills
Additional material Elementary

1.1 Small talk

C SPEAKING

Student A
Find someone who doesn't like football.

Student C
Find someone who drives to college/work.

Student B
Find someone who lives with his/her family.

Student D
Find someone who likes working long hours.

TASK

A

Name: ....
(use your own name or choose another name)

Job: Sales Manager
(or you can use your own job title)

Company: Devo Electronics. A global company based in Warsaw, Poland.
(or you can use your own company)

C

Name: ....
(use your own name or choose another name)

Job: Accountant
(or you can use your own job title)

Company: Bardo Group. An international consulting company based in Caracas, Venezuela.
(or you can use your own company)

B

Name: ....
(use your own name or choose another name)

Job: Product Manager
(or you can use your own job title)

Company: Vent Furniture. A global company based in Oslo, Norway.
(or you can use your own company)

D

Name: ....
(use your own name or choose another name)

Job: Research Analyst
(or you can use your own job title)

Company: GA Investment Bank. A global company based in New York, USA.
(or you can use your own company)

© Pearson Education Limited 2016

Market Leader Extra: Business skills
Additional material Elementary

2.1 Meetings

Student A

You want to go to this trade fair. Your partners want to go to different trade fairs.

Fair: Extrapresent **Location: Hong Kong, China** **Exhibitors: 24,000**

Key points:
- Very large exhibition
- Big choice of gifts
- China becoming very fashionable
- Never been to Hong Kong before

2.2 Presentations

E SPEAKING

Student A

1 **Present the information below.**

   Name: Lloyd Erskine Sandiford Centre
   Location: Barbados, Caribbean
   Travel: On the main ABC Highway and 15 minutes from the Grantley Adams International Airport
   Rooms: 11 meeting rooms, 50 to 1,000 people
   Food: Four restaurants, for up to 250 people, local food and seafood

2 **Listen to your partner's presentation. Take notes on the Durban International Convention Centre.**

   Location: ....
   Travel: ....
   Rooms: ....
   Food: ....

Market Leader Extra: Business skills
Additional material Elementary

2.2 Presentations

PRE-TASK

Group A

The Adelaide Convention Centre, Adelaide, Australia

Welcome to the 20-minute city – Australia's only city designed to make conferences easier for you, where no journey lasts more than 20 minutes.

- We can offer a large main hall, with space for 3,500 people seated.
- Our 14 meeting rooms can take 30–200 people for breakout sessions.
- Transport is easy – enjoy free tram travel within the city mile.
- The train station is one minute away, and you can check in at the airport, leave your bags at your hotel, and be in the convention centre within 20 minutes.
- Our Regatta Bistro & Bar has excellent views of the gardens.
- The outdoor coffee cart encourages visitors to enjoy the wonderful weather and fresh air.
- Around the conference centre there is a range of restaurants for every taste.
- Nearby – visit the beautiful Botanic Gardens, or enjoy Adelaide Zoo. If you have an extra day, visit Kangaroo Island.

Group B

The Hong Kong Convention Centre, Hong Kong

Enjoy this award-winning convention centre, one of the largest in the world. The front wall, which is made of glass, offers stunning views of the river, and was the largest glass wall in the world at the time of construction.

- We have two main halls, each seating 6,100 people.
- Our two smaller theatres are available for smaller groups of 1,000.
- We have seven restaurants offering a range of Chinese, Italian and Japanese food. There is space for 1,700 guests in our restaurants.
- Car parking for 1,300 cars and 50 large vans.
- Access to the centre is by bus or by the Star River Ferry.
- Nearby – enjoy the shopping malls and nightlife of Hong Kong. If you have time, visit Ocean Park to see the natural wildlife.

© Pearson Education Limited 2016

Market Leader Extra: Business skills
Additional material Elementary

2.1 Meetings

Student B

You want to go to this trade fair. Your partners want to go to different trade fairs.

Fair: Supergift   **Country: Spain**   **City: Madrid**   **Exhibitors: 2,050**

Key points:
- Not too many exhibitors
- High quality products
- Travel to Spain not expensive
- Want to visit the Prado Museum

2.2 Presentations

E SPEAKING

Student B

1 **Listen to your partner's presentation. Take notes on the Lloyd Erskine Sandiford Centre.**

   Location: ....
   Travel: ....
   Rooms: ....
   Food: ....

2 **Present the information below.**

   Name: Durban International Convention Centre
   Location: Next to the beautiful beaches of Durban, South Africa
   Travel: Good roads and a regular bus ride from the airport (30 minutes)
   Rooms: Guests can choose the room size from 10 people to 1,680
   Food: Four garden restaurants with local barbecue food, or a sit-down dinner inside for up to 5,000

3.2 Meetings

Meeting participants

Prepare your questions and ideas for the meeting, using these prompts.

1 **Be prepared to talk about your favourite toy. Think about the following:**
   - How old were you?
   - What was it? Can you describe it?
   - Why was it special?
   - Did you play on your own, or with other people?

2 **Be prepared to ask your team about their favourite toy. Which questions can you ask?**

3 **Be prepared to suggest a toy or game for the relaunch celebration.**

4 **Listen to your colleagues' ideas. Disagree with them, politely, if you want to.**

Meeting Review notes

1 Did you make requests for information/ideas? What did you say? What did you hear?

2 Did you disagree? What did you say? What did you hear?

3 Did you suggest ideas? What did you say? What did you hear?

4 Did you use past expressions with was/were? What did you say? What did you hear?

Market Leader Extra: Business skills
Additional material Elementary

2.1 Meetings

Student C

You want to go to this trade fair. Your partners want to go to different trade fairs.

Fair: Supercadeau   **Country:** France   **City:** Paris   **Exhibitors:** 4,300

- Good number of exhibitors
- Low quality of products
- Travel to Paris not expensive
- Paris very beautiful in autumn

3.1 Negotiations

TASK Parts 1 and 2

The buyer

- You are a buyer of electronic chips. You are negotiating face to face with an international supplier. You have an urgent order for some electronic cards for a major bank.
- You want the chips on 15th July, but no later than 18th. Suggest a delivery date for the supplier. Make sure you ask questions. You can ask open questions:
  When can you deliver? What's the best date for you? What about the 12th?
  Or yes/no questions:
  Can you deliver on the 12th? Is that all right?
- Make suggestions, check understanding and confirm.
- Look again at audio script BSA3.1.12 on page iii to help you.

4.1 Interviews

E SPEAKING

Work with your partner. Take turns and practise answering some common interview questions.

Tip: You can talk about a job you have done or a job you would like to do.

Student A

1 **Ask Student B these questions.**
   1 Tell me about yourself.
   2 What did you do in your last job?
   3 What are your weaknesses?

2 **Answer Student B's questions. Remember to talk about your past experiences in your answers.**

© Pearson Education Limited 2016

Market Leader Extra: Business skills
Additional material Elementary

3.1 Negotiations
TASK Parts 1 and 2

The supplier

- You are an international supplier of electronic chips. You are negotiating face to face with an important international client. Suggest possible dates for the delivery. However, you usually have to confirm with the warehouse manager before you confirm 100%. Your client always has urgent orders and you would like to plan more in advance next time.

- Check understanding, e.g. *I'm sorry. Did you say 13th or 30th?*

- You find it difficult to say 'no' in your culture. Say, for example, *'Perhaps/Maybe, I need to check with the warehouse, I'll think about it. I'm afraid that's a little early for us.'*

- Look again at audio script BSA3.1.12 on page iii to help you.

4.2 Presentations
E SPEAKING

Student A

1 Present the points on the slide below. Think about how to signal the three points (*the first skill is ...* , etc.). Give some more information for each point, think about:

- knowing when to talk and when to be quiet
- being able to answer questions
- planning one lesson, one week and one year and administration work

> **Key skills for a teacher**
> - Have good communication skills.
> - Understand your subject.
> - Be organised.

2 Listen to your partner and make notes.

© Pearson Education Limited 2016

Market Leader Extra: Business skills
Additional material Elementary

3.1 Negotiations

TASK Part 3

Student A: The buyer

- You are a buyer of electronic chips. You are negotiating face to face with your international supplier. You have an urgent order for some electronic cards for a major bank. You need 1,000 chips. Check the supplier can delivery this quantity on the agreed date.
- If your supplier says 'no', insist that you need 750 chips on the agreed date. They can send 250 later.
- Make sure you ask questions, check understanding and confirm.

4.1 Interviews

E SPEAKING

Work with your partner. Take turns and practise answering some common interview questions.

Tip: You can talk about a job you have done or a job you would like to do.

Student B

1 Answer Student A's questions. Remember to talk about your past experiences in your answers.
2 Ask Student A these questions.
   1 What job do you want to do in future? Why?
   2 What are your strengths?
   3 What are your weaknesses?

© Pearson Education Limited 2016

Market Leader Extra: Business skills
Additional material Elementary

3.1 Negotiations

TASK Part 3

Student B: The supplier

- You are an international supplier of electronic chips. You are negotiating face to face with your international client. Your client wants a large quantity for this urgent order. But your warehouse manager says they prefer to send 500 chips on the agreed date and 500 more chips at a later date. If you send more than 500 chips, the workers in the factory have to work over-time and this is more expensive for your company.

- You find it difficult to say 'no' in your culture. Say, for example, *'I need to check with the warehouse. I'm afraid that's a lot for us.'*

- Make suggestions, check understanding and confirm, e.g. *Sorry, did you say 100 or 1,000? So, that's, ...*

4.2 Presentations

E SPEAKING

Student B

1. Listen to your partner and make notes.
2. Present the points on the slide below. Think about how to signal the three points (*the first skill is ...* , etc.). Give some more information for each point using the list below:

    - listen carefully to everything
    - work on your weaknesses
    - learn and understand completely

    Key skills for a student
    - Listen well.
    - Know your strengths and weaknesses.
    - Ask the right questions.

Glossary

> - **noun** (*n.*) The codes [C] and [U] show whether a noun, or a particular sense of a noun, is countable (*an agenda, two agendas*) or uncountable (*awareness, branding*). Note that some nouns in the examples are used as part of a noun phrase.
> - **verb** (*v.*) The forms of irregular verbs are given after the headword. The codes [I] (intransitive) and [T] (transitive) show whether a verb, or a particular sense of a verb, has or does not have an object. Phrasal verbs (*phr.v.*) are shown with their participle.

abroad *adv.* in a foreign country or going to a foreign country
How often do you travel abroad?

access *v.* [T] to find and use information, especially on a computer
I use the Samsung for social contact and to access Facebook.

adapt *v.* [T] to change something so that you can use it for a different purpose
How do international fast-food companies adapt their menus for Indian customers?

advertising agency *n.* [C] a business that designs advertisements for other companies
Volkswagen asked the US advertising agency Deutsch, L.A. to create a TV commercial to launch the 2012 Beetle.

advertising campaign *n.* [C] a planned series of advertisements to advertise a product or to persuade people to do something
The new advertising campaign cost 900,000 euros.

aim *v.* [T] If something is *aimed* at a particular group of people, it has been made or designed for them.
Our new bags are aimed at stylish women.

aisle seat *n.* [C] a seat on a plane that is next to the long space between the rows of seats
Would you like a window seat or an aisle seat?

alarm call *n.* [C] a telephone call made to your hotel room by hotel reception in order to wake you up
Can I have an alarm call at 6.45, please?

ambitious *adj.* determined to be successful or powerful
I like to work with ambitious people because they give me energy.

annual leave *n.* [U] time that you are allowed to be absent from your work, equal to a particular number of days per year
How many days' annual leave do you get in your company?

apply for *phr.v.* to make a formal, usually written, request for something, especially a job, a place at university or permission to do something
In 2011, Martin began to apply for jobs abroad.

appointment *n.* [C] an arrangement to meet someone at a particular time and place
Selim likes to be on time for appointments, but I like to be early.

assistant *n.* [C] someone who helps someone else do their job
My assistant answers the phone and arranges meetings.

attend *v.* [T] to go to an event such as a meeting
When he is away, he attends meetings.

award *n.* [C] a prize for something good that you have done
The 3T group won an award last year for the best magazine advert.

benefit *v.* [T] to have a good effect on someone or something, or to give someone or something an advantage
By the end of my talk, you will understand how the new system benefits us all.

bill *n.* [C] a list showing how much you have to pay for services or goods received
I'm checking out today, so can I have the bill, please?

billboard *n.* [C] a large sign used for advertising
I think our competitors are using a lot of billboard advertising. I saw two huge ads on my way to work this morning.

board *v.* [T, I] to get on a plane, ship, train or bus
Flight BA 125 is now boarding at gate 17.

bonus *n.* [C] an extra amount of money added to an employee's wages, usually as a reward for doing difficult or good work
I'd like to talk to you about the bonus scheme.

book *v.* [T] to arrange to have or do something at a particular time
I need to book a hotel room today.

branch *n.* [C] an individual bank, shop, office, etc. that is part of a large organisation
You will need to set up a new branch in Amsterdam.

briefing *n.* [C] a meeting at which information or instructions are given
Face-to-face communication includes one-to-one meetings, team meetings, forums, briefings, etc.

budget *n.* [C] a detailed plan made by an organisation or a government of how much it will receive as income over a particular period of time, and how much it will spend, what it will spend the money on, etc.
In 2010, Toptek spent about 32 per cent of its budget on print advertising.

GLOSSARY

business *n. [C]* an organisation that produces or sells things
He runs his own business.

business *n. [U]* **1** the work that you do as your job to earn money
She travels on business one week a month.
2 the production, buying and selling of goods or services for profit
The store is open for business 24 hours a day.
How's business?

business card *n. [C]* a card that shows a businessperson's name, company, address, etc.
I usually wait until the person I'm meeting offers me a business card before I offer them mine.

business trip *n. [C]* a journey to a place for business
He doesn't get up early, especially after a business trip.

busy *adj.* having a lot of work or other things to do
I'm very busy in the morning.

candidate *n. [C]* someone who is being considered for a job or is competing to be elected
Last year, she set up and ran summer internship programmes for 60 candidates.

career *n. [C]* a job or profession that you have been trained for and intend to do for your working life, and which offers the chance to be promoted (= move up through different levels)
Tim says working in a call centre is just a job, it's not a career.

casual Friday *n. [C]* a Friday when employees are allowed to wear clothes that are comfortable and usually worn in informal situations
We don't have to wear business suits at the end of the week. My company has a system of casual Fridays.

CEO *n. [C]* **Chief Executive Officer** the person with the most important position in a company
What is a typical day in the life of the CEO of a big company?

chairperson *n. [C]* someone who is in charge of a meeting or who directs the work of a committee or organisation
In meetings, do you prefer to not speak much or to be the chairperson?

change *v. [T]* to give some money to someone and receive the same amount back from them, but in different notes or coins
A customer is changing dollars into euros.

channel *n. [C]* a system that is used for supplying information or goods
There are various channels of communication which can be used.

charge *n. [U]* when someone controls something or is responsible for something
In this exciting job, you will need to be in charge of a team of 25.

check *n. [C]* the American word for a restaurant bill
In New York, you ask for the check at the end of a meal, but in London you ask for the bill.

check *v. [T]* to do something in order to make sure that everything is safe, correct or working properly
How often do you check your work e-mails when you are on holiday?

check-in desk *n. [C]* a place where you go to show your ticket and give in your bags before you get ready to board the plane, train, boat, etc.
I don't like queuing at the check-in desk.

check in *v. [I]* to go to the desk at a hotel, airport, etc. and say that you have arrived
We have to check in two hours before the flight leaves.

childcare *n. [U]* the activity of looking after children while their parents are working
We provide childcare facilities for working parents.

client *n. [C]* someone who pays for services or advice from a professional person or organisation
Jeremy's clients sometimes have quite complicated problems.

colleague *n [C]* someone you work with, used especially by professional people or managers
My colleagues are really nice and I like my boss.

collect *v. [T]* to go to a place and get someone or something
You can collect your luggage at baggage claim.

commercial *n. [C]* an advertisement on television or radio
A typical TV commercial is 30 seconds long.

company *n. [C]* an organisation that makes or sells goods or services in order to make a profit
Burberry isn't an American company, it's British.

compare *v. [T]* If you *compare* things, you examine them in order to find out how they are similar or different.
I'd like to compare prices with Emmerson's, but I'll contact you again this afternoon.

competitive *adj.* used to describe situations and behaviour in which businesses are trying very hard to be more successful than others, for example by selling their goods or services more cheaply than others
Germany is a competitive market for cars.

competitor *n. [C]* a person, product, company, country, etc. that is competing with another
Laurence and Tracy are talking about an advertising campaign by one of their competitors, Palmer and Mason.

complain *v. [I]* to say that you are not satisfied with something or not happy about something
When they arrived, they were complaining loudly about the morning's bad traffic.

complaint *n. [C]* a written or spoken statement by someone complaining about something
The receptionist is listening to a customer's complaint and trying to solve the problem.

conference *n. [C]* a large formal meeting, usually lasting a day or several days, where people discuss things in order to exchange information or to come to an agreement
I met an interesting person at a conference in Singapore.

GLOSSARY

conference call *n. [C]* a telephone call in which several people in different places are able to talk together at the same time
Conference calls are useful, especially for keeping up to date on projects.

confirm *v. [T]* to tell someone that an arrangement is now definite
It's a good idea to confirm your flight before you go to the airport.

confusing *adj.* difficult to understand
The instructions are not always clear, and they are sometimes very confusing.

consultant *n. [C]* someone whose job is to give people or businesses advice or training in a particular area
I think my strengths come from my work as a consultant over the last 20 years.

consumer *n. [C]* a person who buys goods, products and services for their own use, not for business use or to resell
Consumers are people who buy products and services.

contact *n. [C]* a person you know who may be able to help or advise you, especially because of the work they do
What do you say when you meet a new business contact?
keep in contact to meet, telephone or write to someone regularly
For Ahrendts, keeping in contact with relatives is important.

cope *v. [I]* to manage a difficult situation successfully
It can be difficult to cope with stress at work.

cost *v. [T]* to have a particular price
How much does the ticket cost?

cost *n. [C]* the amount of money that you have to pay in order to buy, do or produce something
Customers want low prices, but companies have increasing costs.

course *n. [C]* one of the parts of a meal
What would you like for your main course?

creative *adj.* producing or using new and interesting ideas
I like working with creative people, people who are willing to find new ways to solve problems.

credit *n. [U]* an arrangement with a shop, supplier, etc. to buy something now and pay for it later
Our company wants to introduce interest-free credit to help sales.

custom *n. [C]* something that people in a particular group or society have done for a long time, and which they continue doing because it is important to them
Before you visit a country for the first time, find out about the most important customs and festivals.

customer *n. [C]* a person or organisation that buys goods or services from a shop or company
It is not easy to talk to customers when they are angry and do not want to understand.

deadline *n. [C]* a date or time by which you have to do or to complete something
Maria is very reliable, she always meets deadlines.

deal with *phr.v.* to do something to make sure a problem no longer exists
In my job, I deal with customers, suppliers and their problems.

delay *n. [C]* a period of time when you have to wait for something to happen
Delivery delays are always a problem.

delay *v. [T]* to make someone or something late
I'm very sorry I missed our meeting this afternoon. My flight was delayed.

deliver *v. [T]* to take goods or mail to a place
We deliver large goods on Monday afternoons.

delivery *n. [C]* the act or process of bringing goods, letters, etc. to a particular place or person
It's about the delivery of mobile phones: I want 50, not 15.

demand *n.sing.* If there is a *demand* for something, people want to buy it.
There is a lot of demand from Indian consumers for fast food.

deposit *n. [C]* part of the price of something that you pay when you agree to buy it
We ask for a 15% deposit on large orders.

dessert *n. [C]* something sweet that you eat after the main part of a meal
I usually have ice cream for dessert.

details *n.pl.* small facts or pieces of information about something
Can I have your credit-card details, please?

develop *v. [I,T]* to grow and improve, or to make something grow and improve
In this exciting job, you will need to develop new products.

discount *n. [C]* a reduction in the cost of goods or services in relation to the normal cost
New customers get a 5% discount for orders over 500 items.

dish *n. [C]* food cooked or prepared in a particular way
Curry is a typical Indian dish.

download *v. [T]* to move computer software or information from one computer to another, usually from a large computer to a smaller one
Employees can download information from the intranet.

earn *v. [T]* to be paid a particular amount of money for the work you do
How much money does Lucy earn?

eat out *phr.v.* to eat in a restaurant, not at home
How often do you eat out?

efficient *adj.* working well, without wasting time or energy
Our new boss is very efficient.

employ *v. [T]* to pay someone to work for you
Walmart employs more people than any other company.

employee *n. [C]* someone who is paid to work for an organisation, especially someone who has a job of low rank
Our employees enjoy having flexible hours.

empower v. [T] to give a person or an organisation the power or the legal right to do something
A positive company culture empowers employees. Staff have a lot of control over their work.

encourage v. [T] to give someone hope and confidence in order to persuade them to do something
A positive company culture encourages trust at all levels. Relationships between employees and managers are open and honest.

enter v. [T] to go or come into a place
Following a decision to enter the Brazilian market, Gamesa set up a subsidiary in São Paulo in early 2010.

entertain v. [T] to invite people to have food or drink with you
We often entertain businesspeople at home.

enthusiastic adj. liking something a lot and being excited about it
Mr Colao is not very enthusiastic about video calling.

equipment n. [U] the things that you use for a particular activity
Each apartment has high-quality kitchen and bathroom equipment.

exchange v. [T] to give something to someone who gives you something similar
You can exchange foreign currency in our currency section.

expansion n. [U] when something increases or is increased in size, amount or number
Following the good results in Japan, Yani decided on global expansion.

export v. [T, I] to send and sell things to another country
Dalotek exports to over 12 countries.

export market n. [C] another country where a company sells its goods
The US is Scotland's second largest export market after France.

face to face adj., adv. meeting and speaking directly to someone
How many people do you speak to face to face each day when you are working?

factory n. [C] a large building or group of buildings where goods are made, using large industrial machinery and usually employing many people
When the machinery in the factory starts, it is very noisy.

fail v. [I] to be unsuccessful
Some business deals fail because of small things like a misunderstood e-mail.

flagship store n. [C] the best and most important store that a company owns
Uniqlo opened a flagship store in New York in November 2006.

flexible adj. able to change or be changed easily to suit any new situation
I enjoy having flexible hours.

flexitime adj., n. [U] a system in which people work a fixed number of hours each week or month, but can change the times at which they start and finish each day
We have a flexitime system in our office. Some people choose to work from 9 a.m. to 5 p.m.; others work from 10 a.m. to 6 p.m.

flight n. [C] a journey by plane
Last call for all passengers for flight SA 238 at gate 12: the gate closes in five minutes.

formal adj. done or given officially and publicly
Companies have an Annual General Meeting (AGM) once a year. It is a very formal meeting, with a lot of people.

forum n. [C] an occasion or place where people can discuss an important subject
Employees can use social media to create an internal community, for example by posting profiles, starting discussion forums, etc.

gesture n. [C] a movement of your head, arm or hand that shows what you mean or how you feel
How important are gestures (hand movements, etc.) for you when communicating?

global adj. affecting or including the whole world
Burberry is a global fashion company.

goods n.pl. things that are made for people to buy
I buy things like electrical goods in the January sales because the discounts and special offers are so good.

guarantee n. [C] a formal written promise to repair or replace a product if it has a fault within a specific period of time after you buy it
They give a three-year guarantee.

hard copy n. [C] information from a computer that is printed out onto paper
If you haven't got a hard copy of the report, I can print one out for you.

hard-working adj. working with a lot of effort
I think a hard-working boss is important.

head office n. [C] the main office of a company
Levi Strauss has its head office in San Francisco.

helpful adj. providing useful help
Juan is very helpful, he likes to do things for other people.

hire v. [T] to pay someone to work for you
Yani hired the German designer Jil Sander in April 2009.

hoarding n. [C] BrE a large board fixed to the side of a building, used to show advertisements
'Hoarding' is a British English word for 'billboard'.

home market n. [C] the country where goods are produced, rather than foreign countries
A home market is in the producer's country.

host n. [C] the person at an event who organised it and invited the guests
Take some gifts for your hosts which are typical of your own country.

GLOSSARY

househusband *n.* [C] a man who works at home doing the cooking, cleaning, etc. for his family
He's a househusband at the moment; he looks after our three children.

human resources *n.* [U] the department in a company that deals with employing, training and helping people
He is the company's Vice-President of Human Resources.

improve *v.* [T] to make something better
Do you think we should redesign our website or just improve it?

include *v.* [T] If something *includes* a person or thing, it has that person or thing as one of its parts.
The price includes postage and packaging.

increase *v.* [I, T] to become larger in amount, number or degree, or to make something become larger in amount, number or degree
The company wants to increase its market share from 10.3 to 11.5 per cent.

in-flight *adj.* provided during a plane journey
I usually watch an in-flight movie when I travel.

informal *adj.* relaxed and friendly
Our department starts every day with an informal meeting. It is very relaxed.

information *n.* [U] facts or details that tell you about something or someone
I need a lot of information about tourist attractions.

intern *n.* [C] someone, especially a student, who works for a short time in a particular job in order to gain experience
Paula will be an intern in the company for three weeks.

internship *n.* [C] a job that lasts for a short time, that someone, especially a student, does in order to gain experience
Helen is responsible for organising summer internships.

introduce *v.* [T] **1** to tell two people each other's names when they meet for the first time, or to tell someone your name for the first time
Let me introduce you to my colleague, John Roberts.
2 to make a new product or service available for the first time
Dalotek introduces one or two new components each year.

invite *v.* [T] to ask someone to go somewhere or to do something with you
Why don't we invite Anita and Karlo for dinner?

invoice *n.* [C] a document sent by a seller to a customer with details of goods or services that have been provided, their price and the payment date
There's a problem with the invoice, the figures are wrong.

jingle *n.* [C] a short song or tune used in advertisements
A short song used in advertising is called a jingle.

join *v.* [T] to become a member of a group, team or organisation
In what ways has your job changed since you joined the company?

lack *n.sing.* when you do not have enough of something
In addition to their small sports facilities, they have a lack of modern equipment.

launch *v.* [T] to show or make a new product available for sale for the first time
Our company launches 12 new products a year.

lead *v.* [T] to be in charge of something such as an important activity, a group of people or an organisation
In this exciting job, you will need to lead a team of 25.

leadership *n.* [U] the position of being in charge of a country or group, or the people who are in charge
What have you done that shows leadership?

leisure *n.* [U] time when you are not working and can relax and do things you enjoy
It is sometimes difficult to find enough time for leisure.

lift *n.* [C] Br.E. a ride in someone's car, taking you to where you need to go
I'll give you a lift to the station if you want to go home.

loan *n.* [C] money borrowed from a bank, financial institution, person, etc. on which interest is usually paid to the lender until the loan is repaid
The Assistant Manager arranges loans for customers.

logo *n.* [C] a design or way of writing its name that a company or organisation uses as its official sign on its products, advertising, etc.
I think we should redesign our company logo.

luggage *n.* [U] the bags that you carry when you are travelling
Can I take this as hand luggage?

luxury market *n.* [C] people who buy expensive products that are not really necessary but are pleasing and enjoyable
Rolex watches sell in a luxury market; they are high-quality and expensive goods.

make *v.* [T] to be able to go to something that has been arranged
Sorry, I can't make Monday or Tuesday. How about later in the week?

manage *v.* [T] to direct or control a business, part of a business or the people who work in it
I manage a large department in the clothing industry.

manufacture *v.* [T] to produce large quantities of goods to be sold, using machinery
Dalotek manufactures car parts.

market share *n.* [U] the percentage of sales in a market that a company or product has
Next year, we want to increase our market share to 11.5% and sell over 2,100,000 units of Sparkle.

mass-market *adj.* designed to be bought by a very large number of people
Coca-Cola is a mass-market product; it sells to large numbers of people.

MBA *n.* [C] **Master of Business Administration** a university degree that teaches you the skills you need to manage a business or part of a business
Danielle did an MBA at the Harvard Business School in 2009.

meal *n.* [C] a time when you eat food, or the food that you eat then
Thanks very much – that was a lovely meal, I really enjoyed it.

menu *n.* [C] a list of all the food that is available to eat in a restaurant
You ask for the menu at the start of a meal.

missing *adj.* not able to be found
We can't use it because there's a piece missing.

motivating *adj.* making people want to do something
The new manager is motivating, he really encourages us to work well.

niche market *n.* [C] a part of a market which is small but may be profitable
Selling special-interest holidays is a niche market; it is a small but often profitable market.

online *adv., adj.* directly connected to a computer network or the Internet, or available on the Internet
How long do you spend online each day?

opportunity *n.* [C] a chance to do something
What's important for me is a friendly boss and travel opportunities.

order *n.* [C] a request by a customer for goods or services
We have a lot of big orders in March.

overseas *adj.* to, in or from a foreign country across the sea
The subject of my presentation is overseas expansion.

overtime *n.* [U], *adv.* time that you spend working in your job in addition to your normal working hours
I don't enjoy doing overtime.

part-time *adv., adj.* only working for part of the week
Do you want to work part-time or full-time?

passion *n.* [U] a very strong belief or feeling about something
Famous for her long black hair, pearl necklaces and her passion for Avon, Jung is one of the world's top business leaders.

passport control *n.* [U] the place at an airport or port where your passport is checked when you leave or enter a country
Excuse me, which way is passport control?

phone *n.* [C] a piece of equipment you use to talk to someone who is in another place
Mr Shi Jiabao is on the phone.

place an order *v.* [T] to ask a shop or business to provide goods
I'd like to place an order.

placement *n.* [C] a job that is found for someone, especially to give them experience of work
When I was at university, I did a placement in an advertising agency.

plant *n.* [C] a factory and all its equipment
A manufacturing plant is a factory that makes machines and equipment.

platform *n.* [C] the raised place beside a railway track where you get on and off the train
Passengers on platform 2, the next train to Manchester is at 14.40.

pleased *adj.* happy or satisfied
Pleased to meet you.

practical *adj.* sensible and likely to be effective
A practical person is good at making things work.

presentation *n.* [C] an event at which someone explains an idea to a group of people
He sometimes gives presentations.

promotion *n.* [C] when you are given a higher job
Fast promotion, flexible hours and some sports facilities are what's important for me.

provide *v.* [T] to give someone something they need
Dalotek provides components for the car industry.

public holiday *n.* [C] an official holiday when banks and most businesses are closed
I am so busy at the moment that I worked on New Year's Day, which is a public holiday.

punctual *adj.* arriving, happening or being done at exactly the time that was arranged
Sorry, I'm late again; I know I need to be more punctual.

purchasing *n.* [U] the act of buying something
As a store manager, she was responsible for all purchasing and stock control.

quiet *adj.* with few customers and not much activity
Business is quiet in the summer.

quit *v.* [T, I] to leave your job, especially because you are annoyed or unhappy with it
Andrea told her parents she didn't like her job and wanted to quit.

receipt *n.* [C] a piece of paper which shows how much you have paid for something
Can I have a receipt, please?

receive *v.* [T] to get something that is given or sent to you
How many e-mails or text (SMS) messages do you receive each day?

recommend *v.* [T] to tell someone that something is good or enjoyable
What do you recommend for the main course?

recruit *v.* [T] to find new people to work for an organisation, do a job, etc.
Gamesa is already expanding the Camaçari plant and plans to recruit more workers.

reduce *v.* [T] to make something less or smaller in price, amount or size
We could reduce each department by 10 workers.

GLOSSARY

refund n. [C] a sum of money that is given back to you
I'm sorry there's a problem with the mobile phone, we can give you a refund.

relaunch n. [C] a new effort to sell a product that is already available, often involving a change in advertising, packaging, etc.
The relaunch of Uniqlo began in November 2006 with the opening of a flagship store in New York.

relaxed adj. calm and not worried about anything
I feel very relaxed today.

reliable adj. able to be trusted or depended on
Reliable people do what they say they are going to do, and do it on time.

report to phr.v. to have a particular person in authority over you who gives you tasks and checks that you do them
I report to Peter, he's my line manager.

research analyst n. [C] someone who studies a subject to find out new things about it or to test new ideas, products, etc.
I am a research analyst for an investment bank in New York.

reservation n. [C] an arrangement in which a place on a plane, in a hotel, in a restaurant, etc. is kept for a customer who will arrive later
I have a reservation for two nights, my name's Burkhard.

respect n. [U] when you admire someone, especially for their personal qualities
Her colleagues have a lot of respect for her work and attitude.

responsibility n. [U] when someone is officially in charge of something and has to make decisions about it
Recently, I have also taken responsibility for our summer internships.

retailer n. [C] a business that sells goods to members of the public, rather than to shops, etc.
What do you know about Uniqlo, the global fashion retailer?

revenue n. [U or pl.] money that a business or organisation receives over a period of time, especially from selling goods or services
Today, Avon's revenues are more than $10bn.

reward v. [T] If you are *rewarded* for something you have done, something good happens to you or is given to you.
A positive company culture rewards good performance. There is an incentive scheme for efficient employees.

run v. [T] to control or be in charge of an organisation, company or system
Martin has run his own training company since 2005.

salary n. [C] money that you receive as payment from the organisation you work for, usually paid to you every month
What's important for me is a high salary, long holidays and helpful colleagues.

sales n. [U] the part of a company that deals with selling products
I'm in sales, but I'm not the manager.

sales assistant n. [C] someone whose job is to help sell things in a company
The sales assistant brought me three more dresses to try on.

sales representative n. [C] a person who sells a company's products or services by speaking to customers on the phone or travelling to meet them
Avon's sales representatives sell cosmetics door to door in more than 120 countries.

sample n. [C] a small amount of something that shows what the rest of it is like
I asked the manufacturer to send me a sample of the product.

schedule v. [T] to plan when something will happen
The seminar was scheduled to start five minutes ago but, like many meetings in Brazil, it did not start on time.

security n. [U] when you have something and are not likely to lose it, or when you are not likely to suffer something bad
What's important for me is a friendly boss and job security.

service n. [U] the work that people who work in a company give you
When I buy a product like a computer or a TV, great after-sales service is important for me.

set up phr.v. to start a company or organisation
They want to set up factories in Africa.

shift n. [C] one of the set periods of time during each day and night when a group of workers in a factory, etc. are at work before being replaced by another group of workers
For two weeks each month, I work at night. I can't sleep during the day. I hate shift work.

single adj. intended to be used by only one person
I can give you a single room on the eighth floor, or a double on the third floor.

single n. [C] a ticket for a journey from one place to another but not back again
A single to Oxford, please.

slogan n. [C] a short phrase that is easy to remember and is used by an advertiser, organisation or other group
'Just do it', 'Always Coca-Cola' and 'Because I'm worth it' are all slogans.

sociable adj. friendly and enjoying being with people
Maria gets on well with her colleagues and has a lot of friends; she's extremely sociable.

solve v. [T] to find a successful way to deal with a problem
My job is to solve our customers' problems.

spend v. [T] to use time doing something
At work, he spends a lot of time in meetings and on conference calls.

staff n. [U] the people who work for an organisation or business
I go to all staff meetings.

starter n. [C] the first part of a meal
Would you like a starter?

in stock adj. If a shop has something *in stock*, it has it available for people to buy there.
Are the goods in stock?

strategy n. [C] a plan or series of plans for achieving an aim, especially success in business or the best way for an organisation to develop in the future
Our management team discuss business strategy, but they don't discuss employee problems.

strength n. [C] something that you are good at
What are your strengths and weaknesses?

stressful adj. making you worried and unable to relax
Working in a call centre is often very stressful.

stylish adj. attractive and fashionable
Our new women's bags are stylish and fashionable.

successful adj. having achieved what you have been trying to do
International fast-food companies need to change their menus to be successful in India.

suit v. [T] to be acceptable to you and not cause you any problems
What time suits you?

supply v. [T] to provide goods or services to customers, especially regularly and over a long period of time
Green Shoots supplies the gardening industry.

support v. [T] to help and encourage someone or something
A positive company culture supports innovation. New ideas and change are welcome.

swap v. [T] to exchange something you have for something that someone else has
I use the BlackBerry for business e-mail and to swap SMS messages with colleagues.

target market n. [C] the people you are trying to sell to
The target market is young women who want to look good.

taste n. [C] Your *taste* in something is what kind of that thing you like.
International fast-food companies know how important it is to adapt their food for Indian tastes.

terminal n. [C] a large building that is part of an airport, bus station or port, where people wait to get onto planes, buses or ships
Which terminal does your flight leave from?

tip n. [C] an additional amount of money that you give to someone who has done a job for you as a way of thanking them
If the service is good, I always leave a tip.

trade show n. [C] an event at which many different companies involved in a particular area of business show and sell their products
He often goes to trade shows.

train v. [T] to teach someone the skills that they need to do something difficult
In my last job, I trained staff to use the new IT system.

travel v. [I] to go from one place to another, usually in a vehicle
I travel to work by bus.

turnover n. [U] the rate at which people leave an organisation and are replaced by others
Nobody stays in the job very long, there's a high staff turnover.

uniform n. [C] a set of clothes that people wear so that they all look the same
In many banks, staff can't wear what they like. They have to wear uniforms.

upload v. [T] to move information or programs from your computer onto another computer, especially onto a larger central computer
Employees may join chat rooms or forums to post comments or upload images and discuss with other employees around the world.

waste v. [T] to use more of something than you need to, or to not use it in a sensible way
We waste a lot of paper, but we don't waste electricity.

work experience n. [U] experience of working that is useful in finding a job
Cindy Tan has no work experience.

workforce n.sing. all the people who work in a particular country, industry or factory
Dalotek has a workforce of 2,500.

workshop n. [C] a meeting at which people try to improve their skills by working together
I run a workshop every Wednesday.

Pearson Education Limited
Edinburgh Gate, Harlow, Essex, CM20 2JE, England
and Associated Companies throughout the world.

www.pearsonelt.com

© Pearson Education Limited 2016

The right of David Cotton, David Falvey, Simon Kent and Nina O'Driscoll to be identified as authors of this Work has been asserted by them in accordance with the Copyright, Designs and Patents Act 1988.

All rights reserved; no part of this publication may be reproduced, stored in a retrieval system, or transmitted in any form or by any means, electronic, mechanical, photocopying, recording, or otherwise without the prior written permission of the Publishers or a licence permitting restricted copying in the United Kingdom issued by the Copyright Licensing Agency Ltd, 90 Tottenham Court Road, London.

First Edition first published 2002
Fifth impression 2019
Third Edition first published 2010

Third Edition Extra first published 2016

ISBN: 978-1-292-13474-1

Set in Meta OT 9.5/12pt

Printed in Slovakia by Neografia

Acknowledgements
The publishers would like to thank the following authors for writing the Business Skills lessons: Margaret O'Keefe, Clare Walsh, Iwonna Dubicka, Lizzie Wright, Bob Dignan, Sara Helm and Fiona Scott-Barrett.

The authors would like to thank the following for their invaluable help during the project: Santiago García Nuez, Elena Gutierrez, Raquel García, and our students at Giesecke & Devrient Ibérica, Albert Prades and family, Walerian Dubicki and the Dubicki-Pipers.

The authors would also like to thank Bill Mascull for writing the Teacher's Resource Book, John Rogers for writing the Practice File and Lewis Lansford for writing the Test File.

The authors and publishers are very grateful to the following people who agreed to be interviewed for some of the recorded material in this book: Dr Bernd Atenstaedt, David Bowen, Ian Brinkley, Philippa Foster Back, Anneliese Guérin-LeTendre, Angus McCrone, Charles Middleton, Dr Jonathan Reynolds, Marjorie Scardino, Peter Sirman, Mike Southon, Tom Taylor. Special thanks from the authors to Chris Hartley for his great work on the interviews.

The publishers and authors are very grateful to the following advisers and teachers who commented on versions of this material and contributed to the initial research: Ian Duncan, Andrew Nathan, Nancy Pietragalla Dorfman, Dr Petra Pointner, Michael Thompson, Benjamin White, Aukjen Bosma, David Kadas, Hans Leijenaar, Sabine Prochel, Ulrich Schuh, Robert McLarty.

We are grateful to the following for permission to reproduce copyright material:

Logos
Logo (p66) from Triodos Bank, reproduced with permission; Toyota logo (p84) reproduced with permission from Toyota (GB) plc; logo (p84) from The Procter & Gamble Company, reproduced with permission; logo (p84) from Google, reproduced with permission; Amazon logo (p84) copyright © 2010 Amazon.com, Inc.

Text
Extract on pp.42-43 adapted from Hilton Hotel, Tokyo, www.hilton.co.uk. Reproduced with permission.

The Financial Times
Extract on p.18 adapted from "Business Diary: Eugene Kaspersky" as told to Mary Watkins, *The Financial Times*, 28/02/2011; Extract on p.71 adapted from "Women at the top: Andrea Jung", *The Financial Times*, 16/11/2010; and Extract on p.78 adapted from "The public image: Volkswagen" by Bernard Simon, *The Financial Times*, 23/05/2011, copyright © The Financial Times Limited, 2010, 2011. All rights reserved.

In some instances we have been unable to trace the owners of copyright material, and we would appreciate any information that would enable us to do so.

Photos
The publisher would like to thank the following for their kind permission to reproduce their photographs:
(Key: b-bottom; c-centre; l-left; r-right; t-top)

123RF.com: 123rf.com A3bl; **Alamy Images:** Ben Welsh 59, Danita Delimont Creative 104tr, dbimages 104tl, Drive Images 77bl, Fancy 14, Helen Sessions 8l, Jeff Greenberg 50, JVPhoto 8cr, Kevin Foy 8cl, Mark Richardson 87tr, Richard Levine 54, Tetra Images 88, Tom Wood 77cl; **Corbis:** Bjorn Lindren 57b, Blend Images / Pete Saloutos 104bl, Bloomimage 17, David Buffington / Blend Images 31, Eric Audras / Photo Alto 89, Guo Jian She / Redlink 44, HBSS / Fancy 57c, Blaine Harrington III 22, Image Source 68, 72, 117, Image Source 68, 72, 117, Image Source 68, 72, 117, Image100 51, 108, 111, Image100 51, 108, 111, Image100 51, 108, 111, John Van Hasselt 82, Jon Feingersh / Blend Images 20, Juice Images 90-91, Kimberly White 70, Lehmann, Joerg(P) / The Food Passionates 87bl, Mast Irham / EPA 74, Murat Taner / Terra 90t, Nik Wheeler / Terra 29, Ocean 49, 60, 80, 83, 110, Ocean 49, 60, 80, 83, 110, Ocean 49, 60, 80, 83, 110, Ocean 49, 60, 80, 83, 110, Ocean 49, 60, 80, 83, 110, Tibor Bognar 85l, Horacio Villalobos A5cl; **Courtesy of Gamesa Corporation:** 134, 141, 134, 141; **Courtesy of Hilton Tokyo:** 40l, 40c, 40r, 40l, 40c, 40r, 40l, 40c, 40r; **Courtesy of Volkeswagen:** 76, 77, 76, 77; **Fotolia.com:** JackF A11-A12, Bartas Miklasevicius A11bc, Minerva Studio A3c, Brad Pict 59cr, Rawpixel.com A15bl; **Getty Images:** 69, Adam Gault / Photodisc 78tr, Agence France Presse 46, Andersen Ross / Digital Vision 78tl, Bloomberg 85r, Cultura / Zero Creatives / Stockimage 12, Datacraft Co. Ltd 73, Digital Vision 99cr, Funkystock / age fotostock 81, Hiroshi Higuchi 43, John Coletti / Photographers Choice 91cr, Jose Luis Pelaez / Blend Images 114, Jupiter Images / Comstock 116, Klaus Vedfelt / The Image Bank 103, Pier / The Image Bank 103br, Robert Harding World Imagery 112, The Age 66, Tony Metaxas / Asia Images 13c, Ullstein Bild 24, Westend61 87cl, Toru Yamanaka 104br, Yellow Dog Productions / Stockbyte 15; **Masterfile UK Ltd:** 50b; **Nike:** 74bl; **Pearson Education Ltd:** Studio 8 A11l; **Photoshot Holdings Limited:** Riccardo Antimiani / MaxPPP 100, Tony Albir / EFE 16; **Press Association Images:** Demotix / Piero Cruciatti 52; **Rex Shutterstock:** 9tr, Steve Meddle 9cl; **Robert Harding World Imagery:** Raga Jose Fuste / age fotostock 21; **Shutterstock.com:** 3Dsculptor 96, Africa Studio A7-A8, Alexander Raths 118, Andrey Armyagov 79, Artmim A11r, Greg Blok A6cr, Digieye 119, Elwynn 13cl, Filip Fuxa A11tc, Martin Good 8r, i359702 13, Jo Crebbin 42, Laurin Rinder 121tr, Levngchopan 13tl, Liudmila Gridina 91tr, Luba V Nel 78tc, Minerva Studio 67, Monkey Business Images A1-A2, A12c, A15-A16, Photobank.ch 28, 43cr, Photobank.ch 28, 43cr, Pkchai A3tl, Pressmaster A5-A6, A9-A10, Robnroll 19, S_oleg A11cl, Sailorr 81br, Stefanolunardi 61, StockLite A13-A14, Vadym Drobot 120-121, Wavebreakmedia A3-A4, Wavebreakmedia Ltd 26, 102, 121tl, Wavebreakmedia Ltd 26, 102, 121tl, Wavebreakmedia Ltd 26, 102, 121tl; **SuperStock:** Rubberball 10; **The Kobal Collection:** DANJAQ / EON / UA 6; **Zuma Press:** Bruce Chambers / Orange County Register 36

All other images © Pearson Education

Video
© Pearson Education